JANE AUSTEN, YOUNG AUTHOR

In her lively and accessibly written book, Juliet McMaster examines Jane Austen's acute and frequently uproarious juvenile works as important in their own right and for the ways they look forward to her novels. Exploring the early works both collectively and individually, McMaster shows how young Austen's fictional world, peopled by guzzlers and unashamed self-seekers, operates by an ethic of energy rather than the sympathy that dominates the novels. A fully self-conscious artist, young Jane experimented freely with literary modes - the epistolary, the omniscient, the drama. Early on, she developed brilliantly pointed dialogue to match her characters. Literary parody impels her creativity, and McMaster's sustained study of "Love and Friendship" shows the same intricate relation of the parody to the work it parodies that we later see with *Northanger Abbey* and the Gothic novel. As an illustrator herself, McMaster is especially attuned to the explicit and sometimes hilarious descriptions of bodies that preceded Austen's famous reticence about physicality. Rather than focusing on the immaturities of the juvenilia, McMaster maps the gradual shifts in tone and emphasis that signpost Austen's journey as a writer. She shows, for instance, how the shameless husband-hunting in "The Three Sisters" and the vigorous partisanship of "The History of England" lead on to *Pride and Prejudice*. Her book will appeal to Austen's critics and to passionate general readers, as well as to scholars working in the fields of juvenilia, children's literature, and childhood studies.

To Christine Alexander,
Director of the Juvenilia Press:
Colleague, Collaborator, Friend

Jane Austen, Young Author

JULIET MCMASTER
University of Alberta, Canada

ASHGATE

Published by
Ashgate Publishing Limited
Wey Court East
Union Road
Farnham
Surrey, GU9 7PT
England

Ashgate Publishing Company
110 Cherry Street
Suite 3-1
Burlington, VT 05401-3818
USA

www.ashgate.com

British Library Cataloguing in Publication Data
A catalogue record for this book is available from the British Library

The Library of Congress has cataloged the printed edition as follows:
McMaster, Juliet.
Jane Austen, young author / by Juliet McMaster.
pages cm
Includes index.
ISBN 978-1-4724-4056-3 (hardcover: alk. paper) — ISBN 978-1-4724-4057-0 (pbk.: alk. paper) — ISBN 978-1-4724-4058-7 (ebook) — ISBN 978-1-4724-4059-4 (epub)
1. Austen, Jane, 1775–1817—Criticism and interpretation. 2. Austen, Jane, 1775–1817—Childhood and youth. 3. Children's writings, English—History and criticism. 4. Women and literature—England—History—19th century. I. Title.
PR4037.M36 2016
823'.7—dc23

2015029928

ISBN 9781472440563 (hbk)
ISBN 9781472440570 (pbk)
ISBN 9781472440587 (ebk – PDF)
ISBN 9781472440594 (ebk – ePUB)

MIX
Paper from responsible sources
FSC
www.fsc.org
FSC® C013985

Printed in the United Kingdom by Henry Ling Limited, at the Dorset Press, Dorchester, DT1 1HD

Contents

List of Figures

Lesley Castle

The Three Sisters

Lady Susan

Love and Freindship

Foreword

Lovers of Jane Austen, and there are many of us, have long been waiting for a book devoted to her early writings: the sparkling torrent of sort fiction, miniature plays, verse, and a mock history that she produced between 1787, when she was 11, and June 1793, when she was 17. Austen preserved these writings in her notebooks, entitled *Volume the First*, *Volume the Second*, and *Volume the Third.* But only since the mid-twentieth century have readers and critics had full access to their remarkably diverse contents. The only full-length study to date is a collection of essays, *Jane Austen's Beginnings*, published in 1989. Juliet McMaster, the world's leading authority on Austen's juvenilia, has now stepped forward with *Jane Austen, Young Author*, a deeply meditated exploration of a body of work that calls out for sustained attention. Books on Jane Austen often begin with a chapter on the early writings before proceeding, with an almost palpable sigh of relief, to the mature fiction. Here, in contrast, the spotlight is on the early work itself; not merely as the precursor of the six published novels that would follow but as a major achievement in its own right.

McMaster surveys Austen's writings s from several vantage points. Having illustrated many of them for editions published by the Juvenilia Press – an innovative company that she founded herself – she is ideally placed to undertake critical analyses that complement her visual interpretations of particular scenes. Some of her illustrations are reproduced here, accompanied by a fascinating discussion of her artistic goals. My favourite among her designs is that used for the cover of the Juvenilia Press "Jack and Alice" (Figure 2.10), which, as McMaster says, encapsulates the story's "burlesque extremes." Several others run it a close second, including the chorus of ploughboys bursting into song (Figure 2.18) in one of Austen's miniature plays, "The First Act of a Comedy."

McMaster's chapter on illustrating Austen's juvenilia addresses the full range of the early writings, from what is perhaps the earliest, "Frederic and Elfrida" to the epistolary novella "Lady Susan," probably written in the mid 1790s, shortly before Austen began drafting her first full-length novels. A quite different take on the juvenilia is provided by a chapter on genre. Many of Austen's early writings are told in letters, a popular fictional device for much of the eighteenth century but becoming passé by the early 1800s: "'Lady Susan' comes at the end of the epistolary tradition. McMaster considers young Austen's fascination with letter fiction, as well as her use of third-person narration from and her experiments in writing comic drama. There is also a chapter on idiolect: the characteristic speech of the astonishing number of figures populating Austen's juvenilia. McMaster has long been interested in talking and conversation in Austen's novels, both as a fictional device and as a subject in itself. Here she shows that the youthful Austen was already fascinated by the idiosyncrasies of individual speech patterns and by different forms and levels of conversation – culminating, as McMaster notes, in "Catharine," the last item in *Volume the Third,* with its heroine "in quest not only of a friend but of conversation that deserves the name."

For McMaster the prize item among Austen's juvenilia is the dazzling epistolary fiction "Love and Freindship," which forms the subject of two of her chapters. Several of Austen's early writings satirise the cult of Sensibility, but here her critique is especially acerbic. McMaster takes particular pleasure in the hyper-refinement of Sophia, one of the heroines of the story, who is so achingly in love with her imprisoned husband that she cannot bring herself to come to his aid. "Alas," she cries, "what would I not give to learn he fate of my Augustus! to know if he is still in Newgate, or if he has been hung. But never shall I be able so far to conquer my tender sensibility as to enquire after him." Not to be overlooked is McMaster's ingenious diagram, "The Genealogies of 'Love and Freindship'" (Figure 5.1), demonstrating the order behind what has hitherto seemed an impossibly complex web of family relationships. McMaster also devotes sustained attention to the relationship between "Love and Freindship" and two epistolary novels that it burlesques: Frances Brooke's *The History of Emily Montague* (1769) and the anonymous *Laura and Augustus* (1784). *Emily Montague* is set primarily in Lower Canada (present-day Quebec) in the 1760s. McMaster, a Canadian scholar, enjoys exploring the links between Austen's early fiction and what has been called the first Canadian novel.

Jane Austen, Young Author comes with a bonus: It would be cumbersome to call a book "Jane Austen, Young Author as well as the relationship between Austen's juvenilia and her mature novels," but that is what is on offer here. McMaster, one of our finest critics of Austen's novels as well as of the juvenilia, is in her element as she draws numerous, often surprising comparisons between Austen in her forties and Austen in her teens. While discussing the presence of amnesia in the juvenilia, for instance, McMaster recalls for us the complementary centrality of memory in the novels, citing Johnson's remark in *Rambler* 14 that "it is indeed the faculty of remembrance which may be said to place us in the class of moral agents." With all of Austen's oeuvre at her fingertips, McMaster excels at finding revealing juxtapositions: among them the valetudinarian Mr. Woodhouse in *Emma*, always eager to deny food and drink to others, beside the unfortunate Sir Arthur Hampton in "The Visit," repeatedly denied nourishment by his wife; and the appallingly snobbish and strident Lady Catherine de Bourgh in *Pride and Prejudice* beside the startlingly arrogant Charles Adams in "Jack and Alice."

The virtuoso concluding chapter continues to draw unexpected but impelling connections between *Pride and Prejudice* and the juvenilia. McMaster is, I believe, the first to notice that the prejudices of Elizabeth Bennet echo those of the narrator of Austen's "The History of England," said on its title-page to be written "by a partial, prejudiced and ignorant Historian." As McMaster observes, Austen will later use a very similar construction in telling us, about Elizabeth, that "of neither Darcy nor Wickham could she think, without feeling that she had been blind, partial, prejudiced, absurd." At the outset of *Jane Austen, Young Author*, McMaster remarks that "we can recognize in the canonical adult work the impress of the less polished but always suggestive early work." By the time we reach the conclusion, the validity of this acute observation has been made abundantly clear.

Peter Sabor
McGill University

Preface

"All great painters, of whatever school," wrote Ruskin, "have been great only in their rendering of what they had seen and felt from early childhood."[1] The same might be claimed for all artists, including writers, for early impressions press deeply on the consciousness, feed the imagination, and form a lasting basis for creativity. Childhood writings are a child's best articulation of the self, and most authentic expression of subjectivity.

The childhood writings of those who become famous authors as adults often hold in perceptible form the seeds of genius, and we can recognise in a canonical adult work the impress of the less polished but always suggestive early work. "Tropes and incidents observable in early work recur insistently in the later work of the same author," writes Christine Alexander, editor of Charlotte Brontë's voluminous juvenilia. So Louisa May Alcott imported chunks from her family's "Pickwick Portfolio" into *Little Women*, and makes an episode out of her teenage play *Norna or the Witch's Curse*; so Charles Dodgson, or Lewis Carroll, drew on his early playful work for his siblings as "the source and model of his later work"; and John Ruskin, late in life, built pieces of his early writings into his autobiography, *Praeterita*, since for him they were an indispensable part of the story of his life (Alexander, *Child Writer* 73, 22).

In Jane Austen's juvenilia we see the same processes at work. Here is a child, then adolescent, committed to literary culture, and committed to making her own contributions to it; and these works, indeed, provide sure intimations of the immortality that was to follow.

As the founder and first General Editor of the Juvenilia Press, I have made juvenilia my critical concern for a number of years. Childhood writings can arguably tell us more about the state of childhood than many a child psychologist or cognitive expert. And in the case of a great author, the early writings are surely worth studying, even if only as a means of learning, as it were, where that brilliant writer came from.

I argue that if you don't know Jane Austen's juvenilia, you can't claim to know Jane Austen. And these early works deserve reading not just for developmental interest: Austen's writings in *Volumes the First*, *Second*, and *Third* are brilliant in their own right, as I intend to demonstrate. These are not merely signposts pointing the way to a destination; they are destinations in themselves, instinct with creative energy and inventiveness. Here is a cornucopia of sharply defined characters, vivid and unbridled action, over-the-top absurdity, crackling and wittily apt dialogue, and all delivered in what we can already recognise as "the best chosen language" (*NA* 38).

---

1 *Modern Painters* I, 229. See also Rob Breton's "Introduction" to *From Seven to Seventeen: Poems by John Ruskin*, ed. Rob Breton and others.

Austen wrote the extant juvenilia, as her editors B.C. Southam and Peter Sabor have shown, between 1787 and 1793, at ages 11 to 17. Each was dedicated to a family member or friend, and presumably came in its own individual handmade volume produced at the time of writing. But these first fine careless raptures being dispersed and lost, our source is the three manuscript volumes, *Volume the First* (now in the Bodleian Library in Oxford), *Volume the Second*, and *Volume the Third* (both in the British Library's manuscript collection). Here the young Austen transcribed her fair copies, in a clear legible hand, often some years after the original composition. In this we can already glimpse the young professional at work. She knew the value of her early productions, and wanted them preserved. But for many years the Austen family kept them under wraps, reluctant it seems to expose these juvenile *jeux d'esprit* – with their irreverent burlesques and rowdy shenanigans – to a Victorian readership that was inclined to canonise "their 'dear,' our dear, everybody's dear, Jane" (in Henry James's phrase). But Austen's fans were eager for ever more Austen, and bit by bit, over several decades, the juvenilia were released to the public, always preserved in the somewhat rough-and-ready way in which she wrote them, spelling errors and all.

In 1987 J. David Grey (one of the founders of the Jane Austen Society of North America, or JASNA) ran a whole conference on the juvenilia, which eventuated in a collection he edited, *Jane Austen's Beginnings*. Fortunately Austen's juvenilia are now published in many editions, including Peter Sabor's Cambridge edition (which I use here), and those of R.W. Chapman, Margaret Anne Doody and Douglas Murray, and Christine Alexander, as well as the editions of individual pieces by the Juvenilia Press. In 2013 a handsome boxed set of *Volumes the First*, *Second*, and *Third* was issued by Abbeville Press, produced in full facsimile of the original manuscripts, and complete with transcripts and excellent introductions to each volume by Kathryn Sutherland; we can check Austen's childhood manuscripts without heading for the Bodleian or the British Library.

It is comforting to reflect that by now "The beautiful Cassandra and The History of England" and the rest have indeed "obtained a place in every library in the Kingdom," as young Austen claimed in the dedication to "Catharine"; and if they haven't yet "run through threescore editions," they have at least made a respectable beginning (*J* 241).

Following naturally on editions come critical studies. And the juvenilia are at last attracting some of the same searching and attentive study and commentary that the novels have long enjoyed. "The tide has turned," writes Christine Alexander in the introduction to her Penguin edition, "and readers and scholars cannot get enough of [Austen's] early writings" (xxxix). As yet, however, there has been no book-length study by a single hand. So that is where I come in, with this book.

I have been an admirer of Austen's novels since my schooldays. But my interest in her early writings arose from a curiosity as to where this wonderful author came from. Since the publication of her juvenilia lagged so far behind that of her novels, it took me a while to discover them. But once I did I was hooked; and I encouraged my students to explore them too. By the time of Jack Grey's conference on "The Juvenilia and 'Lady Susan'" I realized that this was a body of writing I wanted to study and write about, and moreover to illustrate; for the juvenilia provide much visual information about bodies, and rambunctious action, and crowded settings. And I have come to know many of the items intimately through editing them for the Juvenilia Press. Here I bring together some adapted versions of my published pieces on the juvenilia with others written specifically for this book-length study, the first of its kind.

The first chapter, "Energy *versus* Sympathy," characterises Austen's juvenilia as being distinct from her novels, though in many respects showing the way to them. The finely responsible moral awareness that informs the novels doesn't pertain in these rowdy short fictions with their greedy self-interested personnel – although of course "morality" is always there as an entity to bounce off. These characters do not recognise responsibility to others. Instead they are galvanised by an energy that drives them to the headlong pursuit of what they want – whether it is a rich husband, material goods, admiration of beauty, or the applause of the world for undeviating "sensibility." We get brief intimations of a more demanding ethic, of care for others, and earned self-approval, in the late unfinished fiction "Catharine, or the Bower," which is almost an achieved Austen novel (though a fragment) of the kind we have come to recognise. But until then the typical figures of the juvenilia, greedy and grabbing and self-interested, claim most of our attention, with their anarchic energy and magnificent independence of scruple.

In the second chapter I take licence to write about my projects in illustrating some of Austen's juvenilia, which began with my turning her short lively piece, "The Beautifull Cassandra," into a picture book for children, with characters turned into small animals à la Beatrix Potter. So Cassandra herself is a mouse, enchanted by a stunning bonnet made by her mouse-milliner mother; and the figures she encounters in her day's adventures include a lounge lizard, a pastry-cook guinea-pig, a frog hackney coachman whose draught animal is a tortoise, and so on. I proceeded to illustrate several other pieces of the juvenilia, including "Jack and Alice," "Lesley Castle," and "The Three Sisters," as volumes for my brainchild, the Juvenilia Press. Illustration is an act of interpretation, as literary criticism is, and in discussing my choices in illustrating Austen's juvenilia, I hope to engage my readers in similar exercises in visualisation.

Henry James famously characterised Jane Austen as an unconscious writer, a "wool-gathering" spinster who happens almost by mistake to achieve greatness. My study of Austen's early writings reveals, for me at least, that right from the beginning she was a highly conscious writer, a budding young professional whose early works, despite their often chaotic playfulness, demonstrate a close attention to different techniques and different genres, as she tests the possibilities of epistolary fictions, drama, and the third-person narration that was to be her chosen mode in her mature work.

Following from a series of essays I wrote on dialogue in Austen's novels, I wanted to explore the dialogue in the juvenilia too, sometimes including the letters (which like speech come in the characters' own words). Here again close study, such as I provide in my fourth chapter, reveals that young Austen's mastery of dialogue was already well developed. As in the novels, the speech in the juvenilia is already closely related to character, and figures like Lady Williams of "Jack and Alice," Charlotte Lutterell of "Lesley Castle," and Camilla Stanley of "Catharine, or the Bower" all have their recognizable idiolects. Moreover, Austen has already learned the uses of a change of register for comic purposes – for instance in the bump-down from the high-flown rhetoric of Edward in "Love and Freindship" to the down-to-earth practical locutions of his sister.

The first four chapters of my study, then, engage the range of the many different pieces of juvenilia, including the epistolary "Lady Susan." In Chapter 5 I move to detailed study of a single work – "Love and Freindship," which is perhaps the best known piece of Austen's early writings. My focus is on teaching this masterful burlesque, and so I suggest various classroom strategies, for various pedagogic contexts. I certainly believe Jane Austen's juvenilia do belong in the classroom, and can even bear study in contexts quite separate from Austen and the novel, such as courses in rhetoric, or romanticism, or women's studies. And here I take occasion to touch on an exercise I have practised with many students in my time – editing; for I have edited (as well as illustrated) a number of these lively works with students, both graduate and undergraduate, for the Juvenilia Press, and it is an exercise that acquaints us deeply with Austen's artistry in these brief but animated texts.

Following on the chapter on teaching "Love and Freindship" I proceed to an exploration of its relation to the novels it principally burlesques, the anonymous *Laura and Augustus* of 1784, and Frances Brooke's *The History of Emily Montague* of 1769 – both epistolary, both offering extremes that an alert young satirist can pounce on for parody. Here, writing with "one eye on the model and the other on the reader," as Rachel Brownstein writes, Austen can develop a kind of complicity with the reader that is based on shared reading experiences (128).

Then, by way of connecting the juvenilia with the classic novels of Jane Austen's maturity, I investigate *Pride and Prejudice* in light of what it inherits from the works of Austen's teenage years – especially "The Three Sisters," which features sisters in want of husbands and a Collins-like suitor who is ready to marry any one of them; "A Collection of Letters," where we find a very recognizable early version of Lady Catherine de Bourgh; and "The History of England," which like *Pride and Prejudice* is a vivid dramatisation of the operation of prejudice.

Austen's brilliant early writings deserve study for many reasons: as a corrective to the wide-spread perception that Austen was always proper and decorous, and wrote about nothing more exciting or surprising than tea-parties and country balls; as our best source of information on Austen's childhood subjectivity and creativity; as an index to her literary and cultural inheritance; and as a place where we can watch a brilliant teenager on her way to becoming a great author. But the best reason is that these rowdy and irreverent narratives are brilliant, funny, artful, and delightful in themselves.

Juliet McMaster
University of Alberta

Acknowledgements

My first and heartfelt thanks go to Peter Sabor of McGill University, editor of the *Juvenilia* volume in the Cambridge University Press Edition of the Works of Jane Austen. He it was who first suggested that I should collect a number of essays and informal pieces I had written on Austen's wonderful early writings and adapt them in the form of a book. He also kindly volunteered to write a Foreword – and without my twisting his arm! – and has given me invaluable help along the way.

Other inspiration has come from generations of students at the University of Alberta who have worked with me, not only in studying Jane Austen at large, but also in editing a number of individual items of her juvenilia as books for the Juvenilia Press – a process that acquaints one deeply with this most delightful and creative of young authors. Some I name when I reference their work; others, who have worked with me on other young authors, include Lesley Peterson (now herself a recognized doyenne of juvenilia studies), Leslie Robertson, Charn Jagpal, Amy Stafford, Kaarina Mikalson, and Ryan McDougall. It has been an education to work with them all.

To Christine Alexander of the University of New South Wales, my friend and co-editor in the collection *The Child Writer from Austen to Woolf*, who took over the Juvenilia Press on my retirement from teaching, I express my gratitude by dedicating this book to her. Besides being a distinguished scholar, especially in her magnificent edition of the extensive early writings of Charlotte Brontë, she is also the editor of the Penguin edition of Jane Austen's juvenilia.

I also hail and thank the many members of the Jane Austen Society of North America, or JASNA, a large and august body of which I am proud to be a founding member. They are the best audience I know, and I hope they will be readers of this book!

In this and in all my literary work I have had the inestimable benefit of support and encouragement from my family – my dear late husband Rowland, as well as my beloved children Rawdon and Lindsey and step-children Geoffrey and Loren, and their spouses and children. Through the years I have rejoiced in being a highly "partial and prejudiced" reader and encourager of *their* juvenilia too. They have inspired me in my lasting critical attention to childhood writings, this fascinating but usually neglected body of literature.

Susan Allen Ford, the editor of the Jane Austen journals *Persuasions* and *Persuasions-on-Line*, has kindly given me blanket permission to use parts or adaptations of some essays I first published there: "'The Beautifull Cassandra' Illustrated" (10, 1988), "Illustrating Jane's Juvenilia" (20, 2004); and "Your Sincere Friend, the Author" (*Persuasions-on-Line*, 2005). Likewise Joanna Penglase, the editor of Australia's Jane Austen journal, *Sensibilities*, allows me to draw on a number of short pieces on illustrating individual Austen works: *Lesley Castle* (17,

1998), *Jack and Alice* (24, 2001), *Frederic and Elfrida* (26, 2003), and *Three Mini-Dramas* (34, 2007). I am grateful to both editors. I also thank Jacqueline Langille for permission to adapt and reuse my brief article in *Eighteenth-Century Fiction*, "Jane Austen in the New World: From *Emily Montague* to 'Amelia Webster' and 'Love and Freindship'" (1:3, 1999).

For permissions to use parts of other essays published previously, I provide footnotes at the appropriate places.

List of Abbreviations

For reference to Jane Austen's works I use the Cambridge Edition of *The Works of Jane Austen*, as below.

E	*Emma*, edited by Richard Cronin and Dorothy McMillan, 2005
EM	*The History of Emily Montague*, by Frances Brooke (1769), A Critical Edition, edited by Laura Moss. Ottawa: The Tecumseh Press, 2001
J	*Juvenilia*, edited by Peter Sabor, 2006
L&A	*Laura and Augustus: An Authentic Story in a Series of Letters*, attributed to Eliza Nugent Bromley. London, 1784
"L&F"	"Love and Freindship"
Letters	*Jane Austen's Letters*, edited by Deirdre Le Faye, Oxford: Oxford University Press, 1995
LM	*Later Manuscripts*, edited by Janet Todd and Linda Bree, 2008
MP	*Mansfield Park*, edited by John Wiltshire, 2005
NA	*Northanger Abbey*, edited by Barbara M. Benedict and Deirdre Le Faye, 2006
P	*Persuasion*, edited by Janet Todd and Amtje Blank, 2006
PP	*Pride and Prejudice*, edited by Pat Rogers, 2006
SS	*Sense and Sensibility*, edited by Edward Copeland, 2006

Chapter 1
Energy Versus Sympathy[1]

Take "Jack and Alice," which Jane Austen wrote when she was about 13. It has three heroines, one with a red face who is "addicted to the Bottle and the Dice," one a virtuous widow "with a handsome Jointure and the remains of a handsome face"; and the third a "lovely young Woman" whom we first encounter lying under a citron tree with a leg broken by a man-trap. The eponymous hero, Jack, barely appears. The other hero is "of so dazzling a Beauty that none but Eagles could look him in the Face." The villainess is "short, fat and disagreeable" (*J* 14, 17).[2] The action includes the breaking and setting of a leg; a masquerade, from which the guests are all "carried home, Dead Drunk" (15); proposals of marriage by a woman; threats and attempts by one lady to cut the throat of another; and a poisoning. Finally the villainess is "exalted in a manner she truly deserved ... Her barbarous Murder was discovered and ... she was speedily raised to the Gallows" (29). Does this sound like the Jane Austen we know? Hardly.

"What Became of Jane Austen?" is the title of Kingsley Amis's 1957 essay on *Mansfield Park*. He was staggered that Austen, with her mastery of irony, should have settled even temporarily for what he sees as the dreary moralism of Fanny Price and Edmund Bertram. But the difference between *Mansfield Park* and *Pride and Prejudice*, startling though it is (even for readers who have learned to admire Fanny), is as nothing to the difference between Austen's juvenilia and the novels of her maturity.

One tradition of critical response, originating in the Austen family, has remained faintly embarrassed by the juvenilia, even to the point of considering they should not be published (J.E. Austen-Leigh 46; J. Austen-Leigh 178). Most readers of Austen discover them late in the day, and are either surprised and delighted or mildly shocked, but the "real Austen" for them will remain the six novels. "What Became of Jane Austen?" for them, was that she grew up and became a great novelist, in that order. But for a few eccentrics, or choice souls (depending on one's point of view), the answer to the "What became of?" question is less positive: she grew up and was tamed. They measure the loss as well as the gains. The Wordsworth of "Tintern Abbey" looks back on the "aching joys" and "dizzy raptures" of his youth, and tries to convince himself, "other gifts / Have followed; for such loss, I would believe, / Abundant recompense." He does not

[1] A version of this essay was first published as "The Juvenilia: Energy *Versus* Sympathy" in *A Companion to Jane Austen Studies*, ed. Laura Cooper Lambdin and Robert James Lambdin. I am grateful for permission to reprint the essay here.

[2] For reference I use Peter Sabor's edition of *Juvenilia* in the Cambridge Edition of *The Works of Jane Austen*, which I reference as *J*, with the page number.

quite succeed, because he continues to be haunted by that sense that "there hath passed away a glory from the earth" (153).

And so with my reading of Jane Austen. The six novels are indeed "abundant recompense" for the exuberance and dizzy raptures of the juvenilia. And it would be mere perversity to "mourn or murmur" at the passing of Jane's juvenility. Nevertheless, the opposite extreme is perversity too. It is worth lingering, after all, over "the hour / Of splendour in the grass, of glory in the flower." Lingering, and exploring – for if the differences are amazing between the juvenilia and the six novels, so are the similarities. I shall be pondering both the discontinuities and the continuities: the juvenilia as their own separate place of dizzy raptures and the juvenilia as offering intimations of the immortality that is to come.

The Jane Austen who has hit the jackpot of critical success is the novelist of restraint. "First and foremost," wrote G.H. Lewes, in 1852, pulling out all the rhetorical stops, "let Jane Austen be named, the greatest novelist that has ever written, using the term to signify the mast perfect mastery over means to her end" (Southam, *Critical Heritage* 140). The qualification about mastery of "means to her end" strikes the keynote of much of the praise that was to come, the claims that she was (surprisingly) great but exact, whereas other great writers, such as Shakespeare, have always been allowed to be great and chaotic. It used to be held one of Austen's great strengths that she knew her limitations: that she never presented a scene between men in which no women were present (because, after all, she was a woman), and that she never followed her couples into the bedroom (because, after all, she was a spinster). It is rather like praising an athlete for how fast she can run in a hobble skirt. Austen *is* brilliant for all she can do despite her limitations. But it is wonderfully liberating to take a look at what she could do before she knuckled under and took to that hobble skirt. Her juvenilia are not elegant and certainly not restrained. But they do show that athlete's extraordinary energy and agility.

"Keats's amazed delight on first looking into Chapman's *Homer* was nothing compared to mine on first looking into Dr. Chapman's edition of the *Minor Works*," records the novelist Reginald Hill of his younger self (79). To a teenage boy who had been thoroughly put off Austen by a compulsory reading of *Mansfield Park*, the juvenilia were a godsend, an awakening to the *proper* way into Jane Austen's work.

What we find in the juvenilia is not an aesthetic of exactness and restraint, but an aesthetic of exuberance, of excess. Here we have no painstaking search for the single *mot juste*, but a gargantuan delight in plethora. Rich Mr. Clifford, we hear, keeps not just a coach and four but "a great many Carriages of which I do not recollect half. I can only remember that he had a Coach, a Chariot, a Chaise, a Landeau, a Landeaulet, a Phaeton, a Gig, a Whisky, an italian Chair, a Buggy, a Curricle and a wheelbarrow" (51). The "beautifull Cassandra," on a single visit to a pastry-cook's, "devoured six ices, refused to pay for them, knocked down the Pastry Cook and walked away" – a lot of action and consumption for a single sentence (54). Charlotte Lutterell of "Lesley Castle," who is also keen on food, goes to her lodgings in Bristol well supplied: "We brought a cold Pigeon-pye, a cold turkey, a cold tongue, and half a dozen Jellies with us, which we were lucky enough with the help of our Landlady, her husband, and their three children, to get rid of, in less than two days after our arrival" (153). Why use one word when a dozen will do as well? Why restrict yourself to a single long-lost relative when, as in "Love and Freindship," with a flourish of the pen you can be so much more generous? "Another Grand-child!" exclaims Lord St. Clair, with theatrically uplifted hands. "What an unexpected Happiness is this! to discover in the space of 3 minutes, as many of my Descendants!" (121); and presently a fourth reveals himself. Charlotte Brontë famously denounced Austen for her paucity of passion and lamented the absence of the "bonny beck" and "bright, vivid physiognomy" in her novels.[3] And indeed the Austen of the novels is notably sparing in details of personal appearance as of landscape. Not so the Austen of the juvenilia. Elfrida and her companions cheerfully discourse on the "forbidding Squint, ... greazy tresses and swelling back" of the otherwise elegant Rebecca (6).

Such boisterous overstatement is not just over the top, but down the other side too. And while hyperbole is the familiar tool of the satirist, this aesthetic of excess has more than a satiric intent. It is Rabelaisian, carnivalesque, born of a youthful jouissance that is one of the clouds of glory that the mature author has had to leave behind. Far from working with a fine brush on a little piece of ivory two inches wide (as the older Austen described her composition process), this young artist wields a broad and laden brush, sloshing her effects over an area as broad as Tom Sawyer's fence, producing much effect after little labour.

Consider one aspect of the notable discontinuities between the juvenile work and the mature work: motion. Stuart Tave memorably characterises the mature Austen as a dancer who can move "with significant grace in good time in a restricted space" (Tave 1). He shows how the characters who take liberties with time and space (like John Thorpe, who boasts that his horse *cannot* go slower than 10 miles an hour in harness, or Mary Crawford, who also stretches distance and duration), are morally tainted. Approved characters observe a strict decorum in these matters. Similarly, the principle that "3 or 4 Families in a Country Village is the very thing to work on" in a novel (*Letters* 275) implies a commitment to the unity of place that is very different from the wildly unstructured peregrinations that are characteristic of the juvenilia. The young Austen, like Catherine Morland before she was "in training for a heroine," seems to have delighted in the dizzying motion of "rolling down the green slope at the back of the house" (*NA* 7, 7).

Free and vigorous motion, in fact, is one of the recurring characteristics of these rollicking narratives. The heroine of "The Beautifull Cassandra" takes a hackney coach to Hampstead, "where she was no sooner arrived than she ordered the Coachman to turn round and drive her back again" (55). Such motion is not

3 See Brontë's letter to G.H. Lewes of 12 January 1848 in Southam, *Critical Heritage* 126.

purposeful and efficient, but gratuitous, undertaken for its own sake, and so simply pleasurable. She is like the grand old duke of York in the nursery rhyme, who

> had ten thousand men;
> He marched them up to the top of the hill,
> And he marched them down again. (Opie 442)

The irrational and repetitive motion in both cases has its nonsensical appeal for the child. In "A Tour through Wales" the narrator explains,

> My mother rode upon our little pony and Fanny and I walked by her side or rather ran, for my Mother is so fond of riding fast that She galloped all the way … . Fanny has taken a great Many Drawings of the Country, which are very beautiful, tho' perhaps not such exact resemblances as might be wished, from their being taken as she ran along. (*J* 224)

When the girls wear out their shoes,

> Mama was so kind as to lend us a pair of blue Sattin Slippers, of which we each took one and hopped home from Hereford delightfully. (224)

(I suspect that this passage inspired the slipper-strewn cover design of Christine Alexander's Penguin edition of the juvenilia.) Fanny's drawings, though not "exact resemblances," might stand as emblems for the juvenilia: the vigorous young artist has priorities more lively than mere realism.

The hero of "Love and Freindship" sets out from Bedfordshire for Middlesex – both counties in the southeast of England – but though he prides himself on being "a tolerable proficient in Geography" he finds himself in Wales, in the Vale of Uske (108). The heroines rattle about all over the country, and the memorable last scene takes place in a stagecoach that shuttles to and fro between Edinburgh and Stirling. These indeed are "dizzy raptures," to appropriate Wordsworth's phrase for his youth: rhythmic and repetitive motion vigorously indulged in for its own sake. It is the sort of high, like the rides in a fairground, for which the adult loses stomach.

There are gender implications to this wild, unrestricted motion. The value for stability and stasis that characterises the six novels makes them very much a woman's world. Woman has traditionally been the "fixed foot" (Donne's phrase), while the man is that part of the compasses that wanders forth and circles round. A recurring trope in Austen's novels shows the heroine posted at a window, engaged in identifying the mounted male who rides toward her from a distance, as Marianne watches and waits for Willoughby, Elinor for Edward, Elizabeth for Darcy, Charlotte Heywood for Sidney Parker (*SS* 99, 405; *PP* 369; *MP* 493, *LM* 206). Not so in the juvenilia. Waiting and watching are not congenial activities for the hyperactive personnel there, female or male. They know no boundaries.

The young Jane Austen was still relatively free of a gendered identity, and she presents characters who are similarly unsocialized. In fact, one of her most gleeful recurring jokes is gender reversal.

In "Henry and Eliza," which she probably wrote at age 13 (Sabor xxviii), she presents a heroine who is a foundling, like Tom Jones, and chronicles the sowing of her wild oats with a Fieldingesque indulgence. Eliza is an adventuress who purloins banknotes, snaps up other girls' fiancés, absconds to France, and survives motherhood and widowhood. Thrown into prison with her two little boys, she escapes down a rope ladder as resourcefully as any Jack Sheppard. And she is never made to repent of her cheerfully self-indulgent behaviour. Among the assumptions built in to the juvenilia is that girls can be as naughty as boys – in fact, are *meant* to be as naughty as boys – and that a good adventure is more fun than a morally pointed tale any day. In the denouement of this tale, after she has been reunited with her cheerfully forgiving parents, Eliza raises an army, demolishes her enemy's stronghold and "gained the Blessings of thousands, and the Applause of her own Heart" (45). No long-suffering forgiveness of enemies for *this* heroine! And rather than being haunted by the sentimental heroine's sense of unworthiness, Eliza, "happy in the conscious knowledge of her own Excellence," takes the time to compose songs in her own praise (34). As Karen Hartnick points out, "Eliza lives out the traditional male adventure – she leaves her family, travels, faces danger, demonstrates cunning and bravery, and defeats her enemies in armed battle" (xiii). The dangerous adversary of the piece is also a woman, the implacable "Dutchess," who maintains a private army and keeps a personal Newgate "for the reception of her own private Prisoners" (42). There is not much left for the men to do except be snapped up and fought over by the martial ladies.

The Jack of "Jack and Alice" is disposed of in a single paragraph, while the ladies commandeer the stage. And here there is further cheerful reversal of gender roles, this time in the courtship situation. The women of Austen's generation had inherited the courtship codes laid down by Richardson and the conduct books, according to which the woman's role in courtship is meant to be not just passive but almost unconscious: she is not to be aware of her own sexuality until the male awakens it by his proposal. In her novels, Austen continues to challenge this ruling (McMaster, *Novelist* 177), but in her juvenilia, especially "Jack and Alice," she has more fun completely reversing it. Charles Adams, the man all the women lust after, is the feminized male – "amiable, accomplished and bewitching" – while it is the heroine who is "addicted to the Bottle and the Dice" (14). Like Richardson's Pamela, though with much less finesse, he finds himself bound in honesty to admit to his own unimpeachable virtue: "I imagine my Manners and Address to be of the most polished kind; there is a certain elegance a peculiar sweetness in them that I never saw equalled and cannot describe" (28). In his behaviour, no less than in his beauty and virtue, he smacks of the heroine. Pursued by love-hungry ladies, he retires to his country estate. This playing hard to get, of course, is very stimulating for the enterprising young women who come a-courting. Lucy, the most persistent of them, will not take no for an answer. Taking over the conventional phraseology of male discourse, she writes to him that she will "shortly do myself the honour of waiting on him" (24). Like Mr. Collins she attributes his "angry and peremptory refusal" of her proposal to "the effect of his modesty" (24). When he will not answer her letters, like Mr. Elton in the carriage with Emma she "choos[es] to take, Silence for Consent" (24). She does not give up until she is caught, appropriately enough, in a man-trap – "one of the steel traps so common in gentlemen's grounds" (24). Almost in chorus, like a trio of courtly lovers, the women moan iambically, "Oh! cruel Charles to wound the hearts and legs of all the fair" (24).

The female suitors who surround the lovely Charles Adams are quite frank about being attracted by his physical charms rather than by the virtues that *he* considers are his best claim to being loved. In the novels it is usually the male who is expected to succumb irrationally to beauty, as Mr. Bennet did. But here Lucy admits, "I could not resist his attractions." And Alice sighs, "Ah! who can" (23).

The same bold reversal of conventional gender attitudes appears in "A Collection of Letters," where a young girl has no scruple in arguing, "It is no disgrace to love a handsome Man. If he were plain indeed I might have had reason to be ashamed of a passion which must have been mean since the Object would have been unworthy" (209). The long and agonized debates among women in *Clarissa* and *Sir Charles Grandison* on the extent to which "person" in a man may legitimately influence a woman's response are cheerfully set at naught in *this* epistolary collection. These females are frankly in pursuit of good male bodies and, by implication, good sex. The long tendency of sentimental fiction to etherealize the heroine can hardly survive against this gust of earthy comedy.

"The Beautifull Cassandra," probably written when Jane Austen was 12 years old (McMaster, *Beautifull Cassandra*), is again interesting for the heroine's bold appropriation of the male adventure and for its switch of gender roles in the parents' generation. Cassandra's mother, the "celebrated Millener in Bond Street," is apparently the breadwinner of the family, but when Cassandra returns from her day of conspicuous consumption and unashamed self-indulgence, it is to her "paternal roof" (54, 56). The devoted mother is the effectual head of the family, but the male, absorbed with his "noble birth," takes the credit. It is an early version, I like to think, of Anne Elliot's family in *Persuasion*.

In her love life Cassandra is boldly experimental. The narrative offers the highly eligible Viscount, who is "no less celebrated for his Accomplishments and Virtues, than for his Elegance and Beauty" (another feminized male). But Cassandra falls in love with "an elegant Bonnet" instead, a female accessory created by her mother, and cheerfully elopes with it. The bonnet, however elegant and desirable, is no permanent commitment, but only one prominent item that contributes to the protagonist's picaresque journey of self-fulfilment. It is mated, used, and discarded, rather like the women in James Bond's path.

In her narrative voice, too, young Austen often takes over traditionally male territory. The great parodists – Fielding, Sterne, Thackeray, Thurber – have usually been male; but she like them initially found her voice in parodic imitation. In "The History of England," useful in being third-person and apparently omniscient narration, she takes off Goldsmith's somewhat pompous tone of authority and turns it into whimsical Shandyism, as in telling her readers that if we don't already know all about the Wars of the Roses, "you had better read some other History, for

I shall not be very diffuse in this" (178). But I shall have more to say on this aspect of her work in later chapters.

Laughter and the comic mode have all too often been alienated to the masculine, while sentiment has been allowed to be the province of the ladies. Anna Letitia Barbauld, in her historic 50-volume *The British Novelists* of 1810, notes that women specialise in the sentimental novel of distress; it is male authors who write the satire and humour. Thackeray, also writing of the Regency, similarly alienates laughter to the men, in the famous curry episode in *Vanity Fair*. Becky Sharp, who is trying to catch the rich Jos Sedley from India, declares "I must have some [curry], if it is an Indian dish." She puts a brave face on it, though "suffering agonies with the cayenne pepper." And when she takes a chilli, "thinking it was something cool, as its name imported," flesh and blood can bear it no longer, and she gasps for water. Her ploy of delighting in all things Indian has collapsed, and the men delight in the joke: "Mr. Sedley burst out laughing … . The paternal laugh was echoed by Joseph, [who] thought the joke capital." On the other hand, "the ladies only smiled a little. They thought poor Rebecca suffered too much" *(Vanity Fair*, chapter 3). (Becky herself gamely turns a joke. She would have much more in common with Austen.)

This is a division of cultural labour that young Austen refuses to accept. "Why is it that women when they write are apt to give a melancholy tinge to their compositions?" Barbauld wondered. "Is it that they suffer more, and have fewer resources against melancholy? … Is it that humour is a scarcer product of the mind than sentiment, and more congenial to the stronger powers of man?" (Barbauld 44). "No way!" one can imagine young Austen responding; and older Austen, too, come to that (Grundy 15), though it is the young writer who most vigorously claims humour for her own. "The liveliest effusions of wit and humour" are among the characteristics of the novel (as most notably practised by women) that Austen lists in *Northanger Abbey* (31). Not for her the "novel of distress" ghetto. Distress and delicate sensibility are among the earliest targets of her parody. In *Volume the First* appears "A beautiful description of the different effects of Sensibility on different Minds," in which everyone is grouped around the bedside of the interestingly ailing Melissa:

> Sir William is constantly at her bedside. The only repose he takes is on the Sopha in the Drawing room, where for five minutes every fortnight he remains in an imperfect Slumber, starting up every Moment and exclaiming "Oh! Melissa, Ah! Melissa," then sinking down again, raises his left arm and scratches his head. (92)

Distress is made matter for laughter.

In this, besides reversing the expectations of a near contemporary like Mrs. Barbauld, Austen differs from a number of other youthful writers. The adolescent writer, particularly the girl, is typically intensely serious. She usually writes romance rather than burlesque and humour. Fourteen-year-old George Eliot in "Edward Neville" writes serious imitation of the historical romances of Scott and

G.P.R. James, with a rebellious swashbuckling hero who employs high rhetoric ("We … would have defended him to the last drop of our blood" [Eliot 7]). Louisa May Alcott at 15 wrote a serious heroic melodrama, *Norna, or the Witch's Curse*, which she herself sent up mercilessly in *Little Women* years later, when as an adult she was ready to laugh at her own youthful earnestness. Charlotte Brontë's Angrian sagas, though they contain humour, are mainly serious romance. Where childhood writings are funny, the humour is usually unintentional, as in Daisy Ashford's classic *The Young Visiters*. By her own avowal, Ashford gave up writing when she found her brothers laughed at her work (xxii).

From the first, however, Austen courted laughter. Instead of imitating the serious history and distressed fictions she read, she made burlesques of them. It is no surprise that, as Reginald Hill attests, the juvenilia appeal to boys. One of two girls in a family largely of boys, young Jane was evidently something of a tomboy, with an ability to cater to boys' tastes (Tomalin 29) – or, indeed, to the tastes of people of either sex who do not like to be restrained. She writes rowdy fiction, with plenty of violence, movement, irreverence, and bad behaviour. She eschews the goody-goody and the snivelling. And the young women in her fiction can be as forgivably bad as the young men, the young men as namby-pamby as the boy's version of a girl. She seems to have been like Jo March of *Little Women*: quite at home with girls and girls' doings, yet liking also boys' pursuits and boys' language and the freedom of movement and thought that their cultures assigned to the privileged sex. When Jo March's father returns at the end of the first part of *Little Women*, though, he notes with satisfaction, "I don't see the 'son Jo' whom I left a year ago … I see a young lady who pins her collar straight, laces her boots neatly, and neither whistles; talks slang, nor lies on the rug, as she used to do" (Alcott 223). Generations of Alcott's readers have felt a sense of loss as the free spirit they admire inevitably knuckles under to the demands of becoming a young lady. Readers who have admired the boisterous overstatement in Austen's juvenilia, as well as the cheerful experiments and reversals that make gender so unstable a category in her early works, may also feel some regret as she moves into responsible young-ladyhood. In the mature novels, it is the unapproved teenager Lydia Bennet who enjoys the cross-dressing joke: "We dressed up Chamberlayne in women's clothes, on purpose to pass for a lady, – only think what fun! … we were forced to borrow one of [my aunt's] gowns; and you cannot imagine how well he looked! … Lord, how I laughed!" (*PP* 245). But Elizabeth and Jane, now fully socialised and proper young ladies, are faintly disapproving. Have the "glad animal movements" all gone by?

But – and Wordsworth again comes in handy – "O joy! that in her embers / Is something that doth live!" (212). Though in doing justice to the juvenilia one inevitably regrets, to some extent, the taming of the free spirit, the dwindling into an adult, to examine the adult work is to recognise that there is still plenty left of the brilliant, unfettered child writer. As the juvenilia are already pregnant (to use a highly inappropriate metaphor) with the promise of the novels to come; so the novels preserve joyful traces of the gusto and irreverence of the juvenilia. Two strands coexist in the juvenilia and the novels, and though the emphasis changes, the continuity is as notable as the discontinuity. I shall call the two strands the ethic of energy and the ethic of sympathy; Jane Austen the satirist espouses the ethic of energy; Jane Austen the novelist develops the ethic of sympathy.

Take "Love and Freindship," which is in many ways the best single work of the juvenilia. Energy is surely the essential value here. Laura and Sophia, twin heroines who supply a wonderful symmetry, hold our interest for their zest and vigour and unshakeable conviction that their sentimental worldview is the correct one. Morality is memorably turned on its head as Sophia, caught "majestically removing the 5th Bank-note" from her host's supply of cash, unblushingly calls her detector the "Culprit," and accuses him of "insolently" breaking in on her retirement (125–6).

If one works hard, one *can* extract a moral pattern from "Love and Freindship," by carefully reversing Laura's and Sophia's principles. The stodgily "sensible" characters they describe, like Sir Edward and Lady Dorothea, can be made the moral norm, while Laura and Sophia, with their overdeveloped sensibility, become the negative examples. But to make such an argument, one has to become pretty stodgy oneself. What makes "Love and Freindship" enjoyable is the huge energy and conviction of the heroines. We know they are crazy – indeed, Laura is proud of her facility in "running mad" – but we take their side anyway, because they are lively and resourceful rather than because they are right. It is no wonder that Gilbert and Gubar chose "Love and Freindship" for their anthology of women's literature. Here is a pair of heroines, created by a young woman writer, who confidently snatch agency for themselves and are never ground in the mill of morality.

Mary Stanhope of "The Three Sisters" is similarly a character we can admire for the unswerving conviction of her quest for an establishment: she never once descends into the bathos of sympathy or moral approval, but keeps gabbling her list of desiderata in the marriage state. Mr. Gower of "Evelyn" is likewise memorable for his endless appetite for food, bride, money, real estate; he moves easily from snack to full dinner with scarcely a pause: "The Chocolate, The Sandwiches, the Jellies, the Cakes, the Ice and the Soup soon made their appearance, and Mr. Gower having tasted something of all, and pocketed the rest, was conducted into the dining parlour, where he eat a most excellent Dinner, and partook of the most exquisite Wines" (*J* 232–3). He is like a bottomless maw.

It is not for their scruples that we admire such rapacious characters, but for their magnificent lack of them. The satire would be biting if it were not so gleefully overdone. As it is, *satire*, with its suggestion of moral agenda, seems almost too heavy a term for the playful gratuitousness of the overstatement.

The juvenilia present many such figures, especially women who are boldly transgressive – outrageous self-seekers who nevertheless delight us by their energy and conviction. These are heroines who act as heroes, claim male privileges and run their worlds with never a moral scruple; and though it is clear we are not meant to approve of them, it is also clear that serious censure would be out of place. I find it interesting that very few punishments are meted out to these bold self-seekers: they either thrive, like Eliza and the beautiful Cassandra, or persist in their unawakened self-seeking, like Laura, or their stories are uncompleted, like those of Mary Stanhope of "The Three Sisters" and Charlotte Lutterell of "Lesley Castle." Indeed, perhaps that is one reason that many of the juvenilia are left unfinished. In the dedication to "Lesley Castle," the young author almost makes a principle of forgoing closure: "That it is unfinished, I greive; yet fear that from me, it will always remain so" (142). Young Jane does not want to turn her fictions into moral tales by visiting closure and poetic justice on her energetic transgressors. The pattern of the moral tale is at any rate resoundingly rejected. In dedicating some "Miscellaneous Morsels" to her niece Anna, "convinced that if you seriously attend to them, You will derive from them very important Instructions, with regard to your Conduct in Life" (*J* 90), the young author clearly has tongue in cheek, since Anna at the time has only just been born.

Sometimes coexisting with the ethic of energy is the ethic of sympathy. The self-seeking protagonists are occasionally juxtaposed with some character who shows some awakened sense of responsibility – for instance, Sophia's cousin Macdonald in "Love and Freindship," who reproaches Laura and Sophia, "Your Freindship for my Daughter has indeed been most powerfully exerted by throwing her into the arms of an unprincipled Fortune-hunter" (127). But such moments of moral wakefulness are rare among a population largely composed of outrageous self-seekers.

"A Collection of Letters," from *Volume the Second*, alternates between the ethic of energy and the ethic of sympathy, and sometimes it is difficult to tell which predominates. The writers of Letters the Second, Fourth and Fifth unwittingly reveal their greed, whether for gossip, food for sensibility, or admiration; while the writer of Letter the Third, "a young Lady in distress'd Circumstances," is fully sympathetic.

"A Collection of Letters" has received little critical commentary, partly no doubt because its lack of continuity leaves us short of Austen's best hold on our attention: developed character. (A. Walton Litz found it one of "the most interesting of [Austen's] juvenilia," but did not elaborate [Litz, "Juvenilia" 51]). Each letter introduces a new character and a new set of circumstances. But in many quite specific ways, it forms a milestone of distance covered, a signpost of things to come. It includes the names Willoughby, Dashwood, Crawford. It incorporates in Lady Greville a very recognizable forerunner of Lady Catherine de Bourgh. Most interesting, it is a more painstaking examination of manners and what may and may not be done in country gentry society than any previous fiction. It begins with a satirical account of coming out – a much-heralded entry into "the world" by two teenage sisters – and ends with the unscrupulous exploitation of an all-too-easily-fooled heiress by a manipulating older woman.

The writer of Letter the Second has been crossed in love: jilted by Edward Willoughby (whose name combines those of Elinor's and Marianne's men in *Sense and Sensibility*), she is very sorry for herself, but she hardly engages much of the reader's sympathy, since Willoughby is only the latest in a string of boyfriends she has loved and lost, "for all of whom," she claims, "I once felt the most lasting affection that ever warmed a Woman's heart" (194). On the principle that misery loves company – "when one is unhappy nothing is so delightful to one's sensations as to hear of equal Misery," she says (197) – she extracts from a new acquaintance, Miss Jane, a life history so harrowing that she becomes quite cheerful.

Maria, the young lady in distressed circumstances of "Letter the Third," is outrageously patronised by the arrogant Lady Greville, and our sympathy is raised by the social realism of the situation of a girl of dubious class standing in company where she is considered an inferior. "Pray Miss Maria," Lady Greville says loudly at the ball, "in what way of business was your Grandfather? for Miss Mason and I cannot agree whether he was a Grocer or a Bookbinder" (200). In "Catharine" of *Volume the Third*, where social realism is more developed still, we have a similar focus on status at a ball. "As an heiress [Kitty] was certainly of consequence, but her Birth gave her no other claim to it, for her Father had been a Merchant" (333–4). Her friend Camilla is therefore outraged that Kitty should be placed above her in the line-up of dancers: "I should not have minded it … if she had been *anybody* else's daughter; but to see her pretend to be above *me*, when her Father was only a tradesman, is too bad!" Being the victim of such snobbery is sure to raise the reader's sympathy. As Austen refines on social realism, so sympathy comes to dominate over the satire of the greedy and energetic self-seekers.

"Letter the Fifth" provides another heiress, and one who is in the process of being fed to a fortune-hunter; but since she is short of self-awareness, she has the less claim on our sympathy. This is a curiously sour presentation: Lady Scudamore, a seasoned society hostess, has a susceptible guest, Henrietta, an heiress whom she proposes to catch for her impoverished and thick-headed cousin Musgrove. It is a theme later handled by serious adult novelists. Trollope, for instance, in the *Way We Live Now* shows Lady Carbury at work in capturing the innocent heiress Marie Melmotte for her ne'er-do-well son Sir Felix. In *Portrait of a Lady* James shows how the subtle Madame Merle dresses Isabel Archer as a dish for her ex-lover Osmond. There is a sinister aspect to both stories, as innocent girls become commodities to be sacrificed to unscrupulous males. In Austen's version there is some comedy attached, since both principals in the courtship are so dense that Lady Scudamore is obliged to do most of their courtship for them. The excesses of sensibility are again a target, as the cunning manipulator invents pathetic dialogue for Musgrove, to bamboozle the gullible Henrietta:

> When I am dead said he, Let me be carried and lain at her feet, and perhaps she may not disdain to drop a pitying tear on my poor remains … . Ah! Cousin imagine what my transports will be when I feel the dear precious drops trickle o're my face! Who would not die to taste such extacy! (211–12)

The girl finds this account highly erotic, indeed irresistible. But we are left in some quandary as to whether to admire the unscrupulous manager or to sympathise with her dupe.

To juxtapose "Catharine, or the Bower," written at 16, with "Lady Susan" (probably written soon afterwards [Southam, *Literary Manuscripts* 46]) is to see the contrast in vivid form. "Lady Susan" in many ways marks the culmination of the ethic of energy, "Catharine" the triumph of the ethic of sympathy.

"Lady Susan" features a totally self-seeking female protagonist whose considerable power lies in her freedom from moral scruple. She commiserates with her bosom friend, for instance, on having a husband who is "just old enough to be formal, ungovernable & to have the Gout – too old to be agreable, & too young to die" (*LM* 62). Unlike the ice-cream-guzzling beautiful Cassandra, the ostentatiously sensitive Laura or the privilege-hungry Mary Stanhope, Lady Susan, though not moral herself, does understand morality. She is like Henry Crawford, a villain of Austen's maturity, in having "moral taste" (*MP* 274). Hence, by a show of tender sensibility and scrupulous conscience, she is able to manipulate the moral folk, rather like Lovelace, whom she also resembles in her "happy command of Language" (*LM* 11).

We are not meant to like Lady Susan, for the moral pattern that is hardly even latent in "Love and Freindship" is here quite patent; but we are allowed to admire her for her intelligence and resourcefulness. And even when her whole elaborate structure of deceit has collapsed, and she is shown up as a shameless vamp and adulteress, she is cheerfully undaunted. "This Eclaircissement is rather provoking," she admits. " … I am undismayed however" (57) One can't but admire such *sang froid* in a crisis. And there is no come-uppance for this engaging villainess: she calmly takes over the rich baronet she had picked for her daughter, and allows her daughter to marry the young man she had planned to reserve for herself. Nor does she proceed to repent and reform. In her last note to her loyal confidante, Mrs. Johnson, she wishes her well rid of her irritatingly moral husband: "May the next Gouty Attack be more favourable" (72). Jane Austen can't put a good, energetic villainess down.

"I never was more at ease, or better satisfied with myself & every thing about me, than at the present hour," she congratulates herself serenely (72). This boldly managing female protagonist, in fact, largely runs the show, except when her female adversary, Mrs. Vernon, the goody-goody, outsmarts her. As in the early fictions like "Henry and Eliza" and "The Beautifull Cassandra," the males are hardly present. Reginald, the *soi-disant* hero, is less an autonomous character than a bag of goods contested over by the women, like the obligatorily obedient feminine heroine in novels of distress.

At the end of the epistolary "Lady Susan." the narrator, "to the great detriment of the Post office Revenue," takes the wind-up of the tale into her own hands. This is a memorable sign-off: as I read it, a farewell alike to the epistolary mode that had dominated the eighteenth-century novel and many of Austen's own fictions, and to the energy-driven personnel who had dominated them. "I leave [the foolish Sir James] to all the Pity that any body can give him" (75, 78), speaks a newly empowered omniscient narrator, deploying an authoritative first-person pronoun that is both reminiscent of the "partial, prejudiced" narrator of "The

History of England" and prophetic of the urbanely ironic narrative voice at the end of *Northanger Abbey*: "I leave it to be settled by whomsoever it may concern, whether the tendency of this work be altogether to recommend parental tyranny, or reward filial disobedience" (*NA* 261).

Young Austen was already confident enough to show her hand and expose the fictionality of her fiction. Epistolary novels do often strain credibility, and her comments on post office revenues cheerfully give the game away. Moreover, she draws attention to her own fictional manipulations. As she winds up her narrative in her omniscient conclusion, she explains, "Mr. Vernon who, as it must have already appeared, lived only to do whatever he was desired, soon found some accommodating Business to call him [to London]" as the plot requires (75). And, in case we have become too enamoured of the "moral" contingent, Mrs. Vernon and her mother, we hear that the ingénue Frederica was "fixed in the family of her Uncle & Aunt, till such time as Reginald de Courcy could be talked, flattered & finessed into an affection for her" (77). Not much sympathy for the sympathy faction!

Sense and Sensibility, converted from the epistolary "Elinor and Marianne," marks a large step in a new direction, but it resembles the earlier fictions in that the male characters, Edward Ferrars and Colonel Brandon, are still very much dominated by the women. Austen was no doubt improving her art and increasing her saleability by granting fuller autonomy to her heroes as her career went on. But her heroines necessarily dwindle at the same time.

"Catharine, or the Bower," probably written a short time before "Lady Susan," is much more like the mature novels both in theme and narrative tone. Kitty, the protagonist, is subject to discipline and morally scrupulous. She does not carry all before her like the energetic self-seekers, and we are called on to sympathise with her doubts and moral gropings rather than to applaud her energy and headlong conviction. And as the female protagonist is relatively disempowered, so the principal male (at least he is the principal male so far as the unfinished narrative goes) gains in authority and self-confidence. "Why, my dear Cousin," the self-satisfied Edward Stanley addresses Kitty, as he takes her to a ball to which he is not invited, "this will be a most agreable surprize to every body to see you enter the room with such a smart Young Fellow as I am" (*J* 271–2). Convinced by his sister that Edward Stanley has fallen in love with her, the susceptible Kitty is destined to suffer many of those "female difficulties" that Frances Burney made the staple of her fiction. When Kitty discovers that his kissing of her hand was only a mockery of love to shock her puritanical aunt,

> She could not help feeling both surprised and offended … . It is true that she had not yet seen enough of him to be actually in love with him, yet she felt greatly disappointed that so handsome, so elegant, so lively a young Man should be so perfectly free from any such Sentiment as to make it his principal Sport. (289–90)

We are in the realm now of human and realistic character, of nuanced and subtle psychology, of an artistic management, by a trustworthy narrator, of a reader called on to sympathise and partially identify with the protagonist. But by the same token, we have left behind those energetic self-seeking heroines (henceforth demoted to the status of minor characters like Lucy Steele) and moved closer to the feminine novel of distress. It is not all gain.

Margaret Anne Doody has written memorably about Austen's renunciation of the bold and free-spirited mode of the juvenilia: "Jane Austen had to change, in short, from a 1790s writer to a 'Regency' writer" (72). She was tamed, she capitulated, she dwindled into the moral mode and she even settled for writing of a congenitally victimized and moralizing heroine like Fanny Price. And it is fascinating to think of the juvenilia as a different kind of writing altogether, and as pointing to a putative Jane Austen quite unlike the one who wrote the six novels.

But there are continuities as well as discontinuities, and many ways to consider the juvenilia as preparation for the novels rather than pointing elsewhere altogether. As I shall demonstrate later, Elizabeth Bennet, with her vital physical energy, her taste for "follies and nonsense" and her refusal to be browbeaten by magisterial authority, is surely a developed creation of the author of the juvenilia: she too "dearly love[s] a laugh" (*PP* 62). Even Anne Elliot, who suffers sore distress, knows very well how to be amused (Grundy 17). Although the novels show no such bold female suitors as Lucy in "Jack and Alice," still these heroines do take their necessary initiatives in courtship (McMaster, *Jane Austen* 186). And if the heroines of the novels have to cede some power and initiative to the males, they still remain among the most vivid and self-determining heroines of fiction.

Among the many characteristics that do carry over from the juvenilia to the novels is the delight in language and what it can accomplish. Austen already has a command of certain figures such as syllepsis, an incongruous yoking of the literal and figurative applications of an idiom: Charles Adams is cruel "to wound the hearts & legs of all the fair" (Burrows 72); the adulterous Louisa Lesley "left [her Husband], her child & reputation a few weeks ago in company with Danvers and dishonour" (*J*, 143). The use of the wickedly well-placed adverb is famous in the account of Charlotte Lucas's campaign to catch Collins: "[she] *instantly* set out to meet him *accidentally* in the lane" (*PP* 121); but it is already familiar in "Love and Freindship," where Laura and Sophia "*instantly* unfolded to each other the most inward Secrets of our Hearts." (*J* 114; my italics).

Already a potent weapon in her linguistic armoury is her power in dialogue. She has already developed a sure sense of register, and an ability to endow her characters with their own idiolects, an assured facility in pitting one voice against another with sharp comic effect. But these attributes I shall examine in another chapter.

The consciousness of medium, and her prestidigitation in switching from epistolary to omniscient narration to drama to history, is again the subject of another chapter. Here I draw attention to the young author's sophisticated awareness of her narrative procedures. Her characters, in the juvenilia as in the novels, comment on each others' speech habits; they novelize each other and sometimes themselves.

Quixote-like, they tend to draw on literature as a model for life. This is art that humorously draws attention to its own fictionality.

The same metafictional consciousness of medium prompts the humorous "Dedications" to the different pieces, which so elaborately mimic the literary etiquette of the author's relation to the patron. "I commend to your Charitable Criticism this Clever Collection of Curious Comments, ... by your Comical Cousin, The Author" (190), reads one. Another claims that previous works, "The Beautifull Cassandra" and "The History of England," "have obtained a place in every library in the Kingdom, and run through threescore Editions" (192). This young writer has a highly developed awareness of her status as author and a developing ambition, however veiled in humour, for professional recognition.

The dedications bring us back to the family audience. There is one work, sometimes more, for each of her brothers (except George), one for each of her parents, several scraps for her nieces, two for one cousin, Jane Cooper, one for another, Eliza de Feuillide, and three for her sister. She is conscientiously covering the ground, making sure no one feels neglected; everyone has a memorial copy. Although she grouped and copied the juvenilia together into her *Volumes the First*, *Second*, and *Third* (aspiring thus to the status of the standard three-decker novel), presumably each work was originally its own entity and presented as a gift to the person it was dedicated to – perhaps in its own small volume not unlike those of the Brontë children. Only her fair copy survives; but it is tempting to think of those original compositions set out individually, in handwriting that would have shown her age at the time. They would no doubt have conveyed even more vividly the sense of a gleeful young professional at work.

Still developing in this young author is the shaping hand, the control and restraint that make for observing the unities of time and place, and adjusting emphasis; and also the patience in developing character and sustaining the narrative to an achieved conclusion. Patience is a virtue, no doubt, and artistic control of this order is rare and precious. But neither would avail without that creative fecundity in the first place – the vigorous imagination, delight in language and its possibilities, and the zest and energy that provide the essential material for the hand to shape. Those are what the young Jane Austen already had in joyous abundance.

"Till the heroine grows up, the fun must be imperfect," the adult Jane Austen wrote to the niece who aspired to follow in her aunt's literary footsteps (*Letters* 275). But the work of the young Jane Austen convinces us that so far as *this* heroine is concerned, by then some of the best fun will be over.

Chapter 2
Jane's Juvenilia Illustrated

The illustrator, like the literary critic, is an interpreter, and I like to believe that the visual interpretation may be interesting and enlightening, as the critic's is. The illustrator's business, of course, must mostly be with characters and action, and she or he should follow such visual information as the author supplies – though of course major gaps must be filled in by invention. But besides action and character the illustrator has the chance to pursue theme, period, surroundings, tone, and emphasis. In illustrating each of young Austen's brilliant and funny narratives I intended to honour her text, but to enlarge and illuminate it too. And just as one critic's take on a text, even if the reader disagrees with it, can lead to the reader's clarifying her own interpretation, so illustrations, even if they do not match another reader's visual experience of the text, may serve to enlarge and clarify too.

In discussing here my intentions in the illustration, I hope to provide legitimate commentary, and a certain visual enlargement that will help to fix Austen's texts in my readers' minds, as they have in mine.

It was *The Beautifull Cassandra* – yes, spelt that way – that first got me into illustrating Jane Austen's juvenilia. I had long admired her early writings. But when I re-read them for the New York conference on the juvenilia and "Lady Susan" organized by J. David Grey, co-founder of the Jane Austen Society of North America, I fell in love with the cheeky tale about a pleasure-loving girl who elopes with a bonnet. Her day's adventures, which include bingeing on six ice creams, refusing to pay for them, knocking down the pastry-cook, and taking a gratuitous hackney-coach trip to Hampstead and back, reminded me of Beatrix Potter's Peter Rabbit and the carrots, and also of Maurice Sendak's Max of *Where the Wild Things Are* ("Let the wild rumpus begin!"). I wanted "The Beautifull Cassandra" to achieve incarnation as a picture book for children. And because I'd been a closet illustrator, I wanted to come out of the closet and make the pictures *mine*.

The Beautifull Cassandra

I turned Cassandra into a mouse (I've always been fond of mice), and the other characters into a lizard, a guinea pig, a frog, a squirrel, and so forth. After fitting in preliminary research and sketches with my life as a scholar and English Prof, I took two weeks off from all other duties, and drew and coloured my pictures. And then I went to market with them.

It makes a difference, I think, that my serious engagement with Jane Austen's juvenilia began in this light-hearted way, with this charming and boisterous tale.

I had long known that Austen's early writings deserve serious scholarly attention, and I have helped to make that happen.[1] I urged Jack Grey, for instance, to collect the papers at his New York conference into the collection *Jane Austen's Beginnings*, which was the first thorough literary look at the content of what R.W. Chapman called *The Minor Works*. But "serious scholarly attention" is not all that the juvenilia deserve. They also merit full and light-hearted enjoyment; and adding pictures to the lively texts has been my way of advancing that enjoyment, and (I hope) engaging youthful readers too. Young Austen's own mood in the writing of this fierce and funny set of narratives, dedicated to her sister, brothers, parents, and friends, was playful and joyful. And if my own tone in writing about the juvenilia is deemed by serious scholars as being too light, it is because I would like my tone to be appropriate to the lively matter I discuss.

How was I to bring that play and joy visibly to the pages of a picture book for kids? And how could one suggest in pictures the wonderful verbal precision that already characterizes this young author? I wanted a flowing but exact line, expressive gesture and attitude, vigour and movement, and bright colour. Turning the characters into small animals dressed in the fashions of the 1780s provided its own opportunity for visual fun and wit. For instance, I made the hackney-coachman's horse a tortoise; and when the frog coachman cracks his whip, the tortoise, safe in its shell, can look its amused immunity. (I write, necessarily, of my own intentions. How far I succeeded in fulfilling them is for others to judge.)

Austen's prose, we know, is finely economic. She packs a load of suggestion into a turn of phrase. And although the juvenilia are in so many ways different from the novels, the young Jane's prose already has this power of suggestion. An illustrator, like a film-maker, has the opportunity to expand the suggestion; and I relished my chance to visualise. *The Beautifull Cassandra* occupies only three pages in the Chapman and Cambridge editions; so in spreading the story with pictures to 30 pages, I could expatiate.

For instance: after Cassandra has appropriated the Duchess's bonnet to her own head, she sallies forth and meets a Viscount, who is "no less celebrated for his Accomplishments & Virtues, than for his Elegance & Beauty." Aha! thinks the trained romance reader, Here comes the Hero. But not in an Austen burlesque. Cassandra has other fish to fry. The text reads simply, "She curtseyed & walked on." In my pictures I could show more. I turned the Viscount into a lounge lizard, togged up in the finery of an eighteenth-century "macaroni" (in a pose borrowed from Rowlandson), and looking as snooty as possible with a nose pointing skywards. First picture shows them facing each other, with Cassandra's deep curtsey, eyes lowered. Next picture shows him solo, making his elaborate bow

[1] Besides founding the Juvenilia Press, with Christine Alexander I co-edited a collection on juvenilia called *The Child Writer from Jane Austen to Virginia Woolf*. It includes essays on Jane Austen by Margaret Anne Doody and Rachel Brownstein, as well as others on the Brontës, George Eliot, Louisa May Alcott, John Ruskin, and other authors whose early writings are extant.

to nobody in particular. Last in the sequence shows him quite crestfallen, still dangling his tricorn, as he sees Cassandra now in the distance, having cheerfully passed by his display. He is the one with the pride and self-conscious status. She is the one with better things to do and more exciting places to go. That's the story I extract from the five words, "She curtseyed & walked on."

Cassandra's adventures occupy a day, from the moment she falls in love with the bonnet and elopes with it, through her cheerful indulgence in six ice creams and a trip to Hampstead, her coping with the importunate coachman and other encounters, back to her parental home and her indulgent milliner mother. It is episodic rather than causally driven. So to supply a visual unity of action I made the journey outward and back my storyboard line. For the first part of the story, after the magical moment of falling in love, Cassandra moves from left to right, forwards like the written narrative line. At Hampstead, her destination in the hackney coach, "she was no sooner arrived than she ordered the Coachman to turn round & drive her back again." I took that as the mid-point of the story, and rendered it in two silhouette compositions on one page, to mark the reversal. (Hampstead is identified by a vignette of Kenwood House in the background: I did some on-the-spot research for that!) For the rest of the story, until the gratifying stasis at the end, Cassandra moves back from right to left. Within this large pattern the rhythm changes briefly: for instance: there's a stalled moment while Cassandra searches her pockets for money to pay the peremptory coachman. ("Peremptory," I've been told, is a word that this story has added to the vocabulary of many a four-year-old.) And the climax of the action, as I take it, is her resourceful and hilarious device of plonking her now wrecked bonnet on his head and running away (Figure 2.1). Jane Austen's little text, written as it appears with such cheerful spontaneity, lends itself to these calculations. It is in fact a fine-tuned and shapely tale.

One problem I faced in turning the characters into small animals: What was to be the relation of the animals to the human world? (Ernest Shepard, in illustrating *The Wind in the Willows* some years after it had appeared as text alone, faced the same problem, for instance in showing Toad disguised in a washer-woman's outfit.) Cassandra's mother, we hear, is a milliner, who makes a beautiful bonnet for a "Dutchess." Was the off-stage duchess also to be an animal?

I decided that there is a parallel world of human activity. Cassandra's mother was to be a mouse-milliner making bonnets for aristocratic human beings who remain off-stage. She is like the mice in Beatrix Potter's *The Tailor of Gloucester*, who busy themselves in helping to sew a new embroidered waistcoat for the human Mayor.

A reel of thread serves her for a stool, and the needle she sews with, in relation to her, is huge. How, then, does Cassandra the mouse, after falling in love with a human-sized bonnet, manage to have "placed it on her gentle head" and sally forth? My decision was that the moment of falling in love effects a magical transformation, after which the bonnet fits her. Otherwise, to her the bonnets are the size of furniture. Before the action we see her swinging on the ribbons of a bonnet as on a swing; and when she has dumped the bonnet that becomes

Fig. 2.1 The coachman gets the bonnet.

her Significant Other, she reverts to mouse size. She delivers her only piece of dialogue, the final satisfied "This is a day well spent," while flopped out in a sofa-sized bonnet, devotedly tended by her doting mother (Figure 2.2).

Through the years since I published the picture book, I have received many comments and questions. But I realize now that no one ever challenged me, "How is it that Cassandra the mouse can actually wear that huge human-sized bonnet?" Nor has anyone complained that the mouse is actually very large in relation to the human bonnets. I have discovered that readers are very ready to take the illustrator's decisions on trust, and they don't get picky about issues of realism

Fig. 2.2 Cassandra at the Milliner's: "This is a day well spent."

that certainly do engage them in a text. The calculations about direction, size, and plausibility are ones that the illustrator must go through, to convince herself of just how the tale works.

The Beautifull Cassandra represents my only set of illustrations in full colour, and; since I'm most at home with line I saw colour as a daunting challenge. My storyboard taught me that you can run into trouble as different characters run into each other in different illustrations; and I wanted each to carry his or her own individual aura. So for minor characters I limited the range: red to purple for the snobbish paternal rat, yellow through orange for the lizard Viscount, yellow and green for the frog coachman, and so on. But my major characters, Cassandra and her sexy bonnet, come in the full range of primary colours, red and yellow and blue, with a purple pelisse thrown in. I wanted those two to be strong and dominant on the page.

These two characters, mouse and bonnet, appear in many pictures, and each must have her/its own visual development. Cassandra as protagonist has action to tell her story – curtseying to the Viscount, knocking down the pastry-cook, and so forth. Mice have tails, and I needed Cassandra's tail to be expressive. Each image of her called for a decision on what the tail would be doing: elegantly curved over her back as she curtseys, totally flaccid when she relaxes at the end, or – when she escapes from the peremptory coachman – hitched over her arm as she makes an athlete's escape.

The bonnet, being mainly passive (like many of the male figures in the juvenilia), has to have an unfolding history too: and I chose to show it participating in Cassandra's adventures. So, having chosen daffodils as the floral decoration, I showed them curtseying when she curtseys, and getting fat as she devours the six ices. What with the fisticuffs and vigorous movement, I calculated, the bonnet through the course of the action must take something of a beating. And sure enough, by the time Cassandra is ready to leave it to the coachman in lieu of his fare, as in Figure 2.1, the bonnet is crumpled, the ostrich feathers broken, the daffodils dangling – so that it is no great sacrifice for Cassandra to abandon it, and proceed bonnetless through the rest of the day's adventures. Character development? Ah, yes – this bonnet, like other major characters, has its own unfolding history, which the illustrator may choose to render visible.

Once I'd made my pictures, I went to market with them. Having at the time some standing as a Jane Austen critic, but none as an illustrator, it took me a long time to find a publisher, despite having Jane Austen as a team-mate. But once I'd found Sono Nis Press, the publisher and I agreed there should be some explanatory text – not an introduction, to put off the child reader before she even gets to the story itself, but an afterword, written in simple language, where I could include some information about who Jane Austen was, when she was writing, and what were her possible aims and achievements in the story. I could also confess that in all probability she had not envisaged her characters as small animals.

I provided a putative date for the story, 1788, when the age of the 15-year-old Cassandra of the story matches that of Jane's actual sister Cassandra. In the summer of that year, we know, the Austens took their two daughters on a trip to Kent and London, where they stayed with the Hancocks in Orchard Street – just round a couple of corners from Bond Street, where the fictional Cassandra's mother has her milliner's shop. I've always imagined that the two Austen girls took a walk, and that Cassandra, enchanted by the Bond Street display of fashion, may have moaned, "Oh, I'm in love with that bonnet!" – the genesis of Jane's story.

The publisher also asked me to add a simple line drawing, more or less realistic, of young Jane at work, an assignment I much enjoyed (Figure 2.3). The face and hair I adapted from the Rice portrait, which appears on this book's cover; the smile of secret satisfaction as she writes was my own inspiration. The dress, I fear, is not authentic for the period. The engaging little girl who consented to sit for me as young Jane Austen had a long dress of her own that she was bound and determined to wear for the occasion. But the writing desk on the three-footed pedestal table was taken from Jane Austen's own desk, which was then in Canada, in the hands of her collateral descendant, Joan Austen-Leigh, co-founder of the Jane Austen Society of North America.[2] Later Joan generously presented it to the British Library, where I have seen it proudly displayed. We illustrators have to find our authenticity where we may!

In the Afterword too I could comment on other aspects of the story – the cheerful feminism that allows Cassandra to march through the streets unaccompanied (as Jane Austen herself was never allowed to do), to hire a hackney coach *in propria persona*, and boldly proceed through the streets bonnetless. She is never punished for her outrageous behaviour, but is allowed – like Maurice Sendak's Max and Mickey but *un*like his girl heroine of *Outside Over There* – to be loudly self-assertive. I could also explore young Jane's own love affair with bonnets, and her opinion on their decoration: "I cannot help thinking that it is more natural to have flowers grow out of the head than fruit. – What do you think on that subject?" (*Letters* 44). That was what decided me to include daffodils among the decorations of Cassandra's bonnet. Daffodils seem to me to be able to blow their own trumpets (Figure 2.4).

I'm glad to say that *The Beautifull Cassandra* picture book has had considerable success in reviews and sales, and it remains in print. In 2007 Joanne Forman composed music for her, for flute and Celtic harp, which has had several live performances – one of them to a large audience at JASNA's 2008 conference in Chicago.[3] It was a treat to hear each of the "six ices" Cassandra devours receive its own fluting phrase as she downs it; and the music in turn inspired a children's ballet, where I saw little kids recognizably togged out as my Viscount, frog coachman, and the others.[4]

---

[2] A drawing of the writing desk and pedestal table is on the cover of number 14 of *Persuasions* (1992), the Society's journal, of which Joan Austen-Leigh was the first editor.

[3] Joanne Forman's music, along with the text and pictures, may be heard on the JASNA web site (www.jasna.org), under "Conference Publications."

[4] See www.jasna.org/publications/cassandra/index/htm.

Fig. 2.3 Young Jane at work.

Fig. 2.4 "She devoured six ices."

When you illustrate a story, you have to think about it long and hard. *The Beautifull Cassandra* taught me much about the young Jane Austen and the themes and techniques she carried forward to the six novels. (Also, what she *didn't* carry forward.) And it was this process that made me realize that getting students to think long and hard about an author's early piece of writing was one vivid way to acquaint them with that author. In two undergraduate courses specialised to Jane Austen and the Brontës, I offered the students the topic of editing and illustrating a piece of juvenilia. We turned the class efforts into modest saddle-stitched volumes, and I found I could actually sell them to recover my expenses.

And from this germ grew my brainchild the Juvenilia Press, which produces scholarly (and illustrated!) editions of early works by known writers, with students working alongside experienced scholars to learn about textual editing, annotation, and writing a critical introduction.

Over the years, besides editions of early works by Austen and the Brontës, we have produced some 50 volumes, and our authors have included Louisa May Alcott, Charles Dickens, John Ruskin, Robert Louis Stevenson, Philip Larkin, and Margaret Atwood. Early in the twenty-first century, the distinguished Brontë scholar Christine Alexander of the University of New South Wales took over the Press, and she remains its Director.

But Austen is still our stand-by and best-selling author, as JASNA has been our best patron. And we have been fortunate that a number of distinguished Austen scholars have taken on the editing of her juvenilia for the Press. Different editors have invited me to do the illustrations – and that's an invitation I find hard to refuse!

Our books are scholarly editions: they come carefully edited from the manuscripts, and copiously annotated. These are not, of course, the only annotated editions. But what the Juvenilia Press has done for Austen's juvenilia, I believe – besides making them more accessible and increasing their distribution – is that we have endowed each work with its own individual identity. In collected editions such as Chapman's or Sabor's, the many different items are inevitably homogenised and undifferentiated. Since they are packed with action and characters, and a number of them are unfinished, the reader who reads them in a bunch, one following another in the same type face, can find that the boundaries between them crumble, and in the memory these glittering little narratives can amalgamate; they become like a string of sausages that has lost its defining divisions. Not so with the Juvenilia Press's little books. Fortunately, we have found excellent and distinguished editors – including Jan Fergus, Joseph Wiesenfarth, Peter Sabor, and Christine Alexander, who bring their own critical insights as well as guiding the students they work with. Each story has been pondered on its own and discussed at length by a team of editors, each comes with its own thoughtful introduction, and commentary in the notes that makes explicit its unique place in the Austen canon. Yes, and with its own set of illustrations, too, which pay attention to each character and each setting.

Though I am first a literary critic, because of the intimacy with these texts that I have gained through illustrating them, it is a pleasure to write, for the moment, from the point of view of the illustrator. More than the mature novels, the juvenilia lend themselves to illustration, particularly of the burlesque sort that is my own mode. The novels of Austen's maturity are subtle and nuanced, and moreover they provide few details about the physical appearance of the characters, beyond the brief hints about Elizabeth's "dark eyes" and "light and pleasing" figure (*PP* 26) or Emma's "true hazle eye" (*E* 39), and so forth. I would never dare to attempt to illustrate them; nor do I much like the works of Hugh Thomson and the Brock brothers, charming though they are. The juvenilia, on the other hand, are crowded with bodies and physical detail: Alice's red face, Sukey's fat body, Charles Adams's divine beauty, Charlotte's alternately hideous and handsome suitors, Rebecca's squint and greazy tresses, Augustus's blue-and-white striped satin waistcoat, Lady Lesley's rouge, fine eyes and fine teeth, Kitty's toothache, Edward Stanley's lingering toilette for the ball. The personnel go in for exaggerated gesture, super-elegant bows, fainting, and running mad, demonstrations of delight and surprise and disgust. There's a slapstick element too: dinner guests are directed to sit on each other's laps, and bodies collide and collapse. All this is grist to the illustrator's mill. And what illustrator could resist having a go at Lord St. Clair of "Love and Freindship," surrounded by his four long-lost grandchildren,[5] or Laura and Sophia's wild antics as their husbands lie "weltering in their blood"?

Frederic and Elfrida

"According to the best evidence Jane Austen wrote *Frederic & Elfrida* when she was eleven or twelve years old," notes Victoria Kortes-Papp in her introduction to the Juvenilia Press edition of this brief and outrageous tale. It "weighs in at just over two thousand three hundred words" (vii) – that is, about 10 pages of print, chapter breaks and all: longer than the highly concentrated *Beautifull Cassandra*, but much shorter than *Love and Freindship*, *Catharine*, or even *Jack and Alice*.[6]

The conventions of courtship, and the myriad "dos" and "don'ts" associated with the formal coming together of a couple, remained one of Austen's principal concerns in the mature novels. Elizabeth Bennet and Charlotte Lucas argue over whether, and how much, Jane Bennet should allow her preference for Mr. Bingley to show; Lady Russell intervenes to end a courtship on the issues of income and youth. Here the interaction of convention with desire is treated with finely measured nuance. But in the juvenilia young Austen can indulge in boisterous overstatement on the same delicate matters.

Richardson is certainly the great authority on the elaborate etiquette of courtship. His villain Lovelace, bent on seduction rather than marriage, can seem to be asking Clarissa to marry him without being in danger of her accepting, because he can make it seem as though acceptance would make her appear too eager. "Methinks I could almost wish it had been in my power to comply with his earnest solicitations," Clarissa writes to her friend. "But … some little punctilio is surely necessary" (Richardson, *Clarissa* 513).

[5] My illustration of this memorable incident appeared in *Jane Austen's Beginnings*, ed. J. David Grey, 147, and it was subsequently used as the cover image for a Japanese book on Austen. My illustration of Laura running mad and Sophia fainting as their husbands welter in their blood appears in the Juvenilia Press edition of *Love and Freindship*, 25.

[6] The usual convention for naming the separate pieces of Jane Austen's juvenilia has been to enclose the titles in quotation marks, and that's the convention I follow in the rest of this book. But for this chapter, since my references are to the Juvenilia Press illustrated volumes, the titles come in italics, because these are books, not just parts of books.

Although her favourite heroine, Harriet Byron of *Sir Charles Grandison*, is allowed to fall in love with the hero before he falls in love with her, young Austen in burlesque mode chose to send up the fine-drawn scruples of courtship conduct that Richardson specialised in. In *Northanger Abbey* she even provides a footnote referencing his *Rambler* 97 letter, when she comments on Catherine Morland's too-ready response to Henry Tilney at Bath. Did Catherine dream of him after the first meeting, the narrator wonders? If so, "I hope it was no more than in a slight slumber, or a morning doze at most; for if it be true, as a celebrated writer [Richardson] has maintained, that no young lady can be justified in falling in love before the gentleman's love is declared, it must be very improper that a young lady should dream of a gentleman before the gentleman is first known to have dreamt of her" (*NA* 22).

In such a passage one catches a lingering note of the juvenilia: the nonsensical notion that propriety should pertain even in dreams recalls the assumption that madness and fainting fits are matters of stylistic choice: "Run mad as often as you chuse," Sophia advises Laura in *Love and Freindship*; "but do not faint –" (*J* 133). And Richardson's taboos against the woman's feeling any faint glimmerings of desire are sent up in the labouring over the significant differences between the dreams of "a slight slumber" or "morning doze," and dreams of deeper and presumably more responsible sleep.

The characters in *Frederic and Elfrida* provide case studies in the protocols of courtship. The hero and heroine, we hear at the outset, "loved with mutual sincerity but were both determined not to transgress the rules of Propriety by owning their attachment" (1). Ergo: progress in the courtship slows down to stasis.

To render this impasse visibly I needed two pictures, "They loved with mutual sincerity" comes first, with a young woman and young man, in full eighteenth-century fig, gazing longingly at each other, framed by a heart, as in a Valentine. The "but" introduces the insurmountable obstacle: "determined not to transgress the rules of Propriety" shows them turned away from each other, chins tilted in proud and proper silence, the framing heart broken (Figure 2.5). They are busy letting "concealment, like a worm i' th' bud, / Feed on their damask cheeks." Very noble; very proper. The "celebrated writer" must approve. Since the principals in this affair can't move it along, the parents must intervene: they arrange for an engagement, and things are on the move again: "the wedding cloathes were bought, & nothing remained to be settled but the naming of the Day" (8). Oh-oh, another obstacle.

We're familiar with the convention that the wedding day can be decided by no one but the bride herself. Even Richardson's Clarissa, whose father won't allow her any choice about whom to marry or even *whether* to marry, is allowed to choose her wedding day. I believe this iron-clad convention derives from the delicate matter of menstruation: in the somewhat public ceremonies connected with the bridal night, it's important to avoid the possible embarrassment of the bride's being in mid-period. But these are matters, fortunately, that the illustrator doesn't have to concern herself with. Since it is only the bride who may decide the day of the wedding, and the bride is not allowed to manifest an iota of eagerness

Fig. 2.5 "Loved with mutual sincerity but …"

about marriage, even naming the day, to the highly refined mind, is itself an impropriety. Hence Elfrida puts it off indefinitely. After the wedding clothes are bought, "Weeks & Fortnights flew away … the Cloathes grew out of fashion" (17).

It is hard for an illustrator to show the flight of weeks and fortnights; but clothes and fashion are visible, and clearly her province. I decided that the changing fashions would be my means of conveying the flight of time.

It takes Elfrida so long to name the day that in the interval her friend Rebecca has married and borne a daughter, and the daughter has reached the attractive age of 18. Those wedding clothes could well have decayed as they go out of fashion; and I envisaged them as something like Miss Havisham's wedding dress, the visible markers of the ravages of time and propriety.

So I had to pay attention to fashion. If we take the date of Austen's writing, late 1780s, as the fictional time at the end of the tale, that puts the early part, when Frederic and Elfrida are young, at about 1770, *Evelina* time: the age for elaborate wigs for the men, high hairstyles, panniers and wide skirts for the women. So that was the mode for my early pictures; and I make the wedding outfits on their male and female dummies elaborately decorative, with ruffled sleeves, gathered flounces, ribbons and bows and embroidered edges.

The togs decay, the togs decay, … / And after many a summer dies the swan (to adapt Tennyson). Like Miss Havisham's, the wedding clothes gather cobwebs and tatters, and yes, a resident mouse (Figure 2.6).

It takes Frederic's attraction to his friend's nubile daughter to awaken Elfrida to the fact that one may pay too high a price for the punctilios of the courtship convention. "She flew to Frederic & in a manner truly heroick, spluttered out to him her intention of being married the next Day" (17). High time!

Meanwhile – and there is plenty of time for other plot developments in that couple of decades – a second heroine has fulfilled the trajectory of another conventional fictional fate. The lovely Charlotte, we hear, is characterised by "a willingness to oblige every one" (3). In contrast to Elfrida, the girl who can't say Yes, Charlotte is the girl who can't say No. And like the girl in the song, she finds herself "in a terrible fix." On a visit to London she receives two proposals in swift succession, and she accepts them both, with dire consequences.

Claudia Johnson has explored the implications of Charlotte's double acceptance, showing how forcefully the conduct books and moral conservatives such as Hannah More insisted on "agreeableness" as the indispensable virtue of the woman. Fanny Price, she points out, suffers from Sir Thomas's expectation that she should agree to the male's demand, no matter what the cost to herself (Johnson 51–3).

Charlotte's two suitors are fine contrasts: the first "an aged gentleman with a sallow face & old pink Coat" (11); the second "a young & Handsome Gentleman with a new blue coat" (13). So they are likewise gifts to the illustrator, even if I couldn't do justice to the pink and blue coats (Figure 2.7).

"Look here upon this picture, and on this," as Hamlet urges Gertrude. It's Hyperion to a satyr, and I made the most of the contrast. Although Charlotte, being involuntarily agreeable, accepts them both, she can't help noticing that "there was

Fig. 2.6 "The Cloathes grew out of fashion."

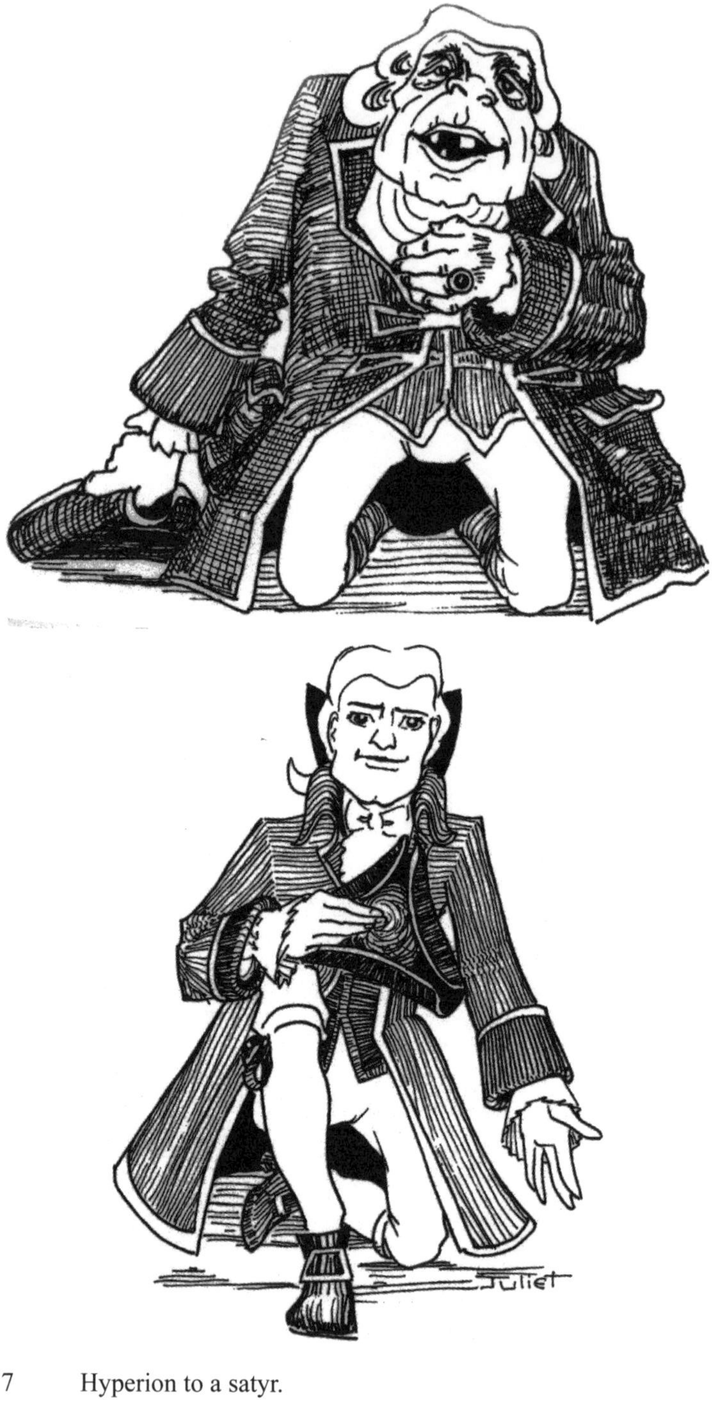

Fig. 2.7 Hyperion to a satyr.

Fig. 2.8 "They did not scruple to kick one another out of the window."

something in the appearance of the second Stranger, that influenced Charlotte in his favour ... : she could not account for it, but so it was" (13). Besides her satire on women's training in agreeableness, Austen jokes about the courtship convention that decrees a woman of delicacy must be blind to a man's sexual attractiveness. Propriety forbids that a man's "person" –or body – should be a factor in her choice.

The contrasts between the formulaic and the natural or realistic pertain in the scenery as among the characters. The landscape is artistically composed: "a Grove of Poplars which led from the Parsonage to a verdant Lawn enamelled with a variety of variegated flowers & watered by a purling Stream" (3) – a wonderful take-off of the jargon of rustic romance. This calls for an idyllic view of the parsonage, complete with poplars, purling stream, and so forth. But presently we hear that the intimacy between these polite friends "grew to such a pitch, that they did not scruple to kick one another out of the window on the slightest provocation" (7). So I could draw again the same idyllic parsonage, but this time with the characters exploding out of the windows – "like popcorn," said the designer (Figure 2.8).

Any incident that recurs in so short a tale gathers the status of a motif. On two occasions the wicked young author tells us of an impromptu speech that is nevertheless delivered in chorus, by three or four characters. The first, a chorus in which three newly-introduced friends deliver vile abuse in an elegantly formal manner, I shall return to later, when I discuss young Austen's dialogue. The second chorus speech involves no less than four characters. It's another courtship crisis. This time it is the parents who cause the delay: "Mrs Fitzroy [Rebecca's mother] did not approve of the match on account of the tender years of the young couple, Rebecca being but 36 & Captain Roger little more than 63" (8). This time the surrounding young people wait only a week before they swing into action with their speech in chorus. They are well rehearsed in the rhetoric of the carrot and the stick:

> "Consent them Madam to their union [they intone] & as a reward, this smelling Bottle which I enclose in my right hand, shall be yours & yours forever .... But if you refuse to join their hands in 3 days time, this dagger which I enclose in my left shall be steeped in your hearts blood." (15)

Fig. 2.9 "This Smelling Bottle … this dagger."

"Such gentle & sweet persuasion," as the narrator characterises the speech, has due effect. For illustration, rather than depicting the speakers, I decided to present the carrot and stick – that is, a line of four smelling bottles crossed with four decorative daggers (Figure 2.9). Other merely decorative images showed a set of make-up bottles from which Rebecca of the "greazy tresses" tries to beautify herself, and a row of masks for the Masquerade sequence in *Jack and Alice.*

A note on placement: for this kind of illustrative decoration one needs careful placement of the image in the text – the bottles and daggers would make no sense unless placed right alongside the speech they belong to. And fortunately, since our designer Winston Pei delights in wedding word with image, he would arrange pages and adjust sizes of pictures to get the images precisely where they need to be.

To make my faces and figures expressive, I have recourse to standard tropes of gesture and facial expression. Frederic and Elfrida in love can lean towards each other; scared off by propriety, their bodies tilt away. The aged Frederic, betrothed to one lady and attracted to another, has his body facing one way, his eyes and face another, and his two feet turned two ways, to indicate his changing mind. Time-worn devices, these; but *Frederic and Elfrida*, after all, is not one of the subtlest of Jane Austen's works! Not subtle; but exuberantly inventive, alert to the nonsense of convention, the intricacies of punctilio, the preposterousness of propriety.

Jack and Alice

The juvenilia present extremes, very often opposite extremes: *Jack and Alice* includes wild rambunctious behaviour over against extremes of formality and decorum: an elegant Masquerade, for instance, from which the guests are presently all "carried home, Dead Drunk" (7). To represent these contrasts, we chose for the cover design the image of Jack at the height of his drunkenness, with jacket unbuttoned, shirt untucked, belly-button exposed for all to see, and still flourishing his wine-class; but carried by two stiffly formal footmen, in wigs and livery, who march in step, elbows stiffly raised, leg muscles braced, and noses in the air; the footmen all firm geometrical lines and curves, Jack's lines rumpled and dishevelled like his clothes (Figure 2.10). For me the image epitomizes the burlesque extremes incorporated in *Jack & Alice.* For the title, I did a forgery job from Austen's manuscript.

How is the illustrator to tackle the stunning Charles Adams, who is "of so dazzling a Beauty that none but Eagles could look him in the Face"? (3). He comes

Fig. 2.10 *Jack and Alice* cover.

to the Masquerade, of course, in "a Mask representing the Sun … The Beams that darted from his Eyes were like those of that glorious Luminary tho' infinitely superior" (5). The beams in fact are so strong that the other guests are forced to retire to the far end of the room. In the illustration I had to make him an Apollo – and not just any Apollo, but the Apollo Belvedere, the classical sculpture in the Vatican, which throughout the nineteenth century was considered the type of male beauty. I could copy his pose from photographs.

There were problems, though. The statue is nude, though in decorous times it was supplied with a fig-leaf. Frontal male nudity in a work by Jane Austen – even one of the juvenilia? I don't think so. So I enlarged the fig-leaf into an elegant little kilt; and was rather proud of my Apollo/Charles Adams. But I ran afoul of the editor, Joseph Wiesenfarth. He pointed out, reasonably enough, that the text reveals that once the Mask has partly closed his eyes to douse his beams, "the Company discovered him to be Charles Adams in his plain green Coat" (5): and Charles Adams in his plain green coat was the image called for. I solved the problem by drawing him again, in the same pose and from the same viewpoint, but clothed this time, and with a mirror in his extended hand wherein to admire his beauty (something he is fond of doing). The editor went for the literal reality; I went for the grand illusion; and the reader gets both. I could provide a small distant figure covering her eyes for the first, an appreciative open-eyed figure for the second (Figure 2.11).

Rodin, we are told, first modelled his sculptural portrait of Balzac nude, before clothing him in that iconic dressing-gown; Goya famously painted both "The Maja Nude" and "The Maja Clothed." Why should I not take similar liberties with Charles Adams?

Jack and Alice presents a plethora of potential heroines, and fortunately for the illustrator they come with clear visual markers. Alice herself, we hear, "has many rare & charming qualities, but Sobriety is not one of them" (18). Her drinking habit gives her a red complexion, which she exacerbates by her heated insistence that "no one can have too much [colour]" in her face (11). In the pictures, then, the red face can be a marker for Alice – not that I had colour at my disposal, but a little cross-hatching on the cheeks did the job.

The imperturbable Lady Williams, "a widow with a handsome jointure & the remains of a very handsome face" (3), likewise provides some visual markers for the illustrator. Lucy, as merely "a lovely young Woman," is not so readily identifiable; but she is first seen "lying apparently in great pain beneath a Citron tree" (15); thus providing attitude and setting for me to latch on to.

The landscape, in fact, contributed to the delectable contradictions between the formal and artful on the one hand, and the down-to-earth realistic on the other. Young Jane imitates and mocks the prettified verbal landscape painting in some of the novels she knew. The "Citron Grove" belongs to the elevated mode of romance. (Factually speaking, there are few Citron trees in England.) This Citron Grove, however, "led from her Ladyship's pigstye to Charles Adams's Horsepond" (12) – associations that bring the elevated tone down with a bump. And just to show that such workaday items can still be co-opted for sentiment, the narrator tells us that the susceptible Alice is "pleased with the prospect of seeing … a Horsepond

Fig. 2.11 Charles Adams / Apollo Belvedere.

Fig. 2.12 “a Lady … in great pain.”

of Charles's" (13). She is like Harriet Smith with Mr. Elton's pencil stub and court plaister, in being able to load even the meanest items with romantic association.

My picture of Lucy, then, makes the most of these stage props. I bring Alice and Lady Williams on their walk away from a bunch of cheerfully observant pigs towards a pond, near which Lucy is posed ("lying apparently in great pain beneath a Citron tree" [15]). Her pose under the fruit-laden tree, mirrored in the horsepond, theatrically renders her pain; and near her bare but elegantly angled foot is the man-trap ("so common in gentlemen's grounds" [17]) that has broken her leg. Again my picture is meant to juxtapose the trappings of romance with the low and the homely (Figure 2.12).

In case the reader becomes as enamoured of Charles Adams's attractions as Alice and the other lovesick ladies, Austen gives us some specimens of his talk and behaviour that are far from attractive. When Alice becomes the heiress to a large fortune, she believes her chances of catching Charles have improved, and she persuades her father to pay him a visit and press his daughter's claims. Mr. Johnson duly presents her case; to which Charles Adams replies,

> "Let me give you a short sketch of yourself and of her. I look upon you Sir to be a very good sort of Man in the main: a drunken old Dog to be sure, but that's nothing to me ... " (21)

While Charles Adams gives his sketch, I provide my own. Old Johnson, though he may indeed be a drunken old dog, has made an effort and got himself spruced up for the occasion (as appears from a contrast with the last picture in which he figures). "Being a man of few words his part was soon performed" (21) – so he delivers his speech standing, with his hat still in his hand. Feet firmly planted for balance and determination, he stands in the background. In the foreground Charles Adams – head and shoulders only, still with handsome Greek profile, but looking suitably surly – addresses him not face to face but arrogantly over his shoulder. For contemporary illustrators of nineteenth-century novels – Phiz illustrating Dickens, for example – the close-up was not among their usual options: a conventional illustration would happen at a fairly standard distance from the viewer, with the characters all in the same plane. But for me the distanced figure and the close-up were my best way of rendering Mr. Johnson's blunt but brave appeal, Charles Adams's outrageous disrespect (Figure 2.13).

Jane Austen's Men: "The Adventures of Mr Harley," "Sir William Mountague," "Memoirs of Mr Clifford," "The Generous Curate"

By 2007 the Juvenilia Press had snapped up the most delectable items in Austen's juvenilia, alongside publishing volumes by Lady Mary Pierrepont (Wortley Montagu), Charlotte and Branwell Brontë, George Eliot, and Louisa May Alcott, besides a number of twentieth-century authors such as Philip Larkin and Margaret Atwood. But aspiring editors and their students were still keen for Austen items, and Sylvia Hunt, who had worked with Peter Sabor in his editions of *Frederic*

Fig. 2.13 "a drunken old Dog to be sure."

and Elfrida and *Evelyn*, was now eager to edit another Austen edition with *her* students. She collected four brief pieces that were still available, and called her volume *Jane Austen's Men*. And I was delighted to be called on to illustrate that edition too.

The text, even of four pieces, being still quite slender, I could spread myself in the illustrations. (Unfortunately, however, I can't spread myself here, as space for reproductions is limited.) And the brief written sketches provide happy opportunities for the illustrator.

"The Adventures of Mr Harley," being dedicated to Jane Austen's brother "Mr Francis William Austen Midshipman on board his Majesty's ship the Perseverance," I ventured my first version of a portrait of an Austen family member, fancifully showing Frank in midshipman's uniform on board an improbably miniature sailing ship, with Nelson as a figurehead. The fact that Harley was "intended by his father for the Church & by his Mother for the sea" allowed me to do my own version of a common eighteenth-century conceit, the half-and-half figure. Harley is a clergyman on his right side, with clerical outfit, a book in hand and a pulpit behind him, complete with a carved angel for the lectern; while on his left side he is barefoot Jack Tar, with tarred pigtail and bell-bottomed trousers. I couldn't resist a grin on the sailor's face, corner of the mouth turned up, which turns downward and solemn on the other side.

"Sir William Mountague" is the most substantial of these pieces. He is the sexually omnivorous baronet who is unable to resist almost any woman whatsoever, and seems to believe himself entitled to them all. The piece begins with a listing of the long line of his ancestors; so I showed him posed in an up-to-date dandy's outfit (which I raided from a fashion magazine of the day) in front of a set of portraits: the first in Elizabethan dress, the next a Cavalier, the next deeply bewigged for early eighteenth century, and the last in mid-eighteenth-century mode; and all the ancestors share Sir William's beak-like phallic nose and protruding lower lip (Figure 2.14). Since the ladies are so smitten with this Lothario, in one picture I presented him among three of them, fairly tiptoed in excitement, one of them clasping her hands to her bosom.

The hero of "Memoirs of Mr Clifford" is the one who fancies vehicles – and possesses "a Coach, a Chariot, a Chaise … " all the way down to a wheelbarrow. Here I had recourse to the splendid volume of *Felton's Carriages*, which I shamelessly plundered (fervently hoping it was out of copyright by now), simply adding my Mr Clifford in various poses to the Felton silhouette.

"The Generous Curate" is a figure Austen probably knew well – an impecunious man of the cloth with slender means and a large family, such as Trollope was to portray in Mr. Quiverful and Mr. Crawley in the Barchester novels. The eldest son, like Austen's brothers Frank and Charles, is sent to sea; and from Newfoundland he sends home a Newfoundland dog, not just once, but every month. Besides Lady Bertram's Pug, Austen doesn't treat us to many dogs; so I took the opportunity to provide a border showing the Curate's children, from the baby to a growing girl, romping with the Newfoundlands.

For the generous curate himself, I resorted to a trope dear to Dickens – the good bald man. Phrenology was only just getting going in Austen's day, though one of its basic texts, Lavater's *Essays on Physiognomy*, already had wide currency. The organ of benevolence is located at the front centre of the head, just above the youthful hair-line: baldness does not itself indicate benevolence, but it does *display* it: hence the long array of kind bald men in Dickens, from Pickwick to Tom Pinch to the reformed Scrooge. So I represent Austen's generous curate as bald too (McMaster, *Dickens* 15–17).

Three Mini-Dramas

The Juvenilia Press edition of *Three Mini-Dramas* was a wide-spread team enterprise, involving co-editors at various academic stages, from me as retired professor to students at a private high school in Toronto, with a graduate student and recent PhD in between. Geographically too we were wide-spread: between western and eastern Canada and Alabama, with the Press's Director Christine Alexander in Australia. But engaging many students from many places in co-

Fig. 2.14 Sir William Mountague and his family portraits.

editing and illustrating a work by a brilliant young author is what the Press was intended for.

Young Austen's three little dramas, though usefully collected together, date form different times. "The Mystery" and "The Visit" come in *Volume the First*, and Sabor dates them at 1788 and1789 respectively ("Introduction" 5–6). "The First Act of a Comedy," however, was probably written in 1793. It comes in *Volume the Second*, and despite being unfinished it is more sophisticated, and for all its cheerful parody shows a developed knowledge of the stage conventions of the day. "The parodies that these playlets constitute are knowing, extremely accurate satire," Penny Gay characterises them in *Jane Austen and the Theatre*; and she notes that "The First Act of a Comedy" parodies "the burletta, or comic opera of the day" (Gay 2).

The illustration for "The Visit" was done by another member of the editorial team. But I was allowed free rein with "The Mystery: An Unfinished Comedy." "Unfinished" it certainly is, so far as audience comprehension is concerned.

"The Mystery" has the distinction of being the first of Austen's juvenilia to be published. Jane Austen's nephew, James Edward Austen-Leigh, in the second and third editions of *A Memoir of Jane Austen*, wrote patronisingly that "Her earliest stories are of a slight and flimsy nature" (42) – this from the man who as a teenager had tried, and failed, to provide endings to his aunt's *Evelyn* and *Catharine* (Sabor, "Note" xix). And he offered "The Mystery: An Unfinished Comedy" as an example of Austen's "juvenile effusions" (42–5), probably – as Peter Sabor suggests – because it is very brief. I like to think that we modern editors and illustrators of Austen's juvenilia know better than to patronise her.

It is a maddeningly tantalising little tour de force, which makes its whole business the withholding of information. For instance:

Fanny	Then t'was to no purpose that I …
Daphne	None upon Earth.
Mrs Humbug	And what is to become of ? …
Daphne	Oh! thats all settled. [*whispers Mrs Humbug*]
Fanny	And how is it determined?
Daphne	I'll tell you. [*whispers Fanny*] (15)

Is the audience privy to the whispers? No.

Do we have any inkling what is going on? No.

Then why would James Edward choose … ? I conclude he must have done it to justify his slighting comments about the "juvenile effusions."

Then how do you illustrate … ? That is the question.

At the best of times, it's harder to illustrate drama than narrative. A narrator is apt to provide much more in the way of description and visual information than the dramatist, who daren't be specific about such matters as height and girth in case there is no actor in the company to match. It's no surprise that the best-known illustration to Shakespeare, Millais's *Ophelia*, draws on Gertrude's narrative speech about Ophelia's suicide in the weeping brook. I have to admit there has been no dearth of illustrations to Shakespeare's plays. But then Shakespeare is a law unto himself.

My first resource in illustrating Austen's play was to go to the stage directions. They, unlike the dialogue, are boldly declarative. Scene the 3rd begins: "[*The curtain rises and discovers Sir Edward Spangle reclined in an elegant Attitude on a Sofa, fast asleep.*]" (15). Ha! "elegant Attitude" I can do – there's a picture in that. "Sofa" I can do. "Sir Edward Spangle" has a name that suggests the get-up of a dandy of the age preceding Beau Brummell: I can do! (Figure 2.15) Moreover, I had lately learned that by 1783 the new "roller-printing machines … produced the distinctive striped designs of the period" (Blank 234). So stripes were in, and could be used for covering new furniture such as the sofa. (Thus I demonstrate the research that goes into illustration!)

Once I have an image, I can even "quote" it; for the following scene introduces Colonel Elliott, who soliloquises,

> There lies Sir Edward … shall I tell him the secret? … No, he'll certainly blab it … But he is asleep and wont hear me … so I'll e'en venture." [*Goes up to Sir Edward, whispers him, & Exit*] (16)

"There lies Sir Edward" allows me to repeat my reclining dandy figure in the background. And the military "Colonel Edward Elliott" surely carries his identity with him in his rank and uniform, and his action within his speech: he addresses the audience; he tiptoes, he hushes, he whispers (Figure 2.16).

My third illustration was a whisper. "I'll tell you," Daphne promises, as she stoops to whisper; and her delight in communicating a secret, and Fanny's in hearing it, are conveyed in their tiptoes poses, their giggles, their hands-over-mouth. Do we share their delight in the secret? Not a chance. The mystery is maintained to the end.

"The First Act of a Comedy," written considerably later than "The Visit" and "The Mystery," is a wonderful mix of different genres within the theatre of Austen's time. It includes pastoral (a pair of lovers called Strephon and Chloe), low comedy (a hostess of an inn, servants, and a cook who speaks in dialect), a rude rustic festival called the "Plough Play," and burletta (the characters break into song at the drop of a hat). The swift changes put one in mind of Dickens's description of the comic drama of his day:

> It is the custom on the stage … to present the tragic and comic scenes, in as regular alternation, as the layers of red and white in a side of streaky bacon. The hero sinks upon his straw bed, weighed down by fetters and misfortunes; in the next scene, his faithful but unconscious squire regales the audience with a comic song. (*Oliver Twist* 118)

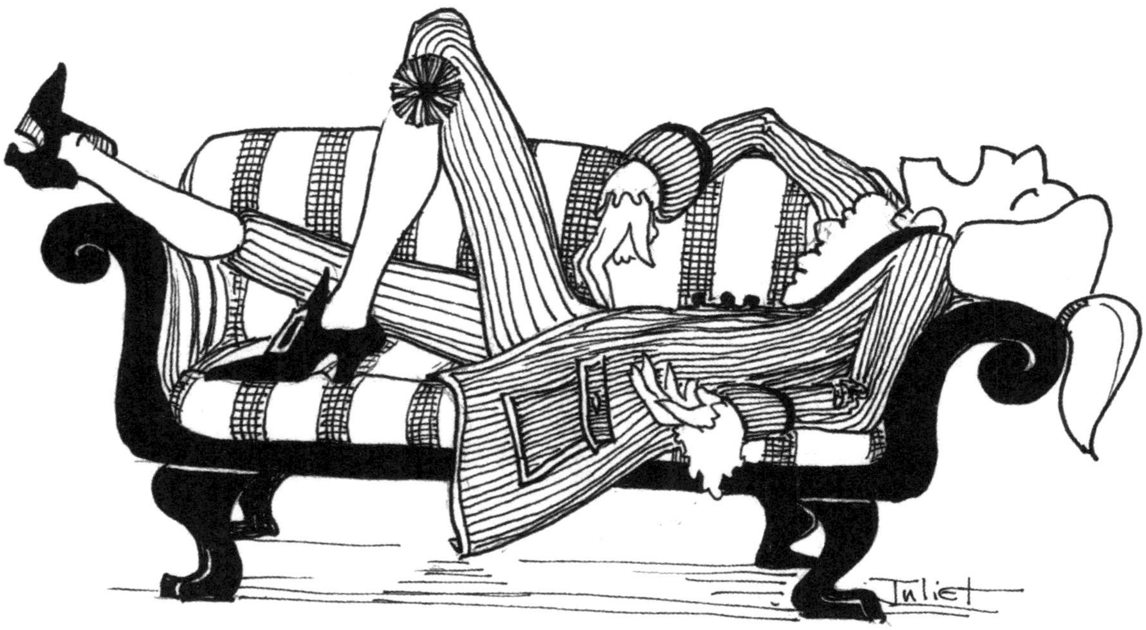

Fig. 2.15 “reclined in an elegant Attitude.”

Fig. 2.16 "He is asleep and wont hear me."

Austen certainly seems to have derived pleasure from her own "streaky bacon" principle here.

Gay's *The Beggar's Opera* seems to have been a model, since a character called Popgun is probably a highwayman on Hounslow heath. And his daughter Pistoletta expects to marry Strephon, although he is already engaged to Chloe. She is like Gay's aggressive Lucy Lockitt. "How happy could I be with either / Were t'other dear charmer away," Strephon might sing with Macheath.

In my picture of Popgun and Pistoletta, the highwayman and his daughter, I provided him with a pistol, plus a many-caped greatcoat, like Tony Weller's or the coachman's in *The Beautifull Cassandra*; and I thought that with a name like Pistoletta, his daughter was likely to pack a rod. I was rather proud of my Popgun figure in his boots and spurs and caped coat. My lines are only two-dimensional,

Fig. 2.17 Popgun and Pistoletta.

but I succeeded in suggesting that he occupies considerable space in a room, as on the page. His genial good humour contrasts with Pistoletta's tense readiness to take offence at almost anything (Figure 2.17).

The "Chorus of Ploughboys" is first mentioned in the list of "Characters"; and inasmuch as a Chorus of Ploughboys is not exactly a group one would expect to meet in a work by Jane Austen, I wanted to pause over them. For this mere mention in a list, I showed them as three dozy rustics in straw hats, smocks, and gaiters; each carries a pitchfork at rest, and each has a straw dangling from his mouth. But when Chloe bursts into song –

> I go to town
> And when I come down
> I shall be married to Stree-phon
> And that to me will be fun – (22)

they are galvanised into action. Chanting their chorus of "Be fun, be fun, be fun" (to rhyme with "Stree-phon" they would need to chant "*Beee* fun … "), they flourish their pitchforks like elegant canes, they wave their straws like top hats, they prance – or clump – in manic imitation of Fred Astaire (Figure 2.18).

A dancing chorus of ploughboys? That to me indeed WAS fun.

Why *three* ploughboys? The text doesn't mention a number, so I was free to provide as many as I liked. But threes lend themselves to firm composition, as Austen's favourite visual theorist William Gilpin had pronounced. When Elizabeth meets Darcy and the Bingley sisters walking in the garden at Netherfield, she refuses to break up the trio. "You are charmingly grouped, and appear to uncommon advantage," she tells them. "The picturesque would be spoilt by adding a fourth" (*PP* 58). So it is with ploughboys.

The History of England

My first essay in illustrating a volume after *The Beautifull Cassandra* was the edition of *The History of England* by Jan Fergus and her students at Lehigh University. It was a challenge to be collaborating not only with Jane Austen but this time with her sister Cassandra Austen too, since she was the first and principal illustrator. But by the same token I hadn't much to do, since she had already provided the portraits of the kings, the villainess Queen Elizabeth, and her heroine Mary Queen of Scots. I touched on the controversy that also engaged Austen – who killed the Princes in the Tower? – they appear as the victims of Richard III *and* "the Monster of Iniquity and Avarice" Henry VII (6). I didn't try to match my portraits of monarchs with Cassandra's, but rather provided caricature versions from historical portraits. My Richard comes with a white rose, my Henry with a red (or rather black, but the viewer is meant to supply the red of his Tudor rose).

Since that edition, the Juvenilia Press has issued a new one, *Jane Austen's The History of England and Cassandra's Portraits*, edited by Annette Upfal and Christine Alexander, which persuasively argues that Cassandra's vignettes of the monarchs are actually portraits of the Austen brothers – James Austen appearing as James I, Henry Austen, the soldier brother, as the warrior king Henry V, and so on. Most interesting – and most contentious – is the argument that wicked Queen Elizabeth's portrait is taken from the girls' mother, Mrs. Austen; and that the portrait of the beautiful and virtuous heroine Mary Queen of Scots is none other than young Jane Austen herself.

Lesley Castle

Just as I am more comfortable with line than colour, so I tend to concentrate on figures and their attitudes and motions rather than their surroundings. Like Mary Crawford, who says she sees "no wonder in this shrubbery equal to seeing myself in it" (*MP* 244), I am anthropocentric: for me, it's the *people* who matter. I can

Fig. 2.18 Chorus of Ploughboys … burst into song.

defend this emphasis, of course: Charlotte Brontë memorably objected that Austen provides "no open country, no fresh air; no blue hill, no bonny beck" (Southam, *Critical Heritage* 126). But for *Lesley Castle*, with settings in Bristol, Paris, and Portman Square in London, besides the Castle in Scotland, I felt I had to provide some markers for location.

There was a particular context for the Juvenilia Press edition of the engaging but unfinished *Lesley Castle*, edited by Jan Fergus and her students. It was commissioned for distribution at the JASNA conference in Quebec City that focussed on *Northanger Abbey*. So the gothic element had to be to the fore. We chose a Gothic script for the cover, and the castle setting was embellished by a dark and stormy night.

In working with Joseph Wiesenfarth on *Jack and Alice* I was limited to line. He has his own informed views on graphic illustration, and he objected to strong areas of black. For *Lesley Castle*, however, it was good to be able to increase my contrasts by strong oppositions of black against white, and I valued this extra element in design.

Lesley Castle itself has some strikingly Gothic qualities. It is "old and Mouldering," and "situated … on a bold projecting Rock" (*Lesley Castle* 3). Craigievar Castle became my model: it is usefully higher than it is wide, so fits our page. I provided a daylight version of Lesley Castle too, as a frontispiece, and added a silhouetted piper in kilt and sporran, as a subtle indication of the Scottish location (Figures 2.19 and 2.20). Kathryn Sutherland has noted "the Scottish flavour" of *Volume the Second* as a whole (Sutherland, *Second* 9); and I was not about to neglect it.

The characters are strongly marked, both mentally and physically, and we hear a lot about bodies, faces, stature, rouge, and so on. Though the romantic Margaret Lesley presents herself as the perfectly beautiful and accomplished heroine of romance in her Scottish fastness, her stepmother de-romanticises: to her the castle is "dismal," and her willowy step-daughters are "two great, tall, out of the way, overgrown, Girls." She complains, "These girls have no Music, but Scotch Airs, no Drawings, but Scotch Mountains and no Books but Scotch Poems – And I hate every thing Scotch" (22). Poor Lady Lesley! She has yet to find out that the family only visits "the M'Leods, the M'Kenzies, the M'Phersons, … the M'Kays, the Macbeths and the Macduffs"! (3)

The oppositions of the romantic and the sceptical allowed me to play with such oppositions in my illustrations. I boldly claim this much kinship with Jane: "I could not sit seriously down to *illustrate* a serious Romance under any other motive than to save my Life." Like her, I must "relax into laughing at myself or other people" (see *Letters* 312). If I attempt the high-flown and heroic, my images inevitably crumble into parody and caricature. So I must make the most of young Jane's gleeful burlesque.

The second pair of sisters, Eloisa and Charlotte Lutterell, epitomise tragedy and comedy, romance and parody; or, one might say, they are extreme versions of Sensibility and Sense. Characters who espouse romance and sensibility, like Edward in *Love and Freindship*, scorn "the mean and indelicate employment of

Fig. 2.19 Lesley Castle by night.

Fig. 2.20 Lesley Castle by day.

Eating and Drinking" (*J* 111). But eating and drinking are almost all that Charlotte cares about. On the other hand her sister Eloisa is all susceptibility and tears. "You must expect from me nothing but the melancholy effusions of a broken Heart," she encouragingly tells her chosen correspondent (31). The first and defining exchange we hear between the sisters comes in Charlotte's voice:

> I never remember any vexation equal to what I experienced on last Monday when my Sister came running to me in the Store-room with her face as White as a Whipt syllabub, and told me that Hervey [her fiancé] had been thrown from his Horse, had fractured his Scull and was pronounced by his Surgeon to be in the most emminent Danger. "Good God! (said I) you dont say so? why what in the name of Heaven will become of all the Victuals? We shall never be able to eat it while it is good." (7–8)

Here was an irresistible occasion for a picture: Eloisa wringing her hands as she delivers the news of Hervey's fatal accident (and I used a speech balloon to provide the content of her speech), while Charlotte, surrounded by pies and fowls and a pig's head, steadily keeps beating her pudding batter (Figure 2.21).

In this story of contrasts I enjoyed fitting the contrasting figures into the same picture, and Charlotte and Eloisa certainly lend themselves for the purpose. Following on the crisis of what is to be done with the wedding food, I showed Charlotte and her mother staunchly eating their way through chicken and sirloin, while Eloisa "continued for some hours in the most dreadful Convulsions" (9). I was rather proud of my Mrs Lutterell, who doesn't otherwise appear: elbows high in the air as she vigorously attacks her sirloin steak (Figure 2.22).

It is tempting to speculate on the source of Charlotte's name: could it be from the staunch and stolid Charlotte whom Goethe's Werther loves and loses? (To have read *The Sorrows of Werther* is one of the qualifications for belonging in the ranks of sensitive souls, according to Laura of *Love and Freindship*.) A generation later than Austen, Thackeray had his own characterisation of Werther's Charlotte, who sounds a lot like Austen's:

> Werther had a love for Charlotte
> Such as words could never utter;
> Would you know how first he met her?
> She was cutting bread and butter. ("Sorrows of Werther," *Ballads* 92)

Agreeable Charlotte of *Frederic and Elfrida* seems cut out of the same cloth; and Charlotte Lucas of *Pride and Prejudice* is another down-to-earth stolidly sensible character, who minds her distaff and her pantry.

In my pictures I have tried to maintain the undercutting that is constantly going on in the text. I try not to sink into what Jane Eyre called "the bathos of sentiment." When Margaret describes her grief-stricken brother taking tearful leave of his two-year-old daughter, after his wife has deserted him, I provide him with tears, as in duty bound; but I represent little Louisa as fed up with his display of emotion. I include her as an extra in other pictures too; but where Margaret inclines to gush over the child's perfections, I represent her as a wayward little brat.

Fig. 2.21 Crisis over the Victuals.

Fig. 2.22 Consumption and convulsions.

The principle of contrast may extend from one illustration to another, as well as within a single design. A picture of Lesley *fils*, tearful and bereft, comes next to one of Lesley *père*, "gay, dissipated and Thoughtless at the age of 57" (3). And – fortunately for the illustrator – physical and visible features are contrasted too. The petite Lady Lesley is an "insignificant Dwarf" to her stepdaughters, while she calls *them* "Scotch Giants" (20, 22). I couldn't resist a picture of their first meeting, in candle-lit *chiaroscuro*, Gothic castle surroundings, with an empty and shadowed suit of armour standing by (21).

Young Lesley's grief at his wife's desertion lasts only between letters 1 and 3. By the time he gets to Paris, "he thinks it very good fun to be single again" (13). He is not the first young man to be consoled from irremediable grief in Paris. In the Preface to *The Ambassadors* Henry James noted "one of the platitudes of the human comedy, that people's moral scheme *does* break down in Paris; … that hundreds of thousands of … persons annually visit the place for the probable catastrophe" (James xiii–xiv). I had to represent this beneficial effect of travel. My young Lesley appears in front of Notre Dame (I avoided the anachronism of the Eiffel Tower), with a Madame-de-Vionnet-like lady on his arm; while a young Parisienne, succumbing to irresistible curiosity, takes a peek at the mysteries beneath his kilt (Figure 2.23). Does that young lady appear in Austen's text? Well, no. But a generous illustrator can throw things in for free – all by way of preserving "the Scottish flavour" of the work.

To highlight the epistolary element, and to remind the reader of the different locations from which the letters are written, I devised a set of letterheads. The designer helpfully inserted outlines at the beginning and end of each letter, to supply the sense of the letters as documents. A letterhead from Lesley Castle was no problem: I simply provided a miniaturised version of the castle as already drawn. Then for Portman Square, another identified location, I provided a version of Montague House, which stands at one end of it. And for Bristol I used the Hotwells, though since that building is long demolished, I had to find images in a Dictionary of Bristol. In each case I formalised the three-quarter view of the building, with diminishing perspectives, into a straight font view, so as to provide a more formal image and emphasise the neo-classical symmetry.

When I ask myself what is my first priority in the illustrating process, my answer is "expressiveness." Just as character interests me more than setting, so the character's state of mind in a given situation (whether writing the "melancholy effusions of a broken Heart" or "fluttering about the streets of London, gay, dissipated and Thoughtless at the age of 57") is what I want to convey. So the poses and facial expressions I give the characters are hyperbolic, overdone, outrageous. Eloisa in her "melancholy effusions" is wallowing in her own drama. Lady Lesley, fully rouged and fed up with her brother's attentions to her stepdaughter, faces the viewer with a really bitchy "*moue*." The gay and dissipated Lesley Senior cavorts in contortions, head turned one way, eyes and body another, as he reaches to pinch the bottom of a conniving coquette (Figure 2.24).

Fig. 2.23 Young Lesley consoled in Paris.

Fig. 2.24 Old Lesley "gay, dissipated and thoughtless."

There are great artists whom I would like to make my models: primarily Hogarth – same century, also mostly in black and white. Those who know his work may notice quotations – St. James's palace in my "gay and dissipated" sketch, for instance, is borrowed from one of the *Rake's Progress* engravings. And in the same scene the randy pug, making advances on a cooperative bitch, is also a reminiscence of Hogarth's many canine characters.[7]

The Three Sisters

Besides being arguably an *ur*-version of *Pride and Prejudice* (a matter I shall return to later) the unfinished epistolary piece *The Three Sisters* invites attention as an early study in sibling relations. And in his Introduction to the Juvenilia Press volume Joseph Wiesenfarth concentrated on the three sisters of the title. It was a subject Austen was to return to in *The Watsons*. There too we hear of sisterly rivalry over a potential husband: the eldest sister Elizabeth was attached to a young man called Purvis, but her sister Penelope "set him against me," says Elizabeth, "with a view to gaining him herself"; and Purvis withdraws altogether. The younger sister Emma is shocked. "Rivalry, treachery between sisters!" she exclaims (*LM* 81).

The treachery between sisters in the earlier work is of a different kind: rather than snatching the man for themselves, the younger sisters thrust him upon Mary by pretending they would marry him if they got half a chance; so Mary, who can't bear the thought of either of them being married – and to a well-to-do husband – before herself, is tricked into accepting the vile but rich Mr. Watts. Hugely greedy and self-interested, Mary doesn't gather much of our sympathy, especially as the story is unfinished, so we don't see the painful result of her choice. But Georgiana, the youngest and most playful sister, does have some moral qualms: "Yet after all my Heart cannot acquit me & Sophy is even more scrupulous" (*Three Sisters* 11).

What, moral scruple in a character of the juvenilia? Such a thing marks *The Three Sisters* as being much later than its placement in *Volume the First* would suggest.[8] Mary, greedy for all she can get whatever happens to anyone else, is a typical figure of the juvenilia; Georgiana, with an awakened moral consciousness, looks forward to the heroines of the mature novels. Georgiana is also one who enjoys a joke. This much self-consciousness and humour made me think of her as in some way close to her author; so I gave her some curls on her forehead and an ironic smile à la Jane.

---

[7] See Kaitlyn Farrell, "A Dog's World: The Significance of Canine Companions in Hogarth's *Marriage A-la-Mode*." "The canines who appear in Marriage-à-la-mode play a vital role in the series by physically personifying the underlying emotions of their masters" (Ferrell 35).

[8] Kathryn Sutherland suggests that Austen inserted "The Three Sisters" into *Volume the First*, despite its being written some time later than the other items there, because she had space that was suitable for this tale but too tight for the longer "Love and Freindship" ("'Love & Freindship': A Writer's Apprenticeship" 16).

In the midst of the fierce bargaining between the two principals in the courtship over jewels, pin-money, and equipages, it is Sophy, the middle sister, who presents the moral norm for a good husband and happy marriage:

> "I expect my Husband to be good tempered & Chearful; to consult my Happiness in all his Actions, & to love me with Constancy & Sincerity." Mr. Watts stared. (12)

The exchange – the serious moral sentiment that is received with incredulous dismissal – has the same mix of satire and morality that we find in Pope's *The Rape of the Lock*, when the sensible Clarissa delivers the moral message about retaining good humour: "So spoke the Dame, but no Applause ensu'd." But Sophy, though more moral than her sisters, lacks the comic self-awareness of Georgiana.

How was I to present the characters? Mr. Watts, we hear from Mary, is "quite an old Man" – that is, about thirty-two! – and "very plain *so* plain that I cannot bear to look at him" (2). So – although the comment may tell us more about Mary than about him – the illustrator has some clue to his appearance. He is at least easier to do than the sisters, as ugliness inevitably comes more readily to the pen than beauty. And he is at his most disgusting when he sets up as a beau: "You see I am come courting in a true Lover like Manner," he tells Mary on his first visit after she has accepted him (22). I presented him in a decorative embroidered waistcoat with a rose in his button-hole: a sight to make Mary shudder, as we imagine. We used that illustration as our cover image, where I had the chance to add a second colour, red, to my black-and-white illustration. Some of the red found its way to his prominent nose (Figure 2.25).

Mary was a challenge. The good old stereotype of bad equals ugly I thought wouldn't work in this case. Granted that Mr. Watts is a thoroughly unpleasant man, and is ready to consider marriage as a matter of bargain and sale as Mary does. Nevertheless, he has a strong sense of entitlement, and thinks any young woman should be his for the asking. So why does he put up with such outrageously insulting behaviour as Mary's? (There is enough psychological realism in this story to make the question worth asking.) I conclude that Mary must be, if not the prettiest of the sisters, at least the most voluptuous and sexually desirable for such a man. Mary herself fully intends when married to keep going to balls and to make full use of the blue and silver carriage she bargains for. But she notes that Mr. Watts "talks a great deal about Women's always Staying at home & such stuff" (4). He imagines her, I suppose, as a bosomy houri lying invitingly on a chaise-longue as she awaits the attentions of her lord and master (Figure 2.26).

He imagines. Once I began to envision a character as someone else sees her, it occurred to me that the two principals in this love affair do a lot of imagining, and their imaginings are usually far removed from reality. The actual action of this piece is mild: the characters visit, talk, write letters. Not much for an illustrator to latch on to, once she has shown two of the sisters at their desks with pens. But the imaginings are vivid indeed: Mary thinks elegant new carriages, jewels, horses, footmen, lady's maids, phaetons, theatres; she imagines going to balls to

Fig. 2.25 Mr. Watts comes courting.

Fig. 2.26 Mary as Mr. Watts sees her.

chaperone her sisters so she can lord it over them. Mr. Watts imagines a docile voluptuous stay-at-home courtesan, a set of sisters merely waiting for him to pop the question.

Besides the literal action, then, I decided to introduce these rich imaginings into my pictures. The idea first occurred to me as I doodled over Mary's wishes. When Mr. Watts threatens to propose to someone else, Mary tells her mother, "I wish I had a Father or a Brother because then they should fight him" (6). This vision appealed to me: a de-wigged Mr. Watts in shirt-sleeves, with his knees knocking together as he faces a handsome brother with a sword. And I made a doodle of same.

Mary's mother replies, however, "They would be cunning if they did, for Mr Watts would run away first." Another cheerful doodle of his making a successful get-away, clutching his wig to his head. I rather liked the sketchy effect. But because this threatened duel was only putative, I enclosed the two pictures in the "thinks balloon" familiar in comic books (Figure 2.27). Thereafter I followed through with various imagined scenes and objects. And to differentiate between her imaginings and his, I supplied the usual cloudy balloon for her, and a manly squared-off structure for his. So he imagines choosing between the three sisters – represented figuratively as three acquiescent dummies on dummy-stands (Figure 2.28); and *she*

Fig. 2.27 Mr. Watts lives to fight another day.

Fig. 2.28 Mr. Watts takes his pick.

imagines all the items in her long list of desiderata (14). It was my way of getting mental activity into my pictures.

For the literal level of action I reverted to eighteenth-century conventions on representing the passions. Many novelists subscribed to the deeply-imbibed doctrine that emotion eventuates in legible gestures of the limbs or facial features (McMaster, *Reading* 12–18). Acting manuals for the stage, and instructions from academies to painters, regularly taught that there are specific motions or "actions" for specific passions, and novelists eagerly picked up on the doctrine. Likewise young Austen eagerly picked up on the novelists' convention. In *The Beautifull Cassandra*, for instance, when Cassandra meets Maria, "They trembled, blushed, turned pale & passed each other in a mutual silence." We are given no clue to what would cause this emotional manifestation; the manifestation itself seems to be the point. So my Maria (a squirrel with a fashionable parasol) provides a full theatrical performance of astonishment and shock – she steps back, turns aside, and clutches her heart. Cassandra drops her eyes and looks demure. This

Fig. 2.29 "We were of course very much surprised."

little charade successfully performed, they pass each other serenely, each going unperturbed about her business.

To perform such actions well was a proof of a certain somatic sincerity that was deemed highly admirable. Margaret Lesley in *Lesley Castle* actually falls in love with a certain gentleman's "polished Manners and Delightful Bow" (36). For the illustrator, as for eighteenth-century actors and artists, this recognized expressive code is very useful; I too want my characters to be vividly and visibly expressive.

Young Austen was already alert to the merely conventional aspects of the code. In *The Three Sisters* there is a moment when the two younger sisters want to fake surprise at something they already know all about. When Mary announces that Mr. Watts has proposed, her sister records, "We were of course very much surprised" (11). Here was my chance to overstate physical motions. John Bulwer, a seventeenth-century authority on gesture, supplies a kind of dictionary of meaningful motions of the hand: "TO THROW THE HANDS UP TO HEAVEN is an expression of *admiration*, *amazement*, and *astonishment*," he writes (Bulwer 33). So in my picture Sophy and Georgiana humorously overact their surprise, with raised hands and widened eyes, as in the manuals. I take full advantage of Austen's tongue-in-cheek descriptions of these theatrical gestures, because they give me a chance to indulge in overstatement too. In the same picture Mary has her own gesture and the self-satisfied facial expression of being the lady who has pulled off a major coup. Austen's overstatement allows for the illustrator's overstatement too.

Lady Susan

The Juvenilia Press edition of *Lady Susan* was edited by Christine Alexander and David Owen, and we were fortunate that JASNA commissioned it for the conference in Milwaukee on "The Letters in Fact and Fiction." Being epistolary, *Lady Susan* filled the bill. It was a successful edition, even praised by Brian Southam as being the first edition "which is faithful to Jane Austen's exact wording and punctuation. In this respect, it must replace R. W. Chapman's edition" (Southam, Review 19).

For the Press's purposes, however, it was rather long (therefore expensive – so JASNA's commission was the more welcome). And where with short pieces like *Frederic and Elfrida* I could spread myself, with illustrations on nearly every page, for *Lady Susan* there was space only for five pages of illustration. I had to think carefully about ways to cover the ground, and a theme that would give coherence to my pictures as an interpretation of Austen's daring and fraught text.

In other sets of illustrations, such as those for *Lesley Castle* and *Jack and Alice*, I had pursued Austen's artistic principle of contrast – contrast between sense and sensibility, or formality and chaos, or reticence and full disclosure. In this more complex text there aren't these simple thematic oppositions. But within each character, I reflected, there are contrary impulses that can conveniently be represented by conflicting characters. Reginald, for instance, the central male character, is torn between the temptations of the siren-like Lady Susan on the one hand, and caution and the family values, as represented by his sister Catherine Vernon, on the other. Lady Susan herself must manage the choice between the physical charms of her lover, Manwaring, and the social security represented by the young heir Reginald. The daughter and juvenile lead Frederica is expected to marry the fatuous Sir James, but is clearly attracted to Reginald, even though he is her mother's suitor. Even Lady Susan's friend and confidante, Mrs. Johnson, must deal with competing claims from Lady Susan – delightful and charming friend – and her troublesome invalid husband.

The only prominent character to feel no such conflict is Reginald's sister, Catherine Vernon: she is on the side of family and morality, which makes her the antagonist of Lady Susan; but without a competing alliance, she is a rather one-track figure, and so comparatively less interesting then the others.

To represent these conflicting alliances, I took Reynolds's famous portrait of Garrick poised between Comedy and Tragedy as my model. Equally accomplished in both modes, Garrick seems to succumb smilingly to the wiles of the nymph-like Comedy on the left, while the Priestess Tragedy on the right, dour and importunate, urges him to moral seriousness.

One reason that I gravitated towards this pictorial allegory was that Thackeray, an author I much admire (and one who has many affinities with Austen) had used a version of Reynolds's design in his cover image for *Pendennis*. Thackeray, who illustrated his own works, shows at large how his hero is torn between the rival charms of social success and dutiful domesticity. In his cover design we see Pendennis with a near-naked mermaid on one side offering the status symbols

Fig. 2.30 Covers for *Lady Susan* and *Pendennis*.

of coach and crown, and a loving wife on the other, who presents the claims of church and children. So my own cover design shows Reginald hesitating between the seductive Lady Susan and his urgently moral sister pulling him in the other direction (Figure 2.30).

Thackeray famously reversed the stereotypes of blonde and brunette: traditionally the wicked temptress is dark, the domestic angel of the house fair; but in *Vanity Fair* he makes the wicked Becky Sharp fair, and his everlastingly moral Amelia dark; and he does the same in *Pendennis*, with the flighty blond Blanche and the serious brunette Laura. I was inclined to go the Thackeray way; and fortunately so was Austen: Lady Susan is described as "delicately fair, with fine grey eyes & dark eyelashes" (11). My Lady Susan wields blond blandishments; moral Catherine Vernon is dark and serious.

And so I proceeded with several further trios: Frederica between Reginald and Sir James, Mrs. Johnson between her husband and Lady Susan, and so on. These designs don't represent any literal encounters in the story. Rather they are little allegories of moral conflicts. So, as with *The Three Sisters*, I found a way in my illustrations for *Lady Susan* to represent mental action rather than literal. It was an added bonus that in providing these mini-allegories, I was also able to provide my own vision of all the prominent characters in their relations to each other.

Working with the juvenilia does indeed give you a special intimacy and a particular angle on Jane Austen as a writer, as those students have found who participated in the editing of these slim volumes. We don't look in the juvenilia for fine moral discriminations or fully realized characters such as we admire in the six novels. But then we don't go to the novels for rambunctious energy and free-fall laughter and brilliant nonsense. What is already there, though, is the wit and intelligence, and especially the wonderful control of language.

As for characters and situations – they come so thick and fast in the juvenilia that they're hard to keep track of, and many readers give up the effort. But as an illustrator I've made it my business to get to know these wild and uninhibited personalities with their gargantuan appetites and manic energy. I agree with Jack Grey, who once shared with me his conviction that there have been two artists who have created world-class works before adulthood: Mozart and Jane Austen.

Chapter 3
Self-conscious Author

"The key to Jane Austen's fortune with posterity has been in part the extraordinary grace of her facility, in fact of her unconsciousness." Thus, in 1905, Henry James, as a pontificating man of letters. "We are hardly more conscious of her process, or of the experience that fed into it," he elaborated, "than the brown thrush who tells his story from the garden bough." Not content with this gentle masculine put-down, he goes on to imagine her at her work-basket, dropping stitches as she is wool-gathering, and picking them up afterwards "as little touches of human truth, … little master-strokes of the imagination" (James, "Lesson" 117–18).

A century has passed, readers and critics have had, and are still having, their ample say; and it is easy to laugh at how wildly wrong the Master could sometimes be. We can pick out our own brief treasures from his rich criticism, the "little touches of human truth," and "master-strokes of the imagination." Yes, he is a deeply sensitive reader. But to emphasise Austen's "facility," as though it all came easily to her, and her "unconsciousness"! – these are times when James forfeits the place awarded to him by the character in Kipling's "The Janeites": Jane Austen "*did* have lawful issue in the shape of one son," one of them claims; "an' 'is name was 'Enery James" (Kipling 163–4).

We of the twenty-first century have had the benefit of the wide-spread knowledge of Austen's letters, and the passage on that "little bit … of Ivory," and the "fine brush" and the "little effect after much labour" (*Letters* 323).[1] We know that each novel, far from being the seemingly spontaneous and unconsidered song of the brown thrush, was actually the product of creative labour long and hard. And of the juvenilia I will claim that though the labour may not have been long or hard – in fact that some of them may have been tossed off as light-heartedly as if she were playing a game – nevertheless this young author was a tough young professional in the making. In this chapter I shall be examining young Austen as a highly conscious writer, busily constructing herself as an "Author," and intensely aware of the formal properties of the various genres she engages.

"Where Edward in the name of Wonder," demands Edward's father, "did you pick up this unmeaning Gibberish? You have been studying Novels I suspect" ("Love and Freindship" (108).[2] So the 14-year-old author, in her own piece of

[1] Mind you, James could have had that too, as it was published among the letters in James Edward Austen-Leigh's *Memoir* in 1870. The letter had been written to him, James Edward, in the first place.

[2] Some parts of this chapter were first published as "Young Jane Austen: Author" in *A Companion to Jane Austen*, ed. Claudia L. Johnson and Clara Tuite, 81–90, and I am grateful for permission from the publisher, Wiley-Blackwell, to use that material here.

fiction, highlights her critical awareness of the genre that she was to make her own. "The following Novel," she writes further, in her dedication to "Catharine, or the Bower," " … I humbly flatter myself, possesses Merit beyond any already published, or any that will ever in future appear, except such as may proceed from the pen of Your Most Grateful Humble Servt. / The Author" (241). Here already is a young writer acutely and delightedly aware of her power with the pen, equally ready to flaunt it, and (to adapt her own praise of novels) to parody by her "contemptuous censure the very performances, to the number of which [she is herself] adding" (*NA* 40). It is this teenager's intense consciousness of medium that informs her youthful *jeux d'esprit*, and requires us to consider her as already not just a writer, but an "Author."

How should we compare these juvenile works to the six famous novels of Austen's maturity? The adjectives applicable to Austen's juvenilia might include: irreverent, rollicking, spontaneous, hyperbolic, violent, indecent, indecorous, outrageous; the very opposite of the familiar descriptors of the canonised work of the mature Jane Austen: balanced, measured, understated, disciplined, decorous, nuanced. However did this mature novelist grow out of that rambunctious child? Some readers shrug their shoulders at this mystery, and elect to neglect the juvenilia and concentrate on the novels. But it is my project to demonstrate that readers of Austen ignore the juvenilia at their peril. All that control, all that restraint in the service of exactness and the *mot juste*, all the fine moral imagination that can trace the delicate intricacies of an evolving relationship and summon full understanding through "the best chosen language" (*NA* 31), are the more remarkable and the more valuable for growing out of the uninhibited gusto of youthful creativity. To the attentive reader of the juvenilia, Jane Austen's beautifully conscious art is charged with the energy of her youthful exuberance, and the brilliant control and precision are informed by the vitality and free-rein prancing dynamism that have been harnessed and channelled into finely articulated narrative.

To listen to that zestful teenage voice is often to hear intimations of the work of the seasoned novelist. The "parties of ladies" in *Northanger Abbey*, with their "important … business, whether in quest of pastry, millinery, or even (as in the present case) of young men" (*NA* 38) are recognizably only one step on from the beautifull Cassandra, who guzzles six ices at the pastry-cook's, and falls in love with a bonnet. When John Thorpe protests his simple taste for the girl he loves and a roof over his head, and claims "fortune is nothing," Catherine Morland agrees with a near-proverbial saying: "Very true … If there is a good fortune on one side, there can be no occasion for any on the other" (*NA* 126). It's a pronouncement that sounds more like wish-fulfilment than truth, like the more famous "a single man in possession of a good fortune, must be in want of a wife" (*PP* 3). Both aphorisms were anticipated m "The Three Sisters," where Mary Stanhope, asked if her affection does not equal that of her fiancé Mr. Watts, replies serenely, "Oh! when there is so much Love on one side there is no occasion for it on the other" (87). The issues of courtship, love, and fortune were already subject to young Austen's satire.

I hear the zest and delight of the young author, too, in the joyful moments in the novels: in Elizabeth Bennet's mock confession to Jane when convincing her that she *does* love Darcy: "I must confess that I love him better than I do Bingley. I am afraid you will be angry" (*PP* 414), or in Anne's and Wentworth's "smiles reined in and spirits dancing in private rapture" (*P* 261). The difference is that in the juvenilia the smiles are not reined in, but given vent in gusts of belly laughs.

We have come far since James Edward Austen-Leigh remarked in his *Memoir* that "The family have, rightly, I think, declined to let these early works be published." (It was only under pressure, it seems, that in 1871, in the second edition of the *Memoir*, he hesitatingly included the playlet "The Mystery" as an example of Austen's "juvenile effusions" (46, 42). We needed the clarion voice of G.K. Chesterton in 1922, when he launched "Love and Freindship" and other works in *Volume the Second.* He memorably announced that young Austen possessed "the inspiration of Gargantua and of Pickwick; it was the gigantic inspiration of laughter" (Chesterton 1922 xv), thus anchoring her early work in a great comic tradition. That is where she belongs.

Austen's Juvenilia comprise several genres – drama and verse, fictions finished and unfinished, in epistolary form and third-person narration; and the consciousness of medium is very much to the fore.

It is in the letters of dedication that young Austen signals most clearly her self-identification as "Author." Characteristically, the work of youthful writers strives to the condition not just of stories, or poems, or plays, but of *books*. The fledgling authors mimic the material form of the volumes they have read – the layout of title, subtitle, author, date, and even publisher. We can see this in the little books of the Brontës. "THE SEARCH AFTER / HAPINESS" reads the title page of one of Charlotte Brontë's little books, "PRINTED BY HERSELF / AND / SOLD BY / NOBODY &c &c" – with the date and year spelt out, "August the seventeenth, eighteen hundred and twenty nine." (She was 13.) Follows a "Preface," numbered chapters, and so on (Brontë *Search*).

Letters of Dedication

For young Jane Austen, in the fair copies she made of the putative volumes that she presumably presented to the dedicatee, the letter of dedication was the clearest signal that this was not just a piece of writing, but a "work," a step in a creative career. Like other authors, she must have a patron. Like other authors, she will be fulsomely flattering. "Madam / You are a Phoenix. Your taste is refined, Your Sentiments are noble, and your Virtues innumerable … " ("Beautifull Cassandra" 53). Like other authors, she will blow her own trumpet: "the following Novel … possesses Merit beyond any already published … " ("Catharine" 241.)

"The earliest letters we have," Rachel Brownstein writes, "are dated 1796" (Brownstein 125). And editions of the letters by Chapman and Le Faye would seem to confirm this. My own view, however, is that the letters of dedication in the juvenilia are also, indeed, letters – written by a real person *to* a real person of her acquaintance, often with personal reference to real things and incidents: to Martha Lloyd, the dedicatee of "Frederic and Elfrida," for instance, she writes of "the gratitude I feel for your late generosity to me in finishing my muslin Cloak" (3). Peter Sabor has convincingly demonstrated that the dedications, wittily tailored to the dedicatee, allude to family interests and events (Sabor, "Dedications" 45). But of course principally the dedications are to draw attention to the piece in hand as a literary work by one who firmly identifies herself as an "Author."

Among her adult letters, we particularly prize those where she writes about her art: that famous "little bit … of Ivory," those oft-quoted "3 or 4 Families in a Country Village" (*Letters* 323, 275). But these early letters of dedication too speak to the young author's art. Here the self-styled Author writes *in propria persona* about her creations, and she also ostentatiously flexes her rhetorical muscles. In her letter of dedication to Jane Cooper for "A Collection of Letters" she produces a *tour de force* of alliteration: "Cousin … with Caution & Care I Commend to your Charitable Criticism this Clever Collection of Curious Comments … by your Comical Cousin / The Author" (190). Here we find the young author frisking and gambolling in her delight in language, laying it on with a trowel. "A Collection of Letters" is indeed a clever collection of curious comments by various characters, and it looks forward, as critics have often noted, to the novels to come.

And the dedications are crackling with irony and mischief. To her niece Anna she writes, "I dedicate to You the following Miscellaneous Morsels, convinced that if you seriously attend to them, [Anna was seven weeks old at the time] You will derive from them very important Instructions, with regard to your Conduct in Life" (90). Needless to say, the morsels that follow are far from seriously inculcating virtue. Jane Austen's was not the Conduct Book mode. And there is no shortage of literary ambition here – as in the "threescore editions" that she claims to have been published of "The Beautifull Cassandra" and "The History of England." There writes an author with a highly developed sense of success and the market.

Running through all her juvenilia is the young author's delight in her medium, her fascination with each genre and its conventions. How does a given genre *work*? she asks herself. What are its divisions and trajectory, its expected content and themes? A novel, now. It comes in chapters. Here we go, then: "The Beautifull Cassandra. A Novel in Twelve Chapters." And 12 chapters there are indeed, even though the whole work, chapter divisions and all, occupies only 3 pages of print. A play? Ah, it comes in acts and scenes. "The Visit: A Comedy in 2 Acts," complete with dedication, Dramatis Personae, "Act the First, Scene the first, a Parlour" (61–3). And yes, characters who have their exits and their entrances, their assigned speeches, their stage directions. An epistolary novel? Ha! It comes in letters; so: "Love and Freindship: a novel in a series of letters … Letter the First. From Isabel to Laura" (122–3). The orderliness that was to be part of the content of Austen's novels – the carefully incremental progress of each relationship, for instance – is here applied to the divisions and physical layout of the different genres she undertakes.

Parody and Burlesque

The parodic element that looms so large in the juvenilia is of course part of this intense consciousness of medium. Parody, we know, doesn't imply contempt. Austen is like her own Henry Tilney, who can parody Ann Radcliffe and still assert, "The person … who has not pleasure in a good novel, must be intolerably stupid. I have read all Mrs. Radcliffe's works, and most of them with great pleasure" (*NA* 107–8). Austen and her family, she announced stoutly in a letter of December 18, 1798, "are great Novel-readers & not ashamed of being so" (*Letters* 26). To parody a genre or a given work, you must know it very well, observe its conventions very closely, and yes, respect it. We can be sure that *Northanger Abbey* has through the years increased the sales of *The Mysteries of Udolpho* rather than the reverse.

To examine "Love and Freindship" in relation to *Laura and Augustus* of 1784, the novel it chiefly parodies (as I shall do at length in a coming chapter), is to recognise that young Austen, like Tilney, was a close and observant reader as well as a mocking one. Both works are subtitled "in a series of letters"; both have a heroine called Laura and a hero called Augustus; both feature (at least in the eyes of the protagonists) grossly tyrannical fathers and nobly resistant children; both have heroines who faint often and run mad at the climax. The most striking difference is that *Laura and Augustus* is a three-volume tear-jerker, "Love and Freindship" a hilarious burlesque of less than 40 pages. For young Austen, brevity is the soul of wit – and its body too.

Austen's strategy in harvesting laughter from tragedy places this one among the best parodies in the language. And I believe it would have been so recognised, had it been published when she wrote it, like, say, Fielding's *Shamela* (which she surely knew) or Thackeray's *Novels by Eminent Hands*,[3] or Byron's "English Bards and Scotch Reviewers." But you can't ride a wave of popularity with a manuscript.

In the case of "Love and Freindship" there is a single identifiable target, and one may trace the parallels. But often the burlesque is generalised, and present only passingly. The excesses of sensibility in much of the fiction of the day comes in for recurring mockery, and not only in "Love and Freindship." In a fragmentary "Beautiful description of the different effects of sensibility on different minds" we have a scene of the apparently dying Melissa, with Sir William in constant attendance: "The only repose he takes is on the Sopha … for five minutes every fortnight … starting up every Moment & exclaiming 'Oh! Melissa, Ah! Melissa'" (*J* 92). Like other figures of sensibility Sir William demonstrates considerable powers of endurance in his manifestations.

Austen also mocks the stilted and conventional description of landscape, the lawns "enamelled with … flowers," "purling" streams (5), and paddocks

[3] To be parodied by Thackeray in this series, originally called "*Punch*'s Prize Novelists" (1847), was a notable form of recognition. His parodies are mentioned in the *Oxford Companion to English Literature* in the entries on Catherine Gore, G.P.R. James, and Charles Lever.

"perfectly even & smooth, and grazed by four white Cows … at equal distances from each other" (231–2). Richardson's *Sir Charles Grandison*, despite its being Austen's favourite novel, comes in for plenty of disrespectful allusion for its incredibly perfect hero. And the mockery of the grandiloquent language of much contemporary fiction is ubiquitous. This was a writer with an ear for what is pompous or overblown, and a gleeful instinct for deflation.

Epistolary Fictions

In "Love and Freindship … in a Series of Letters" the epistolary convention itself comes in for Austen's satire. The great virtue of the convention was its immediacy – what Samuel Richardson called "writing to the moment." But in "Love and Freindship" Austen throws this advantage to the winds. Far from writing "to the moment," her Laura chronicles the events of her youth more than three decades after the event; she delivers her narrative in letters, yes, but it is simply chopped into arbitrary chunks, letter by letter. This is one way of poking fun at a convention that had become too fashionable.

Young Austen's sharp consciousness of medium makes her an excellent parodist of the form; but even as she sends it up, in works like "The Three Sisters" and "Lesley Castle" as well as "Love and Freindship," she was also honing her skills, no doubt in preparation for "Elinor and Marianne," the first version of *Sense and Sensibility*, and perhaps "First Impressions" too (though we don't have hard evidence that this was epistolary).

"Amelia Webster, an Interesting & well written Tale," as she called it, is perhaps the best epistolary parody. At just over two pages of print, it is short enough to make its point tellingly. For the long-drawn-out courtships in such works as *Sir Charles Grandison* and *Emily Montague* Austen substitutes lightning exchanges of letters, but nevertheless accomplishes no less than three courtships. In a later chapter I shall discuss *Emily Montague* as a likely target for the parody in "Love and Freindship" as well as in "Amelia Webster."

Austen laughs at a convention that is so constantly concerned with the *process* of communication that communication itself languishes. The laborious issues of the writing, delivery, and reception of letters have to become part of the narrative. In Richardson's *Pamela*, for instance, the numerous letters that Pamela keeps writing to her parents (even though she can't deliver them) have to become material objects that claim their own subsidiary narrative: concealed in this or that place, sewn into Pamela's garments, discovered by Mr. B (in whom they precipitate a moral revolution), and so forth. Pamela's clandestine letters to Mr. Williams must be concealed between two tiles, by the sunflower, in the garden; and moreover he must be secretly informed of where they are secreted. In "Amelia Webster" young Austen neatly shines the spotlight on the awkwardness of all this, in a letter from Benjamin Barr to the girl he is courting, Sally Hervey, and gives us a laugh at the same time:

> Dear Sally [he writes]/ I have found a very convenient old hollow oak to put our Letters in; for you know we have long maintained a private Correspondence. [She would hardly need to be told this!] It is about a mile from my House and seven from Yours. You may perhaps imagine that I might have made choice of a tree which would have divided the Distance more equally – I was sensible of this at the time, but as I considered that the walk would be of benefit to you in your weak and uncertain state of Health, I preferred it to one nearer your House, and am yr faithfull BENJAMIN BARR (*J* 59)

One imagines the delicate Sally collapsing on the way to collect her mail.

In a later novel we get full debate on Jane Fairfax's imprudently walking to the post office in the rain; like Sally and Benjamin Barr she is maintaining a secret correspondence – with Frank Churchill: and she has to defend herself against Mrs. Elton's officious insistence that she will send a servant for Jane's mail. "The post office is a wonderful establishment!" she exclaims, to change the subject; and the conversation proceeds with wonder that so few letters are lost of all the thousands posted, despite "the variety of hands, and of bad hands too": and so on, to the issue of handwriting generally (*E* 320). An epistolary novelist must pay attention to the large subject of letter-writing; and young Austen, with her many epistolary fictions, draws her reader's attention to such matters, and so provides an extra dimension for her humour.

Of course there were also positive aspects of epistolary narration, by which young Austen was to hone her skills: a virtue of the technique that she made full use of was the letter's potential for self-articulation, and the opportunity it provides for developing character and consciousness though voice. There wasn't space for such things in "Amelia Webster." But in "The Three Sisters" we find Mary Stanhope debating whether or not to accept the proposal of the odious Mr. Watts, and in the process presenting the stalemate between her revulsion and her greed: "He has a large fortune and will make great Settlements on me; but then he is very healthy … I wont have him I declare" (74–5). Mary Stanhope is all before us, with her vanity and envy and acquisitiveness, and her inability to sort out the pros and cons of the decision before her.

Epistolary novels abound in characterisations of one character by another; and in case we need to know more of a character's beauty or virtue than he or she should declare, Richardson's Pamela can *relay* flattering descriptions of herself by other characters. But Austen clearly enjoyed allowing her characters to carol their own praises. Laura of "Love and Freindship" thus describes her youthful self:

> Lovely as I was the Graces of my Person were the least of my Perfections. Of every accomplishment accustomary to my sex, I was Mistress. When in the Convent, my progress had always exceeded my instructions, my Acquirements had been wonderfull for my Age, and I had shortly surpassed my Masters.
>
> In my Mind, every Virtue that could adorn it was centered; it was the Rendezvous of every good Quality and of every noble Sentiment. (*J* 104)

The elements of this description – graces of person going with graces of mind, swiftly exceeding the masters in all talents and performance, and so on – are familiar attributes of the heroine of many a novel – for instance, Emily Saint Aubert of *The Mysteries of Udolpho*. The delicious difference is in the change of person. To substitute "I" for "she" is to change a routine catalogue of qualities into uproarious satire.

In "Lesley Castle" the joke goes a step further, from the "lovely as I am" version to the "lovely as I am, unlike you" put-down. Margaret Lesley, writing to the homely Charlotte Lutterell, advances her discourse from a description of the oppressive admiration she receives in London "in Public, in Private, in Papers, & in Printshops," to regretting the beauty that makes her irresistible. "How often have I wished that I possessed as little personal Beauty as you do; that my figure was as inelegant, my face as unlovely; and my Appearance as unpleasing as yours!" (172).

The fragment ends before we get Charlotte's response to this confidential confession. But she seems to take such revelations in stride. Charlotte Lutterell has sometimes been seen as an on-sage Jane Austen for her ability to be amused by the follies and nonsense of others. She is even good and frank at describing herself, in contrast with her sister, and witty too:

> We both loved Reading. *She* preferred Histories, and *I* Receipts. She loved drawing Pictures, and I drawing Pullets. No one could sing a better Song than She, and no one make a better Pye than I. (164)

Charlotte here shows young Austen's own mastery of language, in contrast, balance, and alliteration. And her culinary artistry, like Austen's literary artistry, makes her independent of the need to catch a husband: she longs to go to Vauxhall not for the opportunities for courtship, but "to see whether the cold Beef there is cut so thin as it is reported, for I have a sly suspicion that few people understand the art of cutting a slice of cold Beef as well as I do" (164).[4] And though she is all for promoting other people's weddings, for the sake of cooking the food, she won't think of marrying herself, "as I very much suspect that I should not have so much time for dressing my own Wedding-dinner, as for the dressing that of my freinds" (156).

It is intriguing to find, in the one brief first-person narrative in the juvenilia, "A beautiful description," that among all the characters surrounding the expiring Melissa, the narrator is the one who cooks: "I am usually at the fire cooking some little delicacy for the unhappy invalid – Perhaps hashing up the remains of an old Duck, toasting some cheese or making a Curry" ([72] – hardly invalid's fare!)

[4] Here I presume to differ from Peter Sabor's reading, "the act of cutting a slice of cold Beef" and opt for the more appropriate "the art of cutting a slice of cold Beef" – despite the fact that I have only a facsimile before me (the Abbeville Press publication of *Volume the Second*, 124), while he no doubt checked the original. Kathryn Sutherland follows the Chapman edition in reading "art," not "act," in her transcription (302).

But before I conclude that Austen shared Charlotte's cooking obsession, I remind myself of the letter of 1816: "Composition seems to me Impossible, with a head full of Joints of Mutton & doses of rhubarb" (*Letters* 321).

It will be apparent that Charlotte Lutterell is my favourite character in the juvenilia: young Austen has produced a small masterpiece of consistent and wittily presented characterisation.

The letters of "The Three Sisters" are sent to various off-stage correspondents who do not reply, so that we miss the sense of an inter-related community of correspondents such as we have, say, in Smollett's *Humphry Clinker*. But in "Lesley Castle" Austen has learned to take advantage of the potential for an exchange of letters within a community, and her sharply differentiated characters interact fully, and define themselves by their responses to one another.

Charlotte Lutterell writes letters and receives them from both Margaret Lesley and Margaret's new stepmother Lady Lesley, and reflects on her position of epistolary confidante to both of them. Before the two meet, she furnishes Margaret with "an exact description of [Lady Lesley's] bodily and Mental charms" (154), and it is indeed sufficiently exact. And it's not all positive. Lady Lesley, she writes, "is naturally pale, but rouges a good deal … remarkably good-tempered when she has her own way, and very lively when she is not out of humour … . She plays, sings and Dances, but has no taste for either" (120). It is typical of Charlotte that she should reflect on her own description: "Perhaps you may … be surprised that one of whom I speak with so little affection should be my particular freind … She is probably by this time as tired of me, as I am of her" (120). This is a thinking, self-aware letter-writer, observing her own pronouncements as she makes them, and adapting her voice to her correspondent.

The stately Lesley sisters resent the intrusion of a new stepmother into their ancestral castle, and consider her, "in comparison with the elegant height of Matilda and Myself, an insignificant Dwarf" (157). Lady Lesley, on the other hand, writing to the same correspondent, denounces her new stepdaughters as "two great, tall, out of the way, over-grown Girls … Scotch giants" (158). As the recipient of both these accounts, Charlotte is "greatly entertained," and recognises "you are both downright jealous of each others Beauty" (163–4).

As Jan Fergus points out, "The letters in 'Lesley Castle' not only tell the story, then, but move the story" (Fergus, *Lesley* viii). Young Austen was learning mastery of the technique. Also among the epistolary works she was developing her skills in the creation of a scene: for like other authors of epistolary fictions she had no qualms about assuming perfect recall among her letter-writers of dialogue and delivery. Her letters, in fact, are small-scale first-person narratives, with the built-in advantage of the possibility of dramatic irony in the writer's distortions through bias or prejudice.

The petite Lady Lesley, who has by now had more than enough of gloomy old Lesley Castle, is irritated to see her brother proceeding to fall in love with one of her big-boned stepdaughters.

> "They are both so horribly tall!" [she objects to him].
>
> "They are *taller* than you are indeed," (said he with a saucy smile) … "Well, … tho' they may be above the common size, their figures are perfectly elegant; and as to their faces, their Eyes are beautifull –"
>
> "I never can think such tremendous knock-me-down figures in the least degree elegant, and as for their eyes, they are so tall that I never could strain my neck enough to look at them."
>
> "Nay (replied he), I know not whether you may not be in the right in not attempting it, for perhaps they might dazzle you with their Lustre." (126).

It is broad, laid on with a trowel for humorous effect; but it shows an author keenly aware of individual bias that informs conversational exchanges, even those that are meant by the speakers to be mere declarations of fact. I hear intimations of Miss Bingley discussing Elizabeth Bennet with Darcy. Lady Lesley is not a prominent character in the fragment; but she like others is already fixed firmly on the page, both by what she reports herself as saying to her brother, and by the way she relays such matters to her immediate reader.

"A Collection of Letters" makes no attempt to connect the five separate letter-writers with each other or with their correspondents. They are simply experiments in catching the voices and tone of the different writers in their different situations, and they could equally serve as narrative journal entries in which a character investigates her own experience. "Letter the Fifth from a Young Lady very much in love" could even be an ironic short story, narrated in all innocence by the dupe of a clever manipulator. There is some subtle manipulation of chronology. We hear first of Henrietta's raptures over the love letter from the fortune-hunter Musgrove. His letter-within-a-letter comes verbatim, as he throws in what he considers are obligatory compliments and raptures, and gets in a muddle over whether to observe the formal third person – "her beauty is encreased in her Musgrove's Eyes" – or to embrace the second and first persons:

> When the lovely Creature first entered the room, Oh! what were my sensations? The sight of you was like the sight of a wonderful fine Thing. I started – I gazed at her with Admiration – She appeared every moment more Charming, and the unfortunate Musgrove became the Captive to your Charms before I had time to look about me … You are an angel. You are Venus herself. In short Madam you are the prettiest Girl I ever saw in my Life." (*J* 205–6)

The bathos of the changed register – from "wonderful fine" to the lame "Thing," or from Venus and angel (strange bedfellows!) to "the prettiest Girl I ever saw in my life" – gives the reader another laugh; and yet we recognise these are probably the most genuine sentiments in the composition: all the rest being more or less conventional formulas clumsily handled. As for the fumbling and inconsistent use of the third person: it's no surprise that much later Austen wrote, on her niece

Anna's debut in fiction, "I do not like a Lover's speaking in the 3rd person: – it is too much like the formal part of Lord Orville, & I think is not natural" (*Letters* 267). She had already had fun satirising that formal practice with her "unfortunate Musgrove," who is certainly no Lord Orville.

Henrietta however is bowled over by this lurching composition; and she is moved to a flashback to recall what led up to it, the interview where Lady Scudamore assesses the susceptible heiress as a useful resource for her impoverished cousin. The manipulation of chronology provides an ironic perspective. And Lady Scudamore's machinations look forward, perhaps, to Mary Crawford's manoeuvres with the necklace and persuasive language to inveigle Fanny into falling in love with Henry Crawford.

"Lady Susan" marks many strides forward in the structuring of epistolary narration. Here we have plots and counter-plots, and the receivers of the letters involve themselves fully on one side and the other. Lady Susan herself, who by her sexual and financial exploits has just made one country estate, Langford, too hot to hold her, proposes to move on to the next, Churchill, the seat of her brother-in-law; Churchill too will soon be a-hum with her devious doings. Lady Susan has her confidante and ally, Mrs. Johnson, in London; and her adversary and sister-in-law Catherine Vernon has hers in her mother Lady de Courcy. In Lady Susan's case especially we need to be privy to her correspondence with her confidante, since here we get the full measure of her duplicity. To her sister-in-law she gushes, in the first letter, "I impatiently look forward to the hour when I shall be admitted to your delightful retirement" (*LM* 3); while to Mrs Johnson, in the following letter, she writes "I take Town in my way to that insupportable spot, a Country Village" (5). One wonders whether Austen recalled Lady Susan when she wrote years later, as a published novelist, "3 or 4 Families in a Country Village is the very thing to work on"! (*Letters* 275).

The two prizes these antagonists contend for are Catherine's brother Reginald and Lady Susan's daughter Frederica. It is a fine symmetrical set-up, for in the duel of deceit and tactics between the two principals – in which Lady Susan's weapons are by far the sharpest – we need to learn what each is *really* working at.

Lady Susan's cheerful self-revelation to Mrs. Johnson in London has convinced me that young Austen knew and to some extent followed *Shamela*, Fielding's devastating parody of Richardson's *Pamela*. Lady Susan, an earl's daughter, is of course immensely superior in social standing to Shamela, a servant girl. But both are outrageously self-seeking heroines who get their way by feigning a delicate morality (or "Vartue," as Shamela calls it). Both reside in the country, with a wily and sexually experienced confidante in London (in Shamela's case, it is her mother, who keeps a bawdy-house in Drury Lane); both prefer a profligate lover (Parson Williams and Manwaring) to their more moral suitors. As writers, both rejoice in the "sentiment," or abstract moral pronouncement, which in Shamela's case is signalled by italics: "*O how foolish it is in a woman, once she has got the reins into her own hands ever to quit them again*," she writes sententiously (Fielding 335); "Consideration & Esteem as surely follow command of Language, as Admiration waits on Beauty," Lady Susan philosophises (268). And the same expression of using skill in language "to make Black appear White" occurs at crucial moments in both works (Fielding 387; *LM* 11–12).

The elegant and effective structure, as managed through the letters from several writers to several mutually interested recipients, makes "Lady Susan" an excellent example of successful epistolary narration. And if it had not been overshadowed by the brilliant and very different novels that were yet to come, it would hold a more prominent place in the canon. As it is we can still trace carry-overs from it to the novels:[5] particularly we see the sinister aspects of Lady Susan again in Mary Crawford. Lady Susan delights in winning over Reginald against his will: "There is an exquisite pleasure in subduing an insolent spirit, in making a person pre-determined to dislike, acknowledge one's superiority" (14); and Mary Crawford rejoices at winning over Edmund to do what he had determined not to do: "His sturdy spirit to bend as it did! Oh! it was sweet beyond –expression" (*MP* 414). Thus Mephistophilis would celebrate the winning of a soul.

Drama

The experience with voice that Austen gathered through her early epistolary fictions, as in the spirited parody "Amelia Webster," seems to have prompted her to further exploitation of voice, indeed towards drama itself. Closely following "Amelia Webster" in *Volume the First* come the two mini-dramas, "The Visit" and "The Mystery."

"Bless me! there ought to be 8 Chairs and there are but 6. However, if your Ladyship will but take Sir Arthur in your Lap, and Sophy my Brother in hers, I beleive we shall do pretty well" (*LM* 55). This is hardly the correct protocol and gracious hospitality of a formal dinner party. But Lesley Peterson, who co-edited the Juvenilia Press edition of *Three Mini-Dramas* and directed what we believe was the world premiere of Austen's playlet "The Visit," discovered that this is a piece of stage business that plays very well. Requiring the guests to sit on each others' laps, besides providing some slapstick comedy, could also be a rather crude ploy in matchmaking, as Miss Fitzgerald plants her brother on the lap of the girl he is courting. "I beg you will make no apologies," says Sophy politely, as one imagines with gritted teeth: "Your Brother is very light" (65).

"The Visit" already provides an early version of those "3 or 4 Families in a Country Village" (*Letters* 275) that Austen more famously espoused later. A brother and sister, who might be considered the Hosts from Hell, throw a dinner party for a local baronet, his lady, a daughter, nephew, and niece. Besides requiring the guests to sit on each others' laps, and accommodating their houseguest with a bed too short for him, they provide a disgusting dinner of cowheel and onion and liver and crow, with home-made wine. Nevertheless, the young people take

[5] Q.D. Leavis has argued at length that "Lady Susan" was "made over" into *Mansfield Park*, and she elaborated many parallels (Leavis 96–125).

it all in stride, and proceed to pair off, as in "Amelia Webster," and accomplish no less than three engagements in as many minutes. Poor doddering Sir Arthur is routinely denied any item of food or drink; his wife peremptorily declares, "Sir Arthur never touches wine"; tripe is "too savoury" for him, pudding "too high a dish," and so on (66–7). All this makes for much amusing stage business.

As she ponders this different form of the drama, with its potential for actual enactment, young Austen busily envisages the physical – not only in the conglomeration of bodies when eight dinner guests must squeeze themselves into six chairs, but also in the progress of courtships over the vile meal. "I am afraid Mr Willoughby … you dont meet with any thing to your liking," says the hostess Miss Fitzgerald to her guest. "Oh! Madam," he responds, presumably gazing into her eyes, "I can want for nothing when there are red herrings on table." Sure enough, after the other couples have paired off, Miss Fitzgerald takes the business of the proposal off the hands of the diffident Willoughby: "Since you Willoughby are the only one left, I cannot refuse your earnest solicitations – There is my Hand" (66–8). Again, brevity is a major part of the joke.

The second playlet, "The Mystery," I discussed in the last chapter in the context of illustrating it. The maddening withholding of information, which is the principal joke of the play, is another means by which Austen teasingly tantalises us with what is not there.

In "The First Act of a Comedy," besides the wild mix of stage modes – pastoral, burletta, and so on – we have the parodic impulse to the fore again, this time in drama. Austen had clearly pondered various aspects of credibility on stage, as in the exchange of letters. A novelist, at least in the novel that is not epistolary, can deliver necessary background information to the reader directly, in the opening paragraphs, perhaps. But a dramatist, being limited to dialogue, is often obliged to put such information into a speech delivered by one character to another who should already know all about the matter. Fully aware of this awkwardness, in "The First Act of a Comedy" young Austen has Popgun reply to a simple question from his daughter in a speech that has as many relative clauses piled up on each other as "The House that Jack Built":

> *Pistoletta*: Pray papa, how far is it to London?
>
> *Popgun*: My Girl, my Darling, my favourite of all my Children, who art the picture of thy poor Mother who died two months ago, with whom I am going to Town to marry Strephon, and to whom I mean to bequeath my whole Estate, it wants seven Miles. (219)

As so often, the young author couldn't resist making fun of the very conventions she was following.

A further foray in drama was "Sir Charles Grandison," the brief stage version of Richardson's long novel, which was initially attributed to Austen's niece Anna Lefroy, with Aunt Jane acting as her amanuensis; but which Brian Southam has convincingly re-attributed to Austen herself.[6] He argues, however, that it is only the first act that belongs among Austen's juvenilia: the 1799 watermarks show that the subsequent acts come later, when Austen was 24 or so. My brief commentary, then, will be largely limited to "Act the First."

To read "Sir Charles Grandison" alongside Austen's brief earlier dramas is to notice some interesting parallels. The first scene, which Austen composed on her own, without an equivalent action in Richardson's novel, has a tantalising gap in the middle that is reminiscent of the maddeningly withheld secrets in "The Mystery." Amid plenty of bustle among servants, a milliner, and the lady of the house, we hear that Harriet Byron's costume for the Masquerade has arrived. ("Oh-oh," says the reader familiar with Richardson; it's from the Masquerade that Harriet gets abducted by the wicked Sir Hargrave Pollexfen.) Her hostess can hardly wait to open up the bandbox. When Harriet herself arrives, we promise ourselves the treat of seeing the outfit. But no, that is not to be, because Harriet says hurriedly, "We will take it up stairs if you please & look at it, for Mr. Reeves is coming, & we shall have some of his Raillery" – and then "Exeunt in an hurry" ("Grandison" 65). It's the kind of deliberate teasing that young Austen seems to have enjoyed.

Female concerns of dress and fashion are to the fore. These ladies don't actually fall in love with bonnets like the beautifull Cassandra, but they would certainly understand the condition. The fact that the first scene is out of Austen's own head, rather than a version of a scene in Richardson, encourages me to look for characteristic incidents, characters, or turns of phrase. She introduces a milliner (there's no milliner in Richardson), and she makes a bustle about dresses and trying them on. The women retreat upstairs as Mr. Reeves arrives, sure that he will plague them with his "Raillery." Sure enough, Mr. Reeves, the first male to appear, congratulates himself on having got "the coast clear of Dresses & Band boxes," and so he can retire to his study unmolested by female fiddle-faddle. That is, from the outset, and in terms more definite than Richardson's, Austen provides a strikingly female setting, and an explicit contrast and antagonism between male concerns and female.

A glance at the "Dramatis Personae" confirms a feminine take on the action. As we all know, the lists of Dramatis Personae in Shakespeare's plays are heavily weighted on the male side. Not here, though. The listing provides nine names under "Men," and no less than 16 under "Women." Austen is feminizing the drama, as in another place she feminized history. Catherine Morland memorably complains of historiography that it consists of "the quarrels of popes and kings, … the men all so good for nothing, and hardly any women at all – it is very tiresome" (*NA* 110). And Jan Fergus points out that in her own "History of England" Austen "includes the very high proportion of seventeen women to twenty-six men" (Fergus, "Introduction" to *History* iv). In her "Grandison" she considerably augmented the proportion of women.

[6] The extent of Austen's authorship of this little play continues to be disputed; but I accept Southam's attribution.

In Frances Burney's first comedy for the stage, *The Witlings* (written around 1779 and never produced in her lifetime) we have a comparably feminized opening – set in a milliner's shop among seamstresses, with orders for cloaks and caps flying about, and strong concerns about lappets and ribbons. Margaret Anne Doody comments on the striking originality of such an opening as an unashamed appeal to female interests (Doody, *Burney* 177).

The expected "Raillery" of Mr. Reeves at women's appurtenances draws attention to opposed male and female interests, not with the usual implication that the male's is the norm and the female's deviant, but with a cheerful acknowledgement that both are legitimate and both amusing; also that the male's usually prevails. Mr. Reeves's soliloquy, as the ladies betake themselves off "in an hurry," puts the male point of view, and his outraged sense of being besieged in his own domain:

> So, for once in a way I have got the coast clear of Dresses & Band boxes & I hope my wife and Miss Byron will continue to keep their Millinery in their own rooms, or any where so as they are not in my way. Why, if I had not had a little spirit the other day, I should have had them in my own study. (65–6)

There is some humour in the patriarch's retreat to his inner sanctum; also some shades of scenes yet to come, such as Mr. Bennet's dismissing his wife and daughter and their concerns: "I shall be glad to have the library to myself as soon as may be" (*PP* 125).

The female concern with dress is matched by another: food. We don't get much about food in the novels: there the character who talks most about food, Mr. Woodhouse in *Emma*, is one who, abstemious himself, seeks to impose his abstemiousness on others, even his guests; so that Emma has to supply them with more apple tart, custard, and wine while he isn't looking (*E* 24–5). It's different in the juvenilia, where references to food abound – as in the beautiful Cassandra's devouring six ices at a sitting. The whole of the longest and final scene of "The Visit" happens at table, with those delectable menu items of fried Cowheel and Onion," red herrings, tripe, "Liver & Crow," and suet pudding, along with mead, warmed ale and nutmeg, and home-made gooseberry wine (66). The fact that the principal male guest, Sir Arthur, is repeatedly denied food and wine by his supervising wife leads me to suspect that perhaps Mr. Woodhouse was to be Sir Arthur's revenge.

In "Grandison" the references to food are not so specific, but much of the action involves the ordering and delivery of tea, broth, and sandwiches, and announcements that dinner is on table. As in the novels, social occasions furnish the big scenes, and these often involve dinners, balls with suppers, and other events that involve the sharing of food in a community. In fact in "Grandison" such "minor" action furnishes more of the matter of the play than the major events in Richardson's novel. In the novel the crisis comes early: the abduction of Harriet Byron on her way home from the Masquerade, and Sir Hargrave's attempt at a forced marriage to her. Then comes Sir Charles's rescue of her, and his fight with

Sir Hargrave and removal of Harriet to the care of his sister. These events we learn, of course, through letters. And in Austen's play? A returning Grandison sister asks the other how Harriet comes to be in their care. Lady G replies "Well, we will go & take a walk in the Garden & talk about it" (92). And off they go. More shades of "The Mystery"! We the audience are meant to know all about it already, because we must have read the novel: so that Austen's "Grandison" is less a re-telling of Richardson's novel than an ornamental play *around* its action.

Austen's juvenilia, I believe, were not addressed *to* children as such.[7] They are addressed to smart reading people like herself, young or old. "Sir Charles Grandison," however, does seem to be intended for children. Brian Southam calls it "a piece of home-theatricals which provided parts for the children as well as for the grown-ups [hence the many brief walk-on parts for servants], and which allowed the youngsters a line or two or the chance to make a brief appearance on-stage to hand round the tea-cups!" (Southam, "Grandison" 12). But I can't accept Southam's breezy dismissal of "The Visit," "The Mystery," and "The First Act of a Comedy" by calling "Grandison" "Jane Austen's only play" (12). As we have seen, she pondered the conventions, strengths, and shortcomings of the drama, as of epistolary narratives, before she embraced her finally chosen mode, third-person narration.

Third-person Narration

Although young Austen evidently enjoyed writing from the point of view of her individual letter-writers, with their differentiated styles and voices, she did not opt for extended first-person narratives of the *Roderick Random* or *Jane Eyre* kind – though Laura in "Love and Freindship" comes close. She chose instead to let dialogue do the work of self-revelation by her characters, while as narrator she could comment omnisciently when she chose. Her narration in the non-epistolary works, however, stops short of the omniscient kind of narrator familiar in Fielding, Thackeray, and George Eliot. Sometimes what the narrator doesn't know is the cream of the joke.

But third-person narration, including some locally limited points of view of her characters, was the mode she was to make her own: and by the time of *Emma* she had perfected the kind of writing that seems omniscient, with the ability to look before and after, but with the more dramatic quality of a point of view mostly limited to Emma's.

Alongside the dramas and the epistolary fictions, then, and from the first, Austen was confident in taking the narrative into her own hands. She was already developing her own narrative voice, and often doing so by negative means, defining her own purposes through burlesquing those of previous writers. The

[7] An exception may be "Mr. Clifford," dedicated to Jane Austen's younger brother Charles, and containing matter, such as Mr. Clifford's addiction to vehicles, which are designed to engage a little boy.

earliest fictions, "Frederic and Elfrida," "Henry and Eliza," and "The Beautifull Cassandra," are all third-person narratives. And in "The History of England" from *Volume the Second*, the young author is almost tyrannically authoritative.

"Frederic and Elfrida" stands first in *Volume the First*, but as we have seen it already has a consistent theme in satirising the extremes of propriety in courtship. Those two or three families in a country village already take centre stage: and young Austen invents playfully gargantuan names for the villages – Crankhumdunberry in "Frederic and Elfrida" and Pammydiddle in "Jack and Alice." The principal couple of this first narrative, Frederic and Elfrida Falknor, live near their intimate friend Charlotte Drummond, and together they visit the newcomers, Mrs. Fitzroy and her two daughters, and develop that enviable degree of intimacy that allows them to kick each other out of the window on the slightest provocation (6). Clothing is already important, with the quest for "a new and fashionable Bonnet" providing the impulse for action, and the decaying wedding clothes providing a marker for passing time. Young Austen's fascination with conventional literary landscape and the manicured look promoted by Repton and others first appears here in the parodic description of the artificially composed scenery: "A Grove of Poplars which led … to a verdant Lawn enamelled with a variety of variegated flowers and watered by a purling Stream" (5). As we have seen, the parody of literary landscape continues in "Jack and Alice" in the incongruous matching of the Citron Grove with pigstye and horsepond, and Austen takes it further still in "Evelyn."

In these early tales the narrator accepts no limitations on her omniscience, and moves readily among families and locations. Nor is she shy of "intruding" as narrator to discuss her own authorial procedures. In "Jack and Alice" she pops in, as it were, to explain:

> It may now be proper to return to the Hero of this Novel, the brother of Alice, of whom I beleive I have scarcely ever had occasion to speak; which may perhaps be owing to his unfortunate propensity to Liquor, which so compleatly deprived him of the use of those faculties Nature had endowed him with, that he never did anything worth mentioning. His Death happened a short time after … . (27)

And that disposes of Jack. Why on earth, in that case, the author should have chosen him as the eponymous hero she chooses not to explain.

The characters' perfect confidence in their own probity and perfection comes in for lively treatment. Eliza in "Henry and Eliza" is so in love with her own virtue that after being dismissed from her benefactors' home for stealing a 50-pound banknote, she sits down under a tree, "happy in the conscious knowledge of her own Excellence," and composes and sings a song:

> Though misfortunes my footsteps may ever attend
> I hope I shall never have need of a Freind
> as an innocent Heart I will ever preserve
> and will never from Virtue's dear boundaries swerve. (39)

It is the most explicit statement of self-approbation among the dozens of self-worshippers of the juvenilia. The narrator, however, does not comment.

"Henry and Eliza" is also a cheerful parody of the birth mystery plot. In the best tradition of *Tom Jones*, *Oliver Twist*, and many others, Eliza is a foundling. The "novel" begins:

> As Sir George and Lady Harcourt were superintending the labours of their Haymakers … they perceived lying closely beneath the thick foliage of a Haycock, a beautifull little Girl not more than 3 months old. (38)

(How a haycock, or pile of hay, comes to have "thick foliage" is not explained.)

"Having no children of their own," we hear, and "touched with the enchanting Graces of her face & delighted with the infantine tho' sprightly answers she returned to their many questions" (an advanced three-month-old, this) they do the Squire Alworthy thing, and take her in, ready to inculcate in her their own "Love of Virtue & Hatred of Vice." It seems they succeed to some extent, for she certainly admires Virtue, and believes she has plenty of it. After her many adventures, including marriage, children, imprisonment and escape with her children, and war with her enemy the "Dutchess," she returns to the place where she was brought up. There – surprise, surprise! – she encounters again her adoptive parents. At seeing her Lady Harcourt all at once remembers that she had borne a baby girl while Sir George was away, "but dreading your just resentment at her not being the Boy you wished, I took her to a Haycock & laid her down" (44) – and then she forgets all about it until this moment of reunion. ("*Just* resentement"? Austen surely includes some irony at the expense of those who consider the mother as responsible for the sex of the child.)

The omniscient narrator could have told us readers about Lady Harcourt's actions at the time. But that would of course spoil the joke.

The birth mystery plot comes in for further burlesque in "Love and Freindship," in the episode where Lord St. Clair discovers a series of long-lost grandchildren.

"Edgar and Emma," another of the early third-person narratives, begins thus:

> "I cannot imagine," said Sir Godfrey to his Lady, "why we continue in such deplorable Lodgings as these … " (*J* 33)

It has a ring that recalls another famous opening speech:

> "My dear Mr. Bennet," said his lady to him one day, "have you heard that Netherfield Park is let at last?" (*PP* 3)

The plunge *in medias res*, and the shorthand of "his lady," as well as the concern with a residence for rent, for me connect the early work with the later much more famous one.[8] "Edgar and Emma" is scarcely known to today's readers; but we can be sure that Austen herself remembered it well, for she continued to allude to her

8 Rachel Brownstein also notices this echo in *Pride and Prejudice* (Brownstein 127).

juvenilia in her letters to Cassandra. I like to think that years later she recalled and echoed the rhythm of that early opening sentence.

Dialogue sets a tone for a work, as Austen knew already; and Sir Godfrey goes on to say they have stayed in lodgings only for his lady's sake; *she* says no such thing, and so on. The narrator steps in with a piece of wisdom: "As, after a few more speeches on both sides, they could not determine which was most to blame, they prudently laid aside the debate" (34). The tone of the marriage counsellor is heard again years later in the unfinished fragment, *The Watsons*. Mr. and Mrs. Edwards have a recurring marital dispute: he likes his bridge nights; she says he stays at them too late. We hear an apparently ritual exchange in which the main points are repeated on each side of the question: "So far, the subject was very often carried; – but Mr. and Mrs. Edwards were so wise as never to pass that point; and Mr. Edwards now turned to something else" (*LM* 91). The narrator has no qualms about evaluating such "prudent" and "wise" behaviour. But when it comes to essential information like whose daughter Eliza is, she would rather leave it to the characters themselves to make the discovery. "Sir George, Sir George," cries Lady Harcourt in excitement, "she is not only Eliza our adopted Daughter, but our real Child" (44). This narrator reserves the right to be omniscient when it suits her, and to limit her knowledge when there's a joke to be made.

There is another case of amnesia in the brief piece called "Mr Harley" in *Volume the First.* Harley goes to sea as a ship's chaplain on board a man of war. (The piece is dedicated to Austen's sea-faring brother Francis, "Midshipman on board his Majesty's Ship the Perseverance" [40].) When Harley returns from his voyage, on the way to his love Emma, he finds he is sharing a coach with a "young Wife … with fine dark Eyes and an elegant Shape" (no, not Elizabeth Bennet, who shares these features), and suddenly recalls, "Inshort Mr Harley soon found out, that she was his Emma & recollected he had married her a few weeks before he left England" (46).

There can hardly be a wider contrast in tone between the juvenilia and the novels than the story of Mr. Harley and his cheerful amnesia about the wife he left behind, and Captain Harville of *Persuasion*, who speaks to Anne so poignantly about the sailor's yearning attachment to wife and family. "[I]f I could make you comprehend what a man suffers when he takes a last look at his wife and children … And then, if I could convey to you the glow of his soul when he does see them again … " But Harville acknowledges, "I speak, you know, only of such men as have hearts!" (*P* 255). There's the difference. The Austen of the juvenilia does not bother herself with such men as have hearts, or women either.

"Mr. Harley" (the similarity of the name to "Harville" is surely not accidental) is so short a piece that the hero's forgetting and belated remembering seem to be the main point. Other figures of the juvenilia are similarly afflicted with amnesia. Laura of "Love & Freindship," for instance, scarcely pauses in her narrative to mention the "trifling Circumstance" of the death of her parents, which she had forgotten before (118). Her forgetfulness is of a piece with that of other characters of the juvenilia.

"It is indeed the faculty of remembrance," Austen's beloved Dr. Johnson declared, "which may be said to place us in the class of moral agents" (*Rambler* 14). Without remembrance, who can keep a promise, honour a commitment, or recognise responsibility? It is Fanny Price, the most unflinchingly moral of Austen's heroines, who delivers an encomium on memory: "If any one faculty of our nature may be called *more* wonderful than the rest, I do think it is memory" (*MP* 243). The personnel of the juvenilia, in lacking memory, likewise lack moral awareness. Hence they have no sense of responsibility, and no power to control or direct their impulses.

This sounds like a severe moral stricture; also an aesthetic reservation, since the moral intricacies pursued in the novels are so indispensable a part of their beauty. But we don't read the juvenilia for moral subtlety. Instead we have free-floating beings who can delight us, and briefly shock us, by their charmed immunity from moral qualms. Only by the time of "Evelyn" does the vision sour, and so mark a turn towards moral engagement.

Driven by their obsessions, notes Spacks, they act mechanically. Hence the relative absence of plot in the juvenilia (Spacks 130). And hence, too, much of the humour, on the Bergsonian principle that man turned machine is funny.

Sir William, the eponymous hero of the short piece "Sir William Mountague," is programmed to fall in love with almost every young woman he meets, and scarcely remembers the last as he proceeds to the next. He falls first for three sisters, and can't make up his mind which one he loves best. Next he falls for a handsome young widow; she consents to marry him. "Vehemently pressed by Sir William to name the Day on which he might conduct her to the Altar, she at length fixed on the following Monday, which was the first of September" – the beginning of the grouse-shooting season! "Sir William was a Shot and could not support the idea of losing such a Day, even for such a Cause" (48). He is sorry to lose his bride, but not so sorry as he would be to lose a day's sport. Like other figures of the juvenilia he is blown hither and yon on the winds of his impulses.

It seems that the ladies he falls for are willing victims; or at least as lacking in purpose and conviction as he is. He next falls for the beautiful Miss Arundel. "But Miss Arundel was cruel; she preferred a Mr Stanhope: Sir William shot Mr Stanhope; the lady had then no reason to refuse him; she accepted him" (48). Sir William might say, with Shakespeare's Richard III (after he has persuaded Lady Anne to marry him even as she follows the husband he has killed to his burial), "Was ever woman in this humour wooed? / Was ever woman in this humour won?" (I.ii). When I illustrated this little piece, I suggested the lady's astonishing precipitance in accepting the man who has just shot her fiancé by showing her picking up her skirts and actually leaping over her fiancé's corpse to join Sir William, whose pistol is still smoking. The lady, it seems, can forget as readily as the gentleman. The narrator, however, has no comment. She has created a world in which this is the way things are; and we can sit back and laugh at them.

A recurring joke, especially in the third-person narratives, is the "life and adventures" interlude. Austen had read enough eighteenth-century novels to know that "interludes," or interpolated tales, were almost obligatory. So it is part of her parody of the genre that her characters call for these narratives at the most inopportune moments. When Alice and Lady Williams find "a lovely young Woman lying apparently in great pain beneath a Citron tree," their first request is "Will you favour us with your Life and adventures?" "Willingly, Ladies," she obligingly responds, "if you will be so kind as to be seated." And "They took their places and she thus began" (20). So a little outdoor theatre is improvised, and the lady with the broken leg performs with aplomb, apparently unhampered by her injury, but helpfully winding up her narrative by accounting for it. Similarly, in "Love and Freindship," Laura has no sooner found her husband "weltering in his blood" after a phaeton accident than she demands,

> "Oh! tell me Edward … I beseech you before you die, what has befallen you since that unhappy Day in which … we were separated."
>
> "I will" (said he) and instantly fetching a Deep sigh, Expired. (130)

The addicted young novelist cheerfully depicts the addiction to narrative in her characters too. Laura's demand for narrative here proves fatal.

In "The History of England" of *Volume the Second* the narrator comes into her own, and her voice is all-important. Here the young author creates a narrator who flaunts and indeed abuses her power. She takes on the dictatorial tone of the historian laying down the law, like her predecessors and butts Goldsmith, Hume, and "the nine-hundredth abridger of the History of England" (*NA* 31; Fergus 1995, i), yet with no pretensions at all to omniscience. Her announcement that she is "a partial, prejudiced, and ignorant Historian" (176) sounds more like a boast than a confession. It certainly signals no crack in her authority, for this narrator assumes all the arbitrary power of the monarchs she chronicles. So of Henry VIII she writes:

> It would be an affront to my Readers were I to suppose that they were not as well acquainted with the particulars of this King's reign as I am myself. It will therefore be saving *them* the task of reading again what they have read before, and *myself* the trouble of writing what I do not perfectly recollect, by giving only a slight sketch … . (130)

The author proposes to share short-cuts with her readers. On other occasions she wields her authorial power more arbitrarily. The dignity of the formal historian is reduced to the capricious antics of a narrator like Sterne's Tristram Shandy, who at the end of his first volume boasts to his reader, "If I thought you was able to form the least judgment or probable conjecture to yourself, of what was to come in the next page, – I would tear it out of my book" (*Tristram Shandy* I, 25). Here, more than in the other third-person narratives, Austen is developing in exaggerated form the personal voice, arch and ironic, and the easy relation with her reader, that is so salient a feature of the finished novels. We are on the way to such friendly intimacies as "my readers … will see in the tell-tale compression of the pages before them, that we are all hastening together to perfect felicity" (*NA* 259).

The insanely self-interested characters of the juvenilia, "who inhabit a world of child-like ego, of greed without boundaries," as Margaret Anne Doody describes them ("Disconcerting," 112), find their epitome in Mr. Gower of "Evelyn" in *Volume the Third.* There are certainly no boundaries to Gower's desires. The difference between him and, say, Mary Stanhope of "The Three Sisters" is that he inhabits a word that is apparently ready to grant them. As we have seen, when Mary lists her requirements of new carriages, horses, jewels, and extra servants, surrounding characters are shocked, and her fiancé Mr. Watts settles down to bargaining, opposing his requirements to hers. But when Mr. Gower gets to the ideal country village, Evelyn, with its manicured symmetrical landscape (there is more parody of the literary "improved" landscape here[9]) he finds a community that that colludes in his "all taking and no giving" philosophy: they earnestly, indeed obsequiously, settle for "all giving and no taking."

He has no sooner arrived, a complete stranger, at the house of the Webbs than they call him "best of Men" and bid him "welcome to this House & and to every thing it contains" – and they mean it, and he takes them at their word. Mrs. Webb orders up chocolate and venison pasty, a basket of Fruit, sandwiches, soup, and jellies and ices, – all while a full meal is in preparation. Not content with offering him hospitality, food and wine, she takes out her purse, and urges him to

> "Accept this my good Sir … I wish my purse were weightier, but Mr Webb must make up my deficiencies –. I know he has cash in the house to the amount of an hundred pounds, which he shall bring to you immediately." Mr Gower felt overpowered by her generosity as he put the purse in his pocket, and from the excess of his Gratitude, could scarcely express himself intelligibly when he accepted her offer of the hundred pounds. (*J* 232)

He likes their house; wants it; gets it. He is attracted by their daughter, wants her, gets her, with a portion of 10,000 pounds; and he generously accepts the parents' apologies that it is not larger.

Nothing is too much for his gigantic sense of entitlement. But this is a judgement the readers must make for themselves, for the narrator presents the facts without moral assessment. But the excesses of his greed and the Webbs' self-abnegation make "Evelyn" an uncomfortable read.

Patricia Meyer Spacks identifies Gower's narcissism, his incapacity for recognising the needs of any other being (Spacks 129). And the Webbs, in catering to his every whim, become co-dependent to his unbounded acquisitiveness.

It seems that his surrounding world adapts itself to his self-interest and burgeoning desires only within the charmed circle of Evelyn and the Webbs' symmetrically constructed estate. Beyond that circle he is subject to fear, denial, and the judgement of others. Victoria Kortes-Papp suggests that the Evelyn sojourn can be read as a narcissistic fantasy (Kortes-Papp x), too improbable to be read

[9] For the implications of this kind of Repton landscape design, see notes 15 to 18 in Jane Austen's *Evelyn*, edited by Peter Sabor et al., 25–6.

except as a wish-fulfilment dream vision. As Anne Elliot might comment, "What wild imaginations one forms, where dear self is concerned!" (*P* 218)

Gower may be said to typify the self-absorbed personnel of the juvenilia, each of them firmly in the centre of their own universe, deserving and demanding everything, owing and giving nothing. They are offered for our amusement as the huge exaggerations of our own egotism. And perhaps young Austen needed to imagine such beings on the way to imagining figures self-absorbed, but struggling towards self-awareness, as she does so memorably in the novels.

Who are the Gowers of the novels? Mr. Woodhouse, though gentle and courteous, is almost infantile in his inability to imagine any need, any subjectivity, that is different from his own. To him the world is a vast mammary gland to keep him supplied with the right proportions of nourishment (or gruel of the correct temperature and consistency), the precise degree of warmth and comfort. And what about Mrs. Bennet, Lydia, Mary Musgrove … the list could keep growing. Emma Woodhouse herself, though her historic struggle from self-absorption to self-awareness occupies most of a great novel, can still declare at the end of it, "I always deserve the best treatment, because I never put up with any other" (*E* 517).

In "Catharine, or the Bower" we find a work on the very threshold of becoming a full-fledged Austen novel, while at the same time, in the person of the heroine's flighty friend Camilla, still including the unthinkingly self-interested characters of the juvenilia. In "Catharine," for almost the first time in the juvenilia, we find a character with a developed subjectivity, a degree of self-awareness and self-judgment that sets her apart from the unreflecting takers and boasters of most of the juvenilia. The opening sentence sets a tone, of looking before and after, of an awakened awareness of the influence of circumstance, that sounds like the opening of *Sense and Sensibility* or *Mansfield Park*, in which the first sentence leads us far into the story and its dependence on social context.

> Catharine [or Kitty, as she is usually called] had the misfortune, as many heroines have had before her, of losing her Parents when she was very young, and of being brought up under the care of a Maiden Aunt, who while she tenderly loved her, watched over her conduct with so scrutinizing a severity, as to make it very doubtful to many people, and to Catharine amongst the rest, whether she loved her or not. (*J* 242)

This narrator, though still self-consciously occupied with genre (the nod to "many heroines" before hers), is also awake to the power of circumstance as a factor in character. Kitty is the way she is partly because of surrounding circumstances; and unlike the glorious guzzlers of the earlier juvenilia, she is morally aware. She lectures herself about the vanity of believing the handsome Edward is attracted to her (though he is another figure who "only consulted his own inclinations" [277]). Nevertheless, on no better evidence than Camilla's passing assertion, she is swiftly convinced he is head over heels in love: "'Charming Young Man! How much must you have suffered … ' Satisfied, beyond the power of Change, of this, She went in high spirits to her Aunt's apartment, without giving a Moment's recollection on the vanity of Young Women" (294–5). In that delightfully ironic "Satisfied, beyond the power of Change" we hear the voice of the Jane Austen that we know from the six novels, just as in Catharine's self-examination, however inaccurate, we recognise a potential protagonist of them.

Camilla Stanley, the visitor of her own age and sex whom Kitty would like to make her friend, is a splendid comic creation of the order of Mrs. Bennet, though in Camilla's case the comedy is broader. She is much like Isabella Thorpe of *Northanger Abbey*, but funnier and less devious. She is not a Mary Stanhope or a Gower, who have no vision beyond their own desires, but somewhat more attuned to the surrounding world. Like Isabella, who seems to regard an estranged fiancé as on a par with the hateful spring fashions (*NA* 90), she is obsessed with dress. Again like Isabella, she makes a point of being vivacious, which for her means having strong responses to everyone and everything, and expressing them emphatically too: of the snobbish Dudley family she exclaims, "Oh, horrid Wretches! I wonder You can endure them … . I declare it is quite a pity that they should be suffered to live. I wish my Father [who is an MP] would propose knocking all their Brains out, some day or other when he is in the House. So abominably proud of their Family!" (255). And like Mrs. Bennet and many characters of the juvenilia, she is a habitual self-contradictor. When Kitty is led to a higher position than hers in the line-up for a dance at the ball, she shows her own sense of precedence is as well developed as the Dudleys': "I am sure," she declares sulkily, "I am not at all offended, and should not care if all the World were to stand above me, but still it is extremely abominable, and what I cannot put up with" (280); and much more in the same vein. But airhead though she is, in her determination to speak in extremes for the sake of effect, she sometimes arrives at speculations of a certain grandeur. When Kitty's toothache prevents her from going to the ball, Camilla is all sympathy: "I wish there were no such things as Teeth in the World; they are nothing but plagues to one, and I dare say that People might easily invent something to eat with instead of them" (261). Austen's humour gets full play in Camilla's attitudes.

Camilla's speculation on how we might learn to masticate our food without teeth is one more reminder that bodies loom large in the juvenilia, desire is unfettered, and the decorum that pertains in the novels is mainly there to be shattered. Food is consumed in large quantities and considerable variety, from chocolate to fried cowheel and onion. Here characters dispute about each others' height and shortness, sit on each others' laps "in the most affectionate manner" (8), set leg-breaking steel traps for each other, throw themselves into streams and drown, and get carried home dead drunk. Eliza of "Henry and Eliza," after escaping with her infants from prison, "began to find herself rather hungry, and had reason to think, by their biting off two of her fingers, that her Children were in much the same situation" (43). There is more bodily violence in "Jack & Alice" alone than in all the six novels, where Louisa's fall from the Cobb is about as violent as it gets. But as in slapstick or in cartoon sequences, the physical collisions and disasters are comic, and one's sympathies are hardly harrowed. Since the narrator and the characters themselves face them serenely, we can too.

A word on scene-setting, something that Austen learned to do brilliantly. The many social occasions in the novels – dinner parties, morning visits, balls, excursions to Sotherton or Box Hill or Lyme – are all exploited to the full as settings for moral growth and moral definition. Each comes with its own protocols, and we learn to read the characters according to their behaviour in such testing grounds. One scene that Austen may be said to have specialised in was the carriage ride; and we already see her experimenting with travel and significant modes of transport in the juvenilia.

Simply the facts of life in the period would make it probable that many narratives would include journeys and scenes of travel. The logistics of the day were undoubtedly complicated, and must have occupied time and thought. But young Austen was clearly enamoured of movement, and had an ear both for what could be absurd and what meaningful about getting from A to B. The number of scenes in carriages, of course, contributes to the rapid pace of the juvenilia. But she was learning how to make the most of journeys, which from the first could be journeys of discovery, potential moral progresses. People in carriages are going somewhere, and the journey is not merely geographical.

The carriage addict Mr. Clifford, with his museum of "a Coach, a Chariot, a Chaise, a Landeau … " and so on (51), all the way down to a wheelbarrow (as in the cherry-stone rhyme, "Coach, carriage, wheelbarrow, cart"), sets a tone for multiple scenes of significant travel, for the novels as for the juvenilia. In "The Adventures of Mr Harley" the hero, confined in a stage coach with "A man without a Hat, Another with two, An old maid and a young Wife" (46), makes the discovery that the young wife is actually his own – the nonsensical collection of passengers suggesting a moral one must travel far to discover: namely, what you really want is already at home. Brief and light-hearted as the tale is, we are to assume that Mr. Harley has a brief epiphany in the crowded coach.

The beautifull Cassandra's gratuitous trip to Hampstead and back in a hackney coach is part of youthful adventure, and lands her in troubles about payment that she has to learn to cope with. In "The Three Sisters" all the ado about the coach that must be "hung as high as the Duttons, and blue spotted with silver" (82) reminds us of the material value of coaches, and their use as status symbols. The ado in *Emma* about whether Mr. Perry is setting up a coach has its social significance in showing the rise in status of the medical man in the period. There is a certain metonymic significance in the coach in "Love and Freindship" which shuttles between Stirling and Edinburgh – constant motion with no progress. Here all the characters of the narrative are coincidentally assembled, as Austen jokes about plot conveniences.

The enforced proximity in a coach provides dramatic possibilities that Austen was to exploit brilliantly, in both the juvenilia and the novels. Maria, the "Young Lady in distress'd Circumstances" of "A Collection of Letters," has to accept a ride to a ball with the arrogant Lady Greville and her daughters. She is required to "sit forwards" – that is, facing forwards – and next to Lady Greville, who considers such a placement as "a great obligation." Lady Greville comments on her gown as too "fine," and actually fingers the fabric of it; then proceeds to make insulting remarks on her family's poverty. With no chance to increase the space between them, Maria's discomfort it exacerbated in the crowded interior. She might say, with Sterne's starling and Maria Bertram, "I cannot get out" (*MP* 115). Fanny Price has a similarly claustrophobic ride in the carriage with her aunt on the way back from Sotherton: fagged and depressed after hours of watching Edmund in the toils of Mary Crawford, accused of having had "nothing but pleasure from beginning to end," and squashed under the cream cheese and other parcels that Mrs. Norris has cadged from the housekeeper at Sotherton, the ride is a sort of crucifixion (*MP* 122).

Almost as bad, perhaps, is Emma's experience in the coach on the way home from Randalls, when Mr. Elton's unwelcome proposal crumbles her best-laid plans for Harriet. Once his disgusting confidence and humiliating talk of "encouragement" and her reproof are over, the two are constrained to complete the journey together, each fuming with resentment, both inescapably tormented by those "little zigzags of embarrassment" (*E* 143). Such scenes were first rehearsed in the juvenilia. Austen was learning all along how to extract the most from each familiar situation.

The subject of carriages and propriety, carriages and dubious sexuality, which appears so memorably in the novels, also began in the juvenilia. In "Catharine, or the Bower," Kitty is unexpectedly rushed into her own family carriage by the handsome stranger Edward Stanley, who takes an astonishingly proprietary stance despite being hardly even a guest, and certainly a gate-crasher at the ball. He keeps *her* waiting, then chivvies her – "[C]ome, the Carriage is ready; so, do not keep me waiting" (*J* 371); he grabs her hand and hurries her away, dismissing her suggestions about the proper way of entering her neighbours' house and her objection that she would "offend against Decorum a second time" (272). She is rushed into acquiescence. The hasty progress of the vehicle figures forth the indecorous speed of the relationship. As in the rest of Austen, everything is significant.

We go on to John Thorpe's abduction of Catherine in *Northanger Abbey*. And though "abduction" may sound too strong a term, in the context of Catherine's limited experience it is nevertheless deeply distressing. He drives her at speed away from her friends, after lying to her to get her to mount his gig. Mr. Allen, who stands *in loco parentis* to Catherine in Bath, emphasises the impropriety of young ladies travelling unchaperoned in open carriages with young men – an instruction that haunts her when she finds herself enjoying such a ride with Henry Tilney later, on another significant journey where he delivers his parody of gothic novels. And when we come to Henry Crawford in *Mansfield Park*, who seems almost able to seduce Julia by driving with her in his curricle, the sexual suggestiveness of the carriage ride is explicit.

Rides with women are less threatening. The first developed scene of *The Watsons* takes place in the family's "old chair," where Elizabeth Watson, the veteran of a decade of local assemblies, drives her sister Emma to the town for the latest ball. Emma, newly returned from adoption by her aunt, is almost a stranger in her own family; but on this pleasantly relaxed journey she learns all about the Watson family dynamics, and so do we. The Watsons are "poor, and [have] no close carriage" (*LM* 79). But the old mare knows the way to Emma's hosts for the evening, and plods on peacefully, "making only one blunder, in proposing to stop at the milleners, before she drew up towards Mr Edward's door" (87). Such little details fill in our knowledge of the Watsons' shabby-genteel situation, and precarious hold on respectability. Another journey of discovery. But it was in the juvenilia that Austen discovered and first exploited the dramatic and symbolic uses of the travel scene. Such a setting lent itself for development in third-person narration, the mode she finally chose for the novels of her maturity.

In exploring the process by which young Austen finds and develops her own authorial voice in the juvenilia through her exuberantly developed consciousness of medium, I don't want to neglect her brilliance in inventing the voices of her characters, in their spoken as in their written language. These grossly greedy, narcissistic, self-aggrandizing personnel define themselves on the page largely by what they say: and from the first Austen was a master of dialogue. She rejoiced in individual speech habits, and she was inventive in concocting means of delivery as well as the style and content of speech. The dialogue is not limited to the dramas and third-person narratives, for the many letter-writers also present developed scenes complete with oral exchanges. But this is a subject to pursue in another chapter.

Jane Austen famously considered *Pride and Prejudice* "too light & bright & sparkling" (*Letters* 203). But earlier the young author felt no need to hide her sparkle under a bushel: and the juvenilia come with their own brilliant flashes of wit – vividly illuminated through narrative, epistle, drama, and dialogue by their young author's gleeful delight in her medium.

Chapter 4
Greazy Tresses, Base Miscreants, and Horrid Wretches: Teenage Jane Does Dialogue

"What is the use of a book … without pictures or conversations?" asks Wonderland's Alice. And many of us will agree with her in the choice of the most delectable parts of a book. I've already discussed some pictures. Now for the conversations.

The speeches in the novels are for me the plums in the pudding. And among the many reasons that we delight in Jane Austen's work, here are two salient ones: she provides a higher proportion of dialogue to narrative than any novelist who preceded her, and most that followed; and the quality of her dialogue is unequalled. And notwithstanding Howard Babb's dismissive comment in his book on Austen's dialogue that "The Juvenilia, of course, are rather barren hunting grounds for the controlled brilliance of Jane Austen's mature conversational effects" (Babb 33), I can claim that these virtues apply in her juvenilia as well as the novels.

Jane Austen's characters are never so much themselves as when they are talking. As critics have often demonstrated, each character has her or his own idiom and speech habits. A novelist like Henry Fielding, who constantly draws attention to the unreliability of what his characters say, insists that "by their *deeds* you shall know them." But Jane Austen's principle is undoubtedly "by their *talk* you shall know them." Moreover, she is intensely interested in talk *as a subject*. Her characters note and comment on each other's speech, and even occasionally parody it, as when Emma takes off the gabby Miss Bates:

> "'So very kind and obliging! – But he always had been such a very kind neighbour!' And then fly off, through half a sentence, to her mother's old petticoat. 'Not that it was such a very old petticoat either …'" (*E* 243)

"For shame, Emma!" Mrs. Weston scolds her. "Do not mimic her. You divert me against my conscience." But she *is* diverted, and we too can be constantly entertained not only by the endlessly varied and appropriate words that issue from the mouths of Austen's characters, but by the critical attention that one character pays to the discourse of another, and also to the varied tones and styles of speech, and of writing too.

The Bennet family can hold a little conference over Mr. Collins's letter announcing his coming visit and his intention of "making amends" to the family for his being next in line in the entail. Mrs. Bennet finds "some sense in what he says about the girls"; Mary considers "In point of composition … his letter does not seem defective" and admires his hackneyed image of the olive branch;

Elizabeth concludes "He must be an oddity, I think … . Can he be a sensible man, sir?" And Mr. Bennet responds delightedly, "No, my dear; I think not. I have great hopes of finding him quite the reverse" (*PP* 71). Thus before he ever makes a personal appearance, Mr. Collins has been variously characterised by the family on the basis of what he says in his letter; and likewise our understanding of *their* characters is advanced by what each says about what *he* says.

In *Pride and Prejudice* Mr. Bennet and Elizabeth present themselves as connoisseurs of character, and take pleasure in discovering the "follies and nonsense" of people in their circle; and in so doing they train *us* readers to become connoisseurs too. In the same way, when characters are alert to each others' speech habits, they make us alert too, so that we become informed critics of talk, of written expression, of speech, of conversation.

"My idea of good company," Anne tells William Elliot in *Persuasion*, " … is the company of clever, well-informed people, who have a great deal of conversation." He gently corrects her – that is not just "good" company; he says; that is "the best" (*P* 162). What qualifies as "conversation" is a subject widely discussed in the novels, and young Austen was already pondering it in the juvenilia too. In a revealing passage in *Northanger Abbey* we hear of Catherine's developing understanding of John Thorpe, after listening to his contradictory remarks about the safety or otherwise of his friend's gig. "All the rest of his conversation, or rather talk, began and ended with himself and his own concerns" (*NA* 63).[1] That is, not all "talk" qualifies as "conversation." Talk may begin and end with the self. But conversation, properly so called, requires exchange between speakers, and the advance of a subject by informed connections between the personal and individual and the general and philosophic. In Austen's novels conversation and other genres of speech are very much a topic of concern, not only practised by the characters but also critiqued and debated.

Most of the characters in the juvenilia are more than satisfied to settle for talk rather than conversation, as we shall see. But Austen was already alert to the rich variety of oral expression as a source both for thought and for laughter. And by the time she was writing "Catharine, or the Bower" she showed a heroine in quest not only of a friend but of conversation that deserves the name.

There are many ways in which young Austen was preparing to be the Austen we know from the novels, and not the least of them is her wonderful ear for spoken idiom, her inventiveness and precision in dialogue, and her determination to provide nothing that is merely bland or convenient, but words that sparkle on the page.

In the novels Henry Tilney is the first of many characters who set up as critics of speech, with his playful objections to the debased colloquial use of words and phrases: "nice," "promised so faithfully," and so on. His sister urges Catherine to correct her usage in self-defence, "or we shall be overpowered with Johnson and

---

[1] Here I go over some ground I have published in a series of essays on dialogue in Austen's novels, including "Talking about Talk" and "The Secret Languages of *Emma*."

Blair" – the dictionary-maker and the rhetorician, Tilney's favourite authorities (*NA* 108). When Sir John Middleton suggests Marianne will be "setting [her] cap" at Willoughby, she delivers her own little homily on "every common-place phrase by which wit is intended." The tendency of such expressions, she says, "is gross and illiberal; and if their construction could ever be deemed clever, time has long ago destroyed all its ingenuity" (*SS* 53). She sounds as though she could write her own version of Blair's *Lectures on Rhetoric*. Sir John only laughs.

In the same way Austen shines the spotlight on other modes of speech by calling on her characters to comment on them. Word games are a resource, and in *Emma* Frank Churchill communicates secretly with Jane Fairfax through the word "blunder" in the game of alphabet; and in a climactic scene, when he calls on those attending the Box Hill party to contribute "one thing very clever … or two things moderately clever – or three things very dull indeed," Miss Bates shows herself capable of self-criticism in language, in saying humbly, "I shall be sure to say three dull things as soon as ever I open my mouth, shan't I?" – with memorable consequences (*E* 403). All this close attention, this intent listening to what people say and how they say it, is part of what educates the characters – those, at least, who are capable of listening.

To be capable of listening – to others, but especially to oneself – is a test of character that many do not pass. Fanny Price is an excellent listener – a quality that others approve and take advantage of – as in the rehearsals for *Lovers' Vows*, when Edmund, Mary, and even Rushworth seek out her help. It is one of Edmund's failings that he is a poor listener, even to matters that concern him closely. When Fanny tries to explain her objections to Henry Crawford – at Edmund's special request – he is dismissive, "scarcely hearing her to the end" (*MP* 406).[2] But Fanny can listen to others and also to herself, coming up with some self-criticism after her outburst on the evergreen, "You will think me rhapsodizing" (244). In the novels, then, the dialogue – including who speaks, how much and in what way, and also who listens – is all deeply involved in the action.

And the same applies in the juvenilia, though there the attentive listeners and enlightened critics of speech are rare.

If we allow what a character writes in a letter to count as speech (and it is still the character's own words), "The Three Sisters" presents an interesting study, especially in Mary Stanhope, the principal character. She has a great deal to say, but is incapable of hearing herself. After announcing her engagement to the vile but rich Mr. Watts on a visit to family friends, the Duttons, she claims,

> "You must know Mr Watts is very much in love with me, so that it is quite a match of Affection on his side."
>
> "Not on his side only, I suppose," said Kitty.

---

2 See my essay, "The Talkers and Listeners of *Mansfield Park*."

> "Oh! when there is so much Love on one side there is no occasion for it on the other. However I do not much dislike him, tho' he is very plain to be sure."
>
> Mr Brudenell stared, the Miss Duttons laughed, and Sophy and I were heartily ashamed of our Sister. (*J* 86–7)

Mary's audience, the Duttons, Mr. Brudenell,and Mary's sisters, hear her and are shocked or embarrassed according to their natures. But Mary can't hear herself. Georgiana, the youngest sister, can not only hear and judge Mary, but is capable of irony. Knowing just how unpleasant Mr. Watts is, she nevertheless presents an ironic defence of him:

> "And then as to his temper; it has been reckoned bad, but may not the World be deceived in their Judgement of it. There is an open Frankness in his Disposition which becomes a Man. They say his is stingy; We'll call that Prudence. They say he is suspicious. *That* proceeds from a Warmth of Heart always excusable in Youth … "
>
> Thus I ran on to the great Entertainment of my Sister. (79)

Georgiana can use language agilely as an instrument for irony and humour, and not just for declarative purposes. It's a rare talent among the figures of the juvenilia. Interestingly, as we have seen, she is also one who can feel moral scruple. As she tricks Mary into marrying Mr. Watts, she reproaches herself: "Yet after all my Heart cannot acquit me and Sophy is even more scrupulous" (80). It seems that moral awareness goes along with control in language.

Readers and critics have long admired the dialogue in Austen's novels for being finely attuned to the speaker. In *Emma*, nobody would mistake a speech by Mr. Woodhouse, or Mrs. Elton, or Miss Bates as being delivered by anyone else. Each has his or her own consistent voice, idiolect, individual manner of speaking. In the novels at large, we learn to recognise Isabella Thorpe by her constant superlatives and striving for effect, Lucy Steele by her bad grammar, Miss Bates by her prolixity (as well as many other more subtle speech habits). Other characters have their identifiable watchwords: Mrs. Bennet's "poor nerves," Mr. Woodhouse's "Poor Miss Taylor," Mr. Elton's "Exactly so," Rushworth's "two and forty speeches." It's as though each character carries a little notice, "*C'est moi qui vous parle*."

In the juvenilia Austen was already developing these skills. These characters too have their idiolects, their recognizable voices. Lady Williams, the "virtuous widow" in "Jack and Alice," is one of several self-contradictors, though she has her own heavily moral discourse. Her verbal strategy seems to be to keep all bases covered. Here she provides what she would claim to be a warm recommendation for her old friend Alice to her new friend Lucy:

> "She has many rare and charming qualities, but Sobriety is not one of them. The whole Family are indeed a sad drunken set … . But she is a charming girl.

> I fancy not one of the sweetest tempers in the world; to be sure I have seen her in such passions! However she is a sweet young Woman. I am sure you'll like her." (*J* 26)

With friends like that, who needs enemies? When the new friend Lucy proposes to move on to Bath, Lady Williams somewhat confusingly encourages her, "I shall be miserable without you – t'will be a most pleasant tour to you – I hope you'll go; if you do I am sure t'will be the Death of me – pray be persuaded" (27). Be persuaded to go? or to stay? one wonders.

As we have seen, self-contradiction is a habit of Mary Stanhope's too, with her shifting determinations: "I wont have him I declare … I believe I must get him while I can" (75). She is one of those unthinking characters who are blown headlong, this way and that, on the wings of their desire. Their desire is strong and unregulated, and they must be emphatic in its expression; but they are incapable of comparing, balancing and reconciling contrary impulses. Such a condition is rich in humour, and young Austen makes the most of its potential.

Austen was already working on idiolects when she wrote "Catherine, or the Bower," which is almost a full-fledged Austen novel. The heroine's aunt, Mrs. Percival[3] (the "Mrs." is a courtesy title, as she is very much a spinster) is like Lady Williams in being heavily moral. And she is so terrified that her niece Kitty will fall in love inappropriately that she eschews the company of young males altogether, so far as she can. Reclusive and fiercely conservative, she is convinced the country is going to rack and ruin. When she sees a young man actually kissing Kitty's hand (he performs the kiss expressly to shock her), she launches into a typical tirade:

> "Oh! Catharine, you are an abandoned Creature, and I do not know what will become of you … But I plainly see that every thing is going to sixes and sevens and all order will soon be at an end throughout the Kingdom." (287)

The generalising from the particular (if Catharine is an abandoned creature all order must be at an end in the nation at large) is typical of her thinking process. And like many memorable minor characters of the novels, she has her signature phrase – everything is going "to sixes & sevens."[4]

Charlotte Lutterell of "Lesley Castle," with her cooking obsession, consciously introduces culinary images into her letters. "My Sister came running to me in the Storeroom with her Face as White as a Whipt syllabub"(146) she writes, evidently with some satisfaction in the simile. She jokes wittily on how her sister "loved drawing Pictures, and I drawing Pullets" (164), and is proud of remaining, when

3 Austen originally called her "Mrs. Peterson," but in changing he name to "Percival" she missed some of the instances of "Peterson."

4 The expression "sixes and sevens" derives from the guild system: the guilds that stood in first to fifth places, such as goldsmiths and mercers, were stable and reliable; but those at the sixth and seventh places were unpredictable.

provoked, "as cool as a Cream-cheese" (165). She is so consistent in such usage that her correspondent notices and imitates it. Margaret Lesley writes to her of a brother's heart "which (to use your favourite comparison) was as delicate as sweet and as tender as a Whipt-syllabub" (151–2). Already young Austen shows her characters picking up on each others' styles of communication.

Charlotte, as we have seen, gets letters from both Margaret Lesley and Margaret's new stepmother Lady Lesley, and is able to compare them – Margaret's complaints about "something so extremely unmajestic in her little diminutive figure" (157) and Lady Lesley's about her "two great, tall, out of the way" stepdaughters, whom she calls "Scotch Giants" (158). Much amused at receiving these two letters in the same week, Charlotte tells Margaret, "I find by them that you are both downright jealous of each others Beauty" (154). She has the enlightenment to say, in effect, "Listen to yourself." Not that Margaret does.

Down-to-earth and sensible as she is, Charlotte is contrasted in style and expression with her sister Eloisa, who is all sensibility, with a writing style to match. Here is the romantic jargon that she shares with Laura of "Love and Freindship" and to some extent with Marianne Dashwood of *Sense and Sensibility*. "I hope you will not think me girlishly romantic," she writes to her new friend, "when I say that to have some kind and compassionate Freind who might listen to my Sorrows without endeavouring to console me was what I had for some time wished for" (168). We are on the way to the effusions of "Love and Freindship," and Laura's meeting with Sophia. "She was all Sensibility and Feeling. We flew into each others arms … and instantly unfolded to each other the most inward Secrets of our Hearts" (114). Margaret Lesley too belongs on the Sensibility side of the spectrum. And it's not surprising that here again we find an echo of "Love and Freindship." Margaret confesses to Charlotte when she is introduced to young Cleveland, "From the first moment I beheld him, I was certain that on him depended the future Happiness of my Life" (173). Her speech is almost an exact quotation of Laura's love-at-first-sight speech in "Love and Freindship" (168). Young Austen has an ear for formulas in speech and writing, and has no qualms in allowing her characters to repeat each other, for what they repeat are expressions already threadbare from their use in novels of sensibility. This is the "unmeaning Gibberish" that Edward's father calls his son's ranting and posturing. It is the standard romantic jargon of the sentimental genre. And Austen was still doing battle against such "thorough novel slang" years later (*Letters* 277), though by this time the formulas have changed, and she was objecting to the "Vortex of dissipation" in her niece Anna's fiction. "I do not object to the Thing, but I cannot bear the expression," she explains. No prude she; only fastidious about language.

And just as the mature Austen chose to deflate, or avoid altogether, the hackneyed and hyperbolic flights and romantic posturing in the dialogue of some current fiction, so as a young writer she was already finding ways to bring language to more down-to-earth, straight-forward use. A joke she learned early was the abrupt change of register, with the humorous incongruity that goes with it.

In the early tale "Frederic and Elfrida" she could already puncture the pretentious by resorting to demotic colloquialisms. This is the tale in which the principals in a courtship are so bedevilled by delicacy that they can't bring themselves to name their wedding day. Only when Elfrida realizes they have reached middle age does she abandon her scruples to announce "in a manner truly heroick" that they will be married next day. Frederic's response is hardly in the "heroick" vein: "Damme Elfrida – *you* may be married tomorrow, but *I* wont" (12). The swearing, the colloquial rhythm and emphasis, and the contraction "wont" bring the register down with a wallop.

In the juvenilia as well as the novels (though here to a more limited extent) Austen wants to give full play to the pointed, the absurd, the ridiculous – passing swiftly over what is merely bland or convenient. Take a delectable passage from *Pride and Prejudice*. The young people are engaged in a spirited conversation on music, and their hostess Lady Catherine butts in:

> "I must have my share in the conversation, if you are speaking of music. There are few people in England, I suppose, who have more true enjoyment of music than myself, or a better natural taste. If I had ever learnt, I should have been a great proficient … . How does Georgiana get on, Darcy?"
>
> Mr. Darcy spoke with affectionate praise of his sister's proficiency. (*PP* 194)

Darcy's speech is merely sensible and to the point, so we get it only in indirect speech. But we get Lady Catherine, with her absurd boasting about how good she *would have* been if she had ever tried, at full length. It is part of the "light, bright, & sparkling" nature of Austen's most light-hearted novel that the witty, pointed, or ridiculous speakers are placed in the limelight, while the merely rational ones give place to them. It's a pattern that began in the juvenilia.

Now consider this piece from "Jack and Alice." I return to the outrageous put-down of Mr. Johnson by Charles Adams for which I provided an illustration, for it deserves quoting more fully in the context of Austen's mastery of dialogue. Mr. Johnson has been persuaded by his daughter Alice to offer her hand in marriage to the stunningly handsome Charles Adams.

> Mr Johnson being a man of few words his part was soon performed & the answer he received was as follows –
>
> "Sir, I may perhaps be expected to appear[5] pleased at and gratefull for the offer you have made me: but let me tell you that I consider it as an affront. I look upon myself to be Sir a perfect Beauty – where would you see a finer figure or a more charming face. Then, sir I imagine my Manners and Address to be of the most polished kind; there is a certain elegance a peculiar sweetness in them that I never saw equalled … . My temper is even, my virtues innumerable, my self

[5] The manuscript here has the error "appeared," but I correct it to allow the passage to flow freely.

> unparalleled. Since such Sir is my character, what do you mean by wishing me to marry your Daughter? Let me give you a short sketch of yourself and of her. I look upon you Sir to be a very good sort of Man in the main; a drunken old Dog to be sure, but that's nothing to me. Your daughter sir, is neither sufficiently beautifull, sufficiently amiable, sufficiently witty, nor sufficiently rich for me –. I expect nothing more in my wife than my wife will find in me – Perfection." ("Jack and Alice," 28)

What a tour de force of a speech! Again the merely routine part of the exchange, Mr. Johnson's proposal, is only summarised; but Charles Adams's brilliantly arrogant answer gets full coverage, verbatim reporting. All we hear from "the drunken old Dog" is "Mr Johnson was satisfied."

I can't help wondering whether Austen remembered Charles Adams's speech, at least in some mischievous part of her mind, when she wrote Elizabeth Bennet's response to Darcy's first proposal. There are certainly parallels in expression.

> Charles Adams: "I may perhaps be expected to appear pleased and gratefull for the offer you have made me:"
>
> Elizabeth: "In such cases as this, it is, I believe, the established mode to express a sense of obligation … "
>
> Charles Adams: "but let me tell you that I consider it as an affront."
>
> Elizabeth: "but I cannot." (*PP* 212)

It's a tempting parallel. But perhaps an expression of gratitude was indeed customary when refusing a proposal. I have not checked the conduct books.

It is worth pausing over the artistry of this 13-year-old. Already she has a fine ear for register, for the varying levels and tones of language use, from highly poetic, through pretentiously formal, on to everyday use, to colloquial or even vulgar and coarse tones.[6] Those who aren't used to Austen's idiom may consider that *all* her dialogue is quite formal, and indeed by the acceptably casual standards of today, much of it is so. But as we get to know Austen and her personnel, we become aware of the fine discriminations: for instance between Lydia Bennet's racy colloquialisms and Mary's pompous formality: "I was ready to die of laughter. And then … we talked and laughed so loud, that any body might have heard us ten miles off," giggles Lydia. "Far be it from me, my dear sister, to deprecate such pleasures," pronounces Mary (*PP* 246).

Charles Adams's speech in "Jack and Alice" already shows young Jane's ability to change register, within a single speech, with hilarious effect. In talking of his own virtues he employs the high-flown rhetoric of heroic drama or the pretentious

---

[6] For a definition of the noun *register* in this sense, *The New Shorter Oxford Dictionary* provides (ll7d.) "*Ling.* A variety of language or level of usage, *spec.* one determined by degree of formality and choice of vocabulary, pronunciation, syntax, etc."

novels of the day, with a flurry of abstracts – "elegance," "temper," "virtue" – and its elaborate parallel structures: "My temper is even, my virtues innumerable, my self unparalleled." But she can also bring us down with a bump to more familiar and colloquial usage: "a very good sort of man in the main," "a drunken old Dog to be sure." And the joke is that she makes Charles Adams employ the high register for his own perfections, the low for the notable *im*perfections of Mr. Johnson and Alice. "Pictures of perfection … make me sick & wicked," Jane Austen said, much later (*Letters* 486–7). In this picture of Charles Adams we see plenty of the "wicked."

As we have seen, Austen has taken the standard novelists' convention of the perfect protagonist, and wickedly sent it up. To begin with, the perfect one, with the beauty, accomplishments, and "peculiar sweetness," is usually the heroine, not the hero. It's already a joke to attach these qualities to a man. And secondly, of course, though a description of the perfections of this person is quite routine, it's normally delivered by the narrator, not the person him- or herself. The simple trick of putting it all in the first person both recalls the familiar convention and deliciously mocks it. Margaret Lesley, aware that self-praise may be frowned upon, adjusts to a more sophisticated version of it, as when she describes herself and her sister: "We are handsome my dear Charlotte, very handsome and the greatest of our Perfections is, that we are entirely insensible of them ourselves" (144).

Pope's aphorism, "The proper study of Mankind is Man," is presented as a piece of wisdom. James Thurber memorably adapted it: "'The proper study of Mankind is Man,' says Man." That is Jane Austen's kind of joke. We always need to listen not just to what is said, but to who says it.

We catch an echo of the self-admiration of Charles Adams and the others, toned down but perceptible, in Lady Catherine de Bourgh's claim: "My character has ever been celebrated for its sincerity and frankness" (*PP* 391). We notice not only the outrageous self-admiration, but also the elevated register. "Ever" is a highfalutin word for "always." "My character has always been celebrated" doesn't have quite the same grand ring.

As I shall demonstrate further in the next chapter, the play with register is again a recurring joke in "Love and Freindship," where the characters of Sensibility similarly espouse the affected high mimetic mode of romance, while the opposing characters of Sense settle for the demotic and prosaic. Edward rants, "Know Sir, that I scorn to marry [Lady Dorothea] in compliance with your Wishes. No! Never shall it be said that I obliged my Father," – the speech that his father calls "unmeaning Giibberish" (108).

The heroines and heroes of "Love and Freindship" scorn down-to-earth workaday language ("scorning" is one of their favourite activities, in fact), and aim at a higher register, using the archaic "thee" and "thou," and other poetic flourishes. And the more practical characters are adept at puncturing this windy rhetoric, often by the use of irony. Young Edward, for instance, is outraged by his sensible sister's suggestion that he and his wife will need some income in order to eat.

> "Victuals and Drink! (replied [Edward] in a most nobly contemptuous Manner) and dost thou then imagine that there is no other support for an exalted Mind … than the mean and indelicate employment of Eating and Drinking?"
>
> "None that I know of, so efficacious" [returns Augusta]. (111)

We hear the same fine control of rhythm and irony, the same canny use of bathos, in the mature novels. Here is Caroline Bingley, trying to impress Darcy with her intellectual powers, on the proposed ball that all the young people are excited about:

> "It would surely be much more rational if conversation instead of dancing made the order of the day."
>
> "Much more rational, my dear Caroline, I dare say [concedes her brother] but it would not be near so much like a ball." (*PP* 61)

Again we have the deft common-sensical put-down of pretension. Young Austen with her sensitivity to register had already mastered many tricks of her trade.

We have seen that Austen enjoyed introducing food in her narratives, even those with characters who purport to scorn it, like Edward with his contemptuous "Victuals and Drink!" Food has its registers as language does. A "feast" or a "banquet" or "ruby-red wine" need not be out of place in heroic literature. But who can be heroic over breakfast, or eggs and bacon, or cabbage, or beer? Young Jane's comestibles are not of the elevated kind; and she knows where to deploy them for bathetic effect. In *Laura and Augustus*, the anonymous novel of 1784[7] that is the main target in "Love and Freindship," the heroine runs pathetically mad when her husband dies, and has a fine speech à la Ophelia, iambic rhythms and all: "Hark! again do you not hear the music of the spheres! See how he rides on yonder cloud!" (III, 137) In her take-off, Austen too provides classical reference and grand iambic rhythms, but adds matter far from heroic: "Look at that Grove of Firs – I see a Leg of Mutton – … they took him for a Cucumber" (130). Pathos and grandly dramatic mad scenes can hardly survive the mention of such low mimetic items as legs of mutton and cucumbers. Thackeray too understood the comic potential of vegetables. In his classic burlesque fairy tale, *The Rose and the Ring*, written for his daughters during a sojourn in Rome, he created the kingdom of King Cavolfiore, whose aristocratic supporters are the Lords Spinacci, Articiochi, Broccoli, and so on (Thackeray X, 394).

Let me explore some more of Austen's changes of register and sharp juxtapositions by which she draws attention to outworn fictional conventions and learns to practise her craft.

She has some wonderful variations on the "first impressions" theme that she developed in *Pride and Prejudice*. "Is it a first love?" Lady Williams tenderly asks the lovesick Alice; and she memorably advises her, "A second attachment

---

7 *Laura and Augustus* is sometimes attributed to Eliza Nugent Bromley.

is seldom attended with any serious consequences; against *that* therefore I have nothing to say. Preserve yourself from a first Love and you need not fear a second" (17–18). We can savour the skewed logic of advancing directly to a second love without having a first.

A joke on first impressions that is more elaborate still comes early, in "Frederic and Elfrida." The heroine, hero, and their friend Charlotte pay a visit to a family newly arrived in the neighbourhood. And here we are treated to notable information on styles of delivery as well as of speech.

> E'er they had been many minutes seated, the Wit and Charms which shone resplendent in the conversation of the amiable Rebecca, enchanted them so much that they all with one accord jumped up and exclaimed,
>
> "Lovely and too charming Fair one, notwithstanding your forbidding Squint, your greazy tresses and your swelling Back, which are more frightfull than imagination can paint or pen describe, I cannot refrain from expressing my raptures, at the engaging Qualities of your Mind, which so amply atone for the Horror, with which your first appearance must ever inspire the unwary visitor." (6)

It is a notable instance of correcting an impression gathered from mere physical appearance!

To unpack this delicious passage a little, and see how it works: The first absurdity, of course, is already there in the context. This is a formal social call on new arrivals in the neighbourhood, so one hardly expects the outrageous personal abuse. And then, although the speech is presented as spontaneous – a speaker who "jumps up" and "exclaims" is surely acting on some compelling impulse of the moment – it is delivered in chorus, by three visitors at once: they *all* jump up and exclaim at once, as though they were a chorus in a musical.

The joke continues in the syntactical intricacy of the speech they are said to declaim spontaneously. After the first formal apostrophe, "Lovely and too charming Fair one," comes the lengthy "notwithstanding" phrase about the squint, greazy tresses, and the rest – formal in tone, but grossly insulting in content. Then follows the main clause, "I cannot refrain from expressing my raptures … "; and there are no less than five subordinate ones, all in one long sentence. Imagine a group of three coming out in chorus with such an elephant of a sentence!

Those greazy tresses and other blemishes loom so large in the first part of the sentence that it's hard to recall that the main purport of the speech, if we read the grammar alone, is highly complimentary. The three speakers are in raptures about the "engaging Qualities of [Rebecca's] Mind." It seems they have been able to rise above their first impressions, founded on her appearance alone, and penetrate to the shining realities beyond. But the sentence doesn't end there, because we move on to a reprise of that daunting first view: the speakers can't leave the damaging part of their response behind, but must remind Rebecca all over again of "the Horror, with which your first appearance must ever inspire the unwary visitor." By now it's not only the three speakers who react this way: they comfortingly assure her that *every* unwary visitor, now and forever more, *must* be inspired with Horror at the sight of her. No wonder poor Rebecca is "abashed"! (6) All that is done in the space of a single sentence: but a sentence which, if read attentively, has its own unfolding history.

One might expect such insulting personal abuse to be delivered in vulgar fishwives' idiom. But no, Austen is above such crudity. And again, she gains her effect by adjusting register. Rebecca has not "greazy hair," but "greazy *tresses*"; not a hump back, but a "*swelling* Back"! "Greazy tresses," in its mix of the low register with the high, becomes a kind of tonal oxymoron.

I apologise for taking so long in explaining a joke that is sufficiently funny without the explanation. But it is worth investigating the art that goes into these squibs, which fall so trippingly from this teenager's pen.

Now that I have lingered over the "greazy tresses" of my title, I shall move on to my next term of abuse, "base Miscreant," which is again in a different register. It comes in "Love and Freindship."

The two heroines, Laura and Sophia, act according to the sentimental code, and never have a moment's doubt that they are right, and the rest of the world is wrong. One element in the code – as in the passage about "Victuals and Drink" – is that one should have a soul above such base considerations as money and food. Since you may not think about money, you're not apt to earn it. But if you don't earn it you may still need it; so you might as well take it off those low-minded people who have it. This is Sophia's principle when she is "majestically removing the 5th Bank-note" from her host's desk to her own purse. When her host catches her in the act, Laura swiftly comes in on her friend's side

> "Base Miscreant! (cried I) how canst thou thus undauntedly endeavour to sully the spotless reputation of such bright Excellence? Why dost thou not suspect *my* innocence as soon?" "Be satisfied Madam (replied he) I do suspect it, and therefore must desire that you will both leave this House in less than half an hour." (126)

There's a nice use of bathos here: to Laura it's unthinkable that *she* should ever be suspected. But her host has already proceeded beyond suspicion to certainty, and he throws her out. Again Austen is having fun with register. Laura and Sophia employ the high rhetoric of melodrama, with the archaic "thee" and "thou," and poetic vocabulary of "base," "Miscreant," "sully," and "spotless." The down-to-earth host responds with "you," not "thou," and with irony and homely prose.

A term of abuse in a different register again from "base Miscreant" is the "Horrid Wretch" of Camilla Stanley in "Catharine, or the Bower."

> "I cannot bear Sir Peter – Horrid Wretch! [exclaims the heroine's new friend Camilla.] He is *always* laid up with the Gout, which is exceedingly disagreeable to the Family."
>
> "And perhaps not very pleasant to *himself*" [responds Kitty, with irony]. (255–6)

Kitty's ironic response registers Camilla's unthinking assumption about Sir Peter's Gout – that because it's inconvenient to others he must be blamed for it. Camilla's "Horrid" in this sense is a colloquialism, the sort of over-used threadbare term that Henry Tilney would disapprove of. In its original meaning of inspiring horror it should belong in the high register. But over-use has devalued it, and it has slipped down to merely childish and colloquial use, as in "When she was good, she was very, very good; / But when she was bad she was horrid." Calling Sir Peter "Horrid Wretch" marks Camilla as childish.

She doesn't notice Kitty's ironic response; for like many other personnel of the juvenilia she is gloriously oblivious of how others might judge her speech. She barges forward in speech and action with never a doubt of her own perfect probity. She can't hear herself, or see herself as others see her; and she is immune from judgement – her own judgement as well as everyone else's – and deaf to irony. Such pushy, unaware characters are very funny, but they don't themselves make jokes, or understand them. We as readers can appreciate young Austen's brilliant irony in presenting them, but they can never participate in our enjoyment of their shortcomings. And they could never recognise, as Elizabeth Bennet does, that they can be "blind, partial, prejudiced, absurd" (*PP* 230). That is, they supremely lack self-knowledge. And without self-knowledge there can be no completed subjectivity.

What happens when there is a dialogue between two characters who can hear each other, but haven't sufficient subjectivity to hear *themselves*? Let me give you some of an exchange between Alice Johnson and Lady Williams. Alice, you remember, is inclined to hit the bottle, and her drinking habit seems to have affected her complexion. Lady Williams, in telling Alice her life story, mentions that her London hostess Miss Watkins was not handsome, for "Her eyes were too small & she had too much colour."

> "How can *that* be?" interrupted Miss Johnson reddening with anger; "Do you think that any one can have too much colour?"
>
> "Indeed I do, and I'll tell you why I do my dear Alice; when a person has too great a degree of red in their Complexion, it gives their face in my opinion, too red a look."
>
> "But can a face my Lady have too red a look?"
>
> "Certainly my dear Miss Johnson and I'll [tell] you why. When a face has too red a look it does not appear to so much advantage as it would were it paler."
>
> "Pray Ma'am proceed in your story." (19)

Lady Williams does proceed, and she gets to the hostess with too much colour, and the argument goes as before, until Alice loses her temper. Moreover, some days later Lady Williams brings up the subject again, apparently to make peace with Alice and to suggest they forgive and forget: "Indeed I was not angry at the time," she assures Alice, "because I saw all along, you were really dead drunk" – an explanation that is hardly placating. She adds her signature self-contraction: "Remember it is all forgot" before proceeding implacably, "I must insist upon not giving you any description of Mrs. Watkins. … It can be nothing to you … if she had too much colour" (21) – so of course the row is renewed. Some jokes improve with repetition, and this circular progress, from red faces to too much colour and back to red faces makes very funny reading.

Sometimes Austen can't resist a funny exchange for its own sake. Early in "Love and Freindship" comes a throw-away scene between Laura and her father and mother. It is not particularly apposite to the large theme of the work, except in demonstrating the total unpracticality of the figures of sensibility; nor does it contribute much to plot or character. It comes just after the set-up of the letters that the romantic Laura is to write to educate the daughter of her bosom friend of yesteryear, and just before the entry of the hero and the beginning of the major action. In its zany implausibility it has the air of being a brief interlude before things get going, while young Jane, hesitating at the outset of Laura's narrative, lets her pen perform a doodle in dialogue.

Laura and her parents hear "a violent knocking at the outward Door of our rustic Cot":

> My father started – "What noise is that," (said he.) "It sounds like a loud rapping at the Door" – (replied my Mother.) "It does indeed," (cried I.) "I am of your opinion (said my Father) it certainly does appear to proceed from some uncommon violence exerted against our unoffending Door." "Yes (exclaimed I) I cannot help thinking it must be somebody who knocks for Admittance."
>
> "That is another point (replied he;) We must not pretend to determine on what motive the person may knock – tho' that someone *does* rap at the Door, I am partly convinced."

A second tremendous rap frightens the mother and gets the family contemplating action:

> "Had we not better go and see who it is? (said she) … "I think we had." (replied I.) "Certainly, (added my Father) by all means." "Shall we go now?" (said my Mother.) "The sooner the better." (answered he). "Oh! Let no time be lost." (cried I.) (106–7)

With the characters so immovably stuck in neutral, it could almost be *Waiting for Godot*. And indeed with the brief assigned speeches this little piece would play very well on stage. Once the servants get on the job and usher in "the most beauteous and amiable Youth," Laura is completely smitten, and we swing into action, leaving behind the little gem of a domestic scene in the rustic Cot in the Vale of Uske. But relevant or not, it provides an irresistible beginning to "Love and Freindship." Like the discussion on red faces in "Jack and Alice," it can stand alone as a brilliantly comic scene of dialogue.

We are told that those who do not study history are doomed to repeat it. In the juvenilia Jane Austen reminds us that those who do not know themselves are stuck with their unreformed identities. They can never grow. And thanks to Jane Austen's comic genius, those characters don't get left behind with the juvenilia. We can still hear them not hearing themselves in the voices of Isabella Thorpe, Mrs. Bennet, Lady Catherine, Mrs. Norris, and Sir Walter Elliot.

In some extended pieces one can listen to a fledgling professional practising her five-finger exercise. That's what "A Collection of Letters" sounds like. Each of the five letters develops a separate narrative in a different tonal range. "Letter the First" I will treat briefly, since although we have the tone of voice of the letter-writer, it contains no dialogue as such. But it firmly sets the series in a social context. It is from a mother about to launch her two daughters on "their entrée into life" – a coming out, no less (150); and the first great occasion is to be having friends in for tea. Austen remained sceptical about the rituals surrounding "coming out," as in *Pride and Prejudice* ("What, all five out at once? Very odd!" comments Lady Catherine [*PP* 187]) and *Mansfield Park* ("The outs and not outs are beyond me," confesses Edmund [*MP* 56]). But being herself about 16 at the time of writing this letter,[8] young Austen was close up to such rites of passage, with her own satirical take on them.

"Letter the Third" introduces in Lady Greville a trial run for Lady Catherine de Bourgh, a connection I shall explore in a later chapter. Here it is worth noting the parallel speech habits of the two shamelessly intrusive characters, for their outrageous arrogance is conveyed as much in the form as in the content of their speech. Their monstrous egotism finds expression in their constant self-reference: "I dare say … I must own … it is not my way … I always think … in my opinion" are phrases by which Lady Greville constantly inhabits her speech as a dominant presence (*MW* 156). Lady Catherine similarly insists "I am not to be trifled with … my character has ever been celebrated … " (*PP* 391).

"Letter the Fifth," about the heiress in love, I have already discussed. But Letters the Second and Fourth are pertinent to my present subject of dialogue, for they provide negative examples of conversation. Both are carefully set in social occasions: in one case a house party at Christmas time, in the other a dinner party; and the letter writer in each case is a woman in "conversation," as she would claim, with another. As writers, of course, both correspondents hold centre stage in their own narratives; but unlike the loud talkers of the Charles Adams or Mary Stanhope kind, each is in urgent search of gossipy information. They are possessed by the same thirst for the "life and adventures" of the people they meet as other characters in the juvenilia, but their curiosity is adapted to these more realistically delineated social circles. John Thorpe's talk is only of himself and his own concerns, and so does not qualify as the considered mutual exchange that deserves the name of conversation. The writers of these two letters are the opposite extreme

[8] In *Volume the Second* "A Collection of Letters" follows immediately after "The History of England," dated 26 November 1791, when Austen was nearly 16.

from those obsessive talkers. They are as thirsty for personal information from the people they address as a vampire for blood.

The writer of "Letter the Second" takes on "Miss Jane," and presently finds herself almost sinking under a plethora of unexpected information. "Miss Jane," it emerges, was actually married for years, but kept the secret from her father, although she was living in his house at the time, with her two children, who pass with her father "as the Children of a Brother (tho' I had ever been an only child)" (196). This improbable story turns tragic: the husband dies, the children sink to early graves, and as for her father, "He died, poor Good old Man, happily ignorant to his last hour of my Marriage" (154). The story-addicted narrator is all gratitude for this staggering account. "Oh! my dear Miss Jane (said I) how infinitely am I obliged to you for so entertaining a Story! You cannot think how it has diverted me!" (196–7) Was she listening? one has to ask. And we are left in doubt as to whether Miss Jane had made the whole thing up, to feed the inquisitive woman a line, or whether we are to take her narrative as true. What is clear is the insatiable appetite of the letter writer, who gluttonously extorts the narrative without apparently hearing it.

The writer of "Letter the Fourth" is "a young Lady rather impertinent" (202). Again, this writer is pumping a woman; but this woman is less forthcoming than Miss Jane. Perhaps young Austen, now "out" herself (or whatever equivalent pertained in the Austen household), was pondering the conversational ploys she observed at the social gatherings she attended; for these accounts, despite the broad and improbable stories, have the air of being drawn from observed experience rather than from other fictions, like so many of the juvenilia.

The writer here, "determined not to remain in ignorance for want of asking" (203), is quite proud of her finesse in extracting information. Instead of boldly asking "Where do you come from?" she cunningly suggests, "You came from Derbyshire?" – and thereby learns the lady actually comes from Suffolk. This exchange is more credible than the one involving Miss Jane, and this lady makes her attempts at turning the question-and-answer exchange into a real conversation.

> "You regret having left Suffolk then Miss Grenville?" "Indeed I do." "You were born there I suppose?" "Yes Ma'am I was and passed many happy years there –."
>
> "That is a great comfort – said I – I hope Ma'am that you never spent any *un*happy one's there."
>
> "Perfect Felicity is not the property of Mortals, and no one has the right to expect uninterrupted Happiness –. *Some* Misfortunes I have certainly met with –." (203–4)

Miss Grenville is making the conversationally correct move, in shifting the subject from the personal to the general. But her questioner won't follow that lead. "'*What* Misfortunes dear Ma'am?' replied I, burning with impatience to know every thing." There is no stopping her, although this character, unlike most in the juvenilia, is capable of being embarrassed – if only passingly. "I was actually silenced," she admits at one point.

Since there are so many obsessive talkers in the juvenilia and novels – Lady Williams, Charles Adams, Mrs. Jennings, Mrs, Norris, Miss Bates, Mrs. Elton[9] – it is of interest to have these sketches of characters who are extracting information rather than delivering it. It takes both kinds to make an *un*conversation. Conversation, as Austen conceives it, involves both the giving and the taking of information, but the activities need to be mutual and shared; and if the content is an artful combination of individual experience with general principle, then such information may open out into knowledge, even wisdom. The hunger for personal history that is dramatised in Letters the Second and Fourth is only a raw substitute.

E.M. Forster, in his discussion of "Story" and "Plot" in the novel, provided a memorable judgement on such people as these two correspondents:

> Curiosity is one of the lowest of the human faculties. You will have noticed in daily life that when people are inquisitive they nearly always have bad memories and are usually stupid at bottom. The man who begins by asking you how many brothers and sisters you have is never a sympathetic character and if you meet him in a year's time he will probably ask you how many brothers and sisters you have, his mouth sagging open, his eyes still bulging from his head. (Forster 94).

Not an exact description of Austen's two cross-questioners, but one sees what Forster means!

Young Austen's sensitivity to register, her ear for the "unmeaning Gibberish" that was all too often the typical speech in novels, and her inventiveness in creating dialogue of her own, equipped her to be a great novelist. The characteristic guzzling gabbing self-satisfied personnel of the juvenilia declaim in their various over-the-top modes because they can't hear themselves or their own absurdity. But *she* can hear them, and she learned to invent characters who can recognise the pretentious – and also the unthinking and the coarse – in speech as in action, in themselves as in others. The Austen of the mature novels created principal characters who are finely self-aware, who could convincingly say with Descartes, "I think, therefore I am." But on the way to Elizabeth Bennet, and Emma Woodhouse, and Anne Elliot, she had gone a progress through a wonderfully varied set of beings who could only claim, "I talk, therefore I am."

"Catharine, or the Bower"

My discussion of "Catharine, or the Bower" belongs here as part of my study of dialogue in the juvenilia, because its heroine Kitty is in quest not only of a friend but of good conversation with ah intellectual equal. But my treatment of

---

[9] See especially two essays in *The Talk in Jane Austen*: My own "Mrs. Elton and other Verbal Aggressors" and Isobel Grundy's "Why do they Talk so Much? How can we Stand it?"

this important work will range beyond the confines of dialogue and conversation to larger issues.

"Catharine" is a fascinating study by a girl on the edge of adulthood about just such another. Jane Austen was 16 when she wrote it, and Kitty may be Marianne Dashwood's age, nearly 17 (*SS* 21) – though with opinions not nearly so settled, and certainly with a livelier sense of humour. And it is tempting to explore to what extent Kitty is young Austen's self-portrait.[10]

> Her Spirits were naturally good, and not easily depressed, and she possessed such a fund of vivacity and good humour as could only be dampened by serious vexation. (242)

That sounds like the writer of the other juvenilia; and not *un*like Austen's humorous self-construction as the "partial, prejudiced" historian of "The History of England." Kitty's very lonely condition, however, as the niece of an over-anxious spinster aunt who denies access to any "Young Men" (246), is unlike Austen's in her large and noisy family, with extra male pupils joining the household; and Kitty's want of female companionship after the loss of the Wynne sisters contrasts with Austen's lasting devotion to her ever-present sister Cassandra. However, each individual is always to some extent alone – hence the plethora of orphans among the heroes and heroines of novels; and young Austen could strip away the accidentals of actual life to imagine herself a single soul in search of true companionship.

As a novel about adolescence, "Catharine" offers the Bower as "an emblematic sign of friendship and happiness for Kitty … In the course of 'Catharine' it becomes a sexualized space, where girlhood and womanhood converge," as Jeffrey Herrle explains (Herrle, ix). Associated initially with her dear friends Cecilia and Mary Wynne, whose intellectually satisfying friendship Kitty sorely misses, once Edward Stanley has kissed her hand there, the Bower's associations shift. We are familiar with Austen's use of significant emblem in the novels, as in – for instance – the barred gate and ha-ha facing Maria Bertram at Sotherton in *Mansfield Park*, or Fanny's cross, gold chain, and necklace, which so economically represent her divided allegiances to William, Edmund, and Henry Crawford. But it is stirring to find so sophisticated a use of symbol and emblem in her juvenilia. "The Bower" as subtitle to the work carries the same sort of symbolic resonance as Henry James's title *The Golden Bowl*.

Young Austen, we know, was a staunch admirer of Gilpin on the picturesque: In *Northanger Abbey* Henry Tilney begins Catherine Morland's education in the picturesque, and informed conversation; and the Bower, which is both natural growth and girl-made, has something of the appeal of the overgrown gothic ruins dear to Gilpin.

The Gilpin allusion is not the only interest that Kitty shares with her author.

Like Burney's *Evelina*, "Catharine" is to some extent "a history of a young lady's entrance into the World." Kitty is not, like Evelina, being introduced to the

---

[10] Christine Alexander draws attention to the fact that "Catharine" is "replete with hidden meanings and private concerns" (Alexander, "Introduction" xxi).

London season. But she is on the threshold of subjectivity, of independent thought, and an awakening to social and sexual awareness. Burney is evidently on Austen's mind, as she names Kitty's early friend Cecilia (probably in allusion to Burney's deeply thinking heroine in *Cecilia* of 1782), and her disappointing new friend Camilla – again an eponymous heroine of Burney's, in the 1796 novel sub-titled "A Picture of Youth."

Kitty's mind has been developed by her close friendship with Cecilia and Mary Wynne, who shared her taste for reading and her romantic attachment to the Bower, which they built together. Having lived an unusually sheltered life with her reclusive aunt, Kitty is eager for company, eager for a friend who is an intellectual equal like her lost friends the Wynnes, and also eager for stimulating conversation and the expansion of the mind that that it can bring; and she has high hopes of her new visitor Camilla. She has suffered long enough from "the tediousness … of her Aunt's conversation" (247).

Despite her inexperience, Kitty bravely tries to open a conversation with Camilla, and she puts her mind to choosing a suitable topic. She decides on books. What kind of books? "She was well read in Modern history herself," we hear – though perhaps she has not written her own "History of England" as her author had. But she chooses "rather to speak first of Books of a lighter kind, of Books universally read and Admired" (249): that is, of course, novels. For a moment we feel we may be reading the famous defence of novels in the fifth chapter of *Northanger Abbey*. And indeed, in many ways "Catharine" does read like an early version of *Northanger Abbey*, as Q.D. Leavis believed it was (Leavis 63). As the topic for this important first conversation Kitty selects Charlotte Smith's novels. She doesn't get far. Camilla claims to know Smith's novels well: "They are the sweetest things in the world," she gushes. *Emmeline* is undoubtedly the best, she claims, evidently mouthing received opinion, and Kitty, eager for a thorough-going literary discussion, invites her to explain the reasons for her preference. But Camilla can't elaborate, and only winds up, lamely,

> "Besides, Ethelinde is so long –" "That is a very common Objection I beleive, said Kitty, but for my own part, if a book is well written, I always find it too short." "So do I, only I get tired of it before it is finished." (249)

Not much chance of an intellectual conversation with *this* friend!

Unwilling to give up, Kitty tries to get Camilla to expand on her description of her London acquaintance. "I cannot bear Sir Peter, he is such a horrid Creature –" But again Camilla is incapable of expanding or explaining, and Kitty "was left in a painful Uncertainty, as to the particulars of Sir Peter's Character; she knew only that he was Horrid and Shocking, but why, and in what, remained to be discovered" (250). Marianne Dashwood, early in *Sense and Sensibility*, has a similar experience when she tries to learn from Sir John Middleton what sort of young man Willoughby is. Sir John's assurance that he is "a very decent shot" and a bold rider doesn't satisfy Marianne:

> "And is *that* all you can say for him?" said Marianne, indignantly. "But what are his manners on more intimate acquaintance? What his pursuits, his talents and genius?"
>
> Sir John was rather puzzled. (*SS* 52)

Like Marianne, Kitty is disappointed to receive so little information of the kind that matters.

Kitty's interests are again like Austen's in her eagerness to talk of history and to argue over her enthusiastic allegiances. The author of "The History of England" fiercely championed Mary Queen of Scots and made a villainess of Queen Elizabeth. And we can hear that Kitty is spoiling for a fight on the same issue. In an attempt to enliven the deadening exchanges between her dreary aunt and Camilla's prosing mother, and stimulate a real discussion, Kitty challenges her aunt, who wishes to restore the manners of Queen Elizabeth's time, "but I hope you do not mean with the times to restore Queen Elizth herself."

> "Queen Elizabeth, said Mrs Stanley who never hazarded a remark on History that was not well founded, "lived to a good old Age and was a very Clever Woman." "True Ma'am said Kitty; but I do not consider either of those Circumstances as meritorious in herself, and they are very far from making me wish her return, for if she were to come again with the same Abilities and the same good Constitution She might do as much Mischief and last as long as she did before." (251)

Kitty can be playful and allusive in her conversational gambits; and in the very structure of her sentence picks up on the cleverness and longevity cited by Mrs. Stanley to emphasize that judgement must depend on what she *does* with these advantages. But her attempt at stimulating a real conversation doesn't get very far. No one in her circle can rise to this challenge. Kitty turns to Camilla and asks, "I hope you will not defend her" (and we can hear Jane Austen's voice here too). "Oh dear," returns Camilla, " … I know nothing of Politics, and cannot bear to hear them mentioned" (251–2). Definitely a conversation-stopper.

We readers can hear that Kitty, like her author, is longing for a stimulating discussion on their favourite topic of whether Queen Elizabeth was right or wrong to have ordered the execution of Mary Queen of Scots. But her conversational gambit is stymied again. Her aunt, Camilla, and Camilla's mother are simply not capable of the light and informed play with a subject that she is hoping for.

At a more personal level, Kitty asks Camilla whether she knows the Halifax girls, to whom her friend Mary Wynne is a companion; and she is delighted to learn that during the season Camilla sees them almost every day. Much gratified, Kitty concludes they *must* be particularly pleasant people, or with such frequent meetings "all conversation must be at an end." For Kitty as for Anne Elliot the test of good company is good conversation. But it turns out that in this case conversation doesn't even *begin*; for Camilla admits that when she and the Halifax girls see each other at a ball or other crowded occasion they don't actually *talk*, being too far apart; "but in that case we always nod and smile" (253). Nodding and smiling across a crowded room is no satisfactory substitute for conversation so far as Kitty is concerned.

The arrival of Camilla's brother, Edward Stanley, with his sophisticated banter and playful self-promotion, is a danger as well as a delight for Kitty. It is not just that he is a man and handsome, though these things have their due weight with her. Rather it is because he has conversation, and can provide the mental stimulation that she has been starving for. He talks about his reading (while Camilla saunters off, "tired of listening to a Conversation … turning occasionally on Books" [285]).

So Kitty takes every opportunity of turning the conversation to her favourite subject of history, and they are soon engaged in a historical dispute, "for which no one was more calculated than Stanley" (285). But it seems he is even *over*qualified for the task; for though he delights Kitty by his spirited defence of Richard III – a perennial issue even today – in fact he has no real convictions, "scarcely a fixed opinion on the Subject":

> He could therefore always take either side, and always argue with temper. In his indifference on all such topics he was very unlike his Companion, whose judgement being guided by her feelings which were eager and warm was easily decided. (285–6)

Here one can surely hear a touch of self-criticism by Austen of her own earlier enthusiasms.

Edward's readiness to take either side of an issue and argue with temper, though initially attractive, will be destructive of the very stimulation that Kitty is seeking in conversation. The easy temper and adaptability are ultimately an arid indifference, as I predict Kitty will discover. For the moment, however, she is enchanted with him and his conversation together. And in pretending to be in love with her, and then abruptly absenting himself, he disappoints more than her hopes of good conversation.

We are privileged to hear some of Catharine's interior monologue about him, and in her shifting positions she sometimes sounds like the self-contradictory characters of the other juvenilia, Lady Williams and Mary Stanhope. These comic minor figures spill their conflicting impulses as they occur, with no awakened sense of incongruity. The incongruity is for *our* delectation, as amused readers. But where the character herself wrestles with her own sense of the different aspects of her desire, and what she considers rational or moral – that's when she rounds out into complexity.

Kitty has a sense of humour: we often hear of her laughing (256, 267, 272). She also has the habit of reflection, and the reflections can be self-contradictory. When Edward Stanley leaves without saying goodbye, she lectures herself:

> "Oh! what a silly Thing is Woman! How vain, how unreasonable! To suppose that a young Man would be seriously attached in the course of four and twenty hours, to a Girl who has nothing to recommend her but a good pair of eyes! …" (291–2)

But when his flighty sister suggests he left precipitately because he was in love, Kitty changes her tune:

> "He could not trust himself to see me –. Charming Young Man! … I *knew* that it was impossible for one so elegant, and so well bred, to leave any Family in such a Manner, but for a Motive like this unanswerable." Satisfied, beyond the power of Change, of this, [writes the narrator drily] She went in high spirits to her Aunt's apartment, without giving a Moment's recollection on the vanity of Young Women. (294–5)

The narrator's irony is there, but so is the character's. Kitty has a developed awareness, a full subjectivity, that not only equips her for real conversation, but also fits her to be the heroine of a complex novel.

In this fragment we find the seeds of issues Austen was to develop, and then set aside, in her later novels. Conversation, as I have shown, was an important subject in itself. But the various topics *within* conversations have their own history, as Austen takes them up, with more or less conviction, to inform the conversations of her characters.

Kitty, who has been starved for conversation, has a tendency to pounce on a topic like a dog on a bone. Rather than letting the conversation simply happen, she prepares for it as though for a lecture or debate. She chooses the subject in advance, and picks one on which she already has knowledge and opinions: As we saw, "Though she was well read in Modern history herself, she Chose rather to speak of Books of a lighter kind" – that is, novels, of course: in this case the novels of Charlotte Smith. (The upper case for the verb "Chose" gives it extra emphasis.) We have seen the failure of that conversational debut. Jane Austen was going to have a say about novels, though, and that happens with some éclat in chapter 5 of *Northanger Abbey*. We have all enjoyed reading and quoting from that famous passage; but such set-piece disquisitions don't happen often, either in authorial commentary or in characters' conversational exchanges. When Elizabeth and Darcy are searching for a topic on the dance floor, "What think you of books?" he proposes. How eagerly would Kitty take up the subject! But Elizabeth responds, "No – I cannot talk of books in a ball-room" (*PP* 104). Austen seems to be training herself in the practice of letting a topic go, in favour of maintaining dramatic appropriateness. The topic of fiction does reappear, though, as a salient topic of conversation and source of inspiration in *Sanditon*, which is as near as Austen came to writing a *roman à clef*.

"[W]ell read in Modern history herself," Kitty denies herself this particular topic on this occasion, but she raises it again, of course, in trying to start a conversation on Queen Elizabeth. And history was to be another "topic" that Austen was to introduce, with diminishing degrees of emphasis, in the later novels. Unlike Kitty, the historical enthusiast, Catherine Morland produces the famous put-down of historiography as consisting only of "the quarrels of popes and kings … the men all so good for nothing, and hardly any women at all" (*NA* 110). Only the heroine's sensible friend, Eleanor Tilney, says quietly, "Yes, I am fond of history," but airs no enthusiasms. That hobby-horse is stabled, and references are kept appropriate to character and dramatic situation.

After Edward Stanley's defence of Richard III, however, a lingering and amusing historical prejudice remains against the name Richard – from Catherine Morland's father, "who was a very respectable man, though his name was Richard" (*NA* 5), to "poor Richard" in *Persuasion*, "a thick-headed, unfeeling, unprofitable Dick Musgrove" (*P* 54).

Similarly, one can trace the fading of young Austen's enthusiasm for the topic of the picturesque. In "The History of England" she names Gilpin as one of her favourite men (*J* 182). Kitty's devotion to her Bower demonstrates her adherence to his theories. In *Northanger Abbey* the conversation between Henry and Eleanor Tilney on a scene's "capability of being formed into pictures" confirms their possession of "real taste," and Catherine listens – all too eagerly – to Henry's "lecture on the picturesque" (*NA* 112). By the time of *Sense and Sensibility* Austen is ready to satirize Marianne for her passion for dead leaves, and her tendency to canonize "him who first defined what picturesque beauty was" (*SS* 113). And in *Pride and Prejudice*, as we have seen, the subject of the picturesque has faded to Elizabeth's playful reference to the threesome at Netherfield as "charmingly grouped" (*PP* 58).

Fanny Price has her enthusiasms on nature and landscape too, and she delivers her own one-sided rhapsodic lectures: on memory, for instance, or the evergreen: "How beautiful, how welcome, how wonderful the evergreen!" But the topic is not taken up for conversational elaboration: Mary Crawford dismisses Fanny's enthusiasm by her egocentric comment, "I see no wonder in this shrubbery equal to seeing myself in it" (*MP* 244). The chosen "topics" for conversation are no longer used as an opportunity for delivering excitement or informed commentary, but as illustration of character.

Another favourite topic that appears in "Catharine, or the Bower" is the issue of accomplishment. Camilla Stanley's youth, we hear, had been "devoted to the acquisition of Accomplishments, which were to be displayed and in a few years entirely neglected" (*J* 248); and the topic finds its way, again with diminishing degrees of emphasis, to the consciously developed debate in *Pride and Prejudice*, where Miss Bingley lays it down that to deserve to be called accomplished "a woman must have a thorough knowledge of music, drawing, dancing, and he modern languages" – with Elizabeth's put-down, "*I* never saw such a woman" (*PP* 43). In *Emma* we hear Mrs. Elton talk of her devotion to music, while being simultaneously "determined upon neglecting her music" now that she is married (*E* 299). And in *Persuasion* we have no debate on the topic; only Anne Elliot's demonstrated accomplishment in her piano-playing, and her competence in translating "inverted, transposed, curtailed Italian lines, into clear, comprehensible, elegant English" (*P* 203). She *is* accomplished, without making a topic of it.

When her "own darling child" had come to hand from the printers, Austen wrote delightedly to Cassandra that *Pride and Prejudice* was "rather too light & bright & sparkling": and she added,

> it wants shade; – it wants to be stretched out here & there with a long Chapter … – about something unconnected with the story; an Essay on Writing, a Critique of Walter Scott – or the story of Bonaparte. (*Letters* 203)

Of course she didn't mean it. She had all along been training herself to excise all that was not intimately and immediately connected with her story, and that included excising disquisitions on subjects dear to her heart: there were to be no more Essays on Novels, or Modern History, or the Picturesque, or Accomplishments. But all these favourite and recurring topics, which were canvassed so variously in the novels that were to come, made their early appearance in this first fragment of a realistic novels.

As the most mature piece of the juvenilia that Austen collected in her three notebook volumes, "Catharine, or the Bower," nevertheless remains unfinished. Its incomplete state is more of a disappointment than that of "The Three Sisters" or "Lesley Castle" (though both of these fragments are tantalising too), because it is so close to being a Jane Austen novel in the league of those famous other six. The characters are developed enough that we have a keen interest in what is to become of them, and how that endearing Kitty, with her questing intelligence, her ironic self-awareness, and her humour will find fulfilment.

When I co-edited "Catharine, or the Bower" with a group of students for the Juvenilia Press, we sought to tease the readers' curiosity by an appendix we called "What Next?" and we played over our own speculations on the probable development and resolution of Kitty's fictional trajectory, and those of her friends, the enlightened Cecilia and Mary Wynne, the ditzy Camilla Stanley, and her charming by irresponsible brother Edward, who first awakens Kitty's sexual interest.

A pattern established in the six novels is that the *first* man of interest always wins the heroine in the end. Catherine Morland meets Tilney before she meets John Thorpe; Elizabeth meets Darcy before she encounters Wickham; Emma knows Mr. Knightley before Frank Churchill ever appears – and so forth. Even Marianne, exceptional in marrying her *second* love, met Brandon before she fell for Willoughby. Mindful of this pattern, one is tempted to predict that Edward Stanley, with all his faults, may yet win Kitty in the end, after some vicissitudes that will suitably reform him. But he is *so* shallow and so frivolous that he inevitably fails the test of being worthy of the heroine. Kitty will surely find his charm fades.

In his defence it needs to be said, however, that though by kissing Kitty's hand in the Bower he plays at being in love with her, he does it in the belief that she knows it is only play: it's his silly sister who convinces Kitty he is in love. In his light-hearted play he is more like a brother or friend to Kitty than a lover.

In fact he is like Frank Churchill with Emma: perfectly happy that others think he is courting her, but with a firm conviction that she is above being harmed by his apparent preference. "Amiable and delightful as Miss Woodhouse is," Frank Churchill writes confessionally to his stepmother,

> she never gave me the idea of a young woman likely to be attached … She received my attentions with an easy, friendly, good-humoured playfulness, which exactly suited me. We seemed to understand each other. (*E* 478)

To seem to be courting Emma (so long as she herself is not too susceptible) suits Frank Churchill's purposes, because he is covering up his secret engagement to Jane Fairfax. And my corollary speculation is that for Edward Stanley to *seem* to be in love with Kitty suits his purposes too, because *he* is covering up his secret engagement to … ? Mary Wynne, of course! – who depends for her upkeep, like Jane Fairfax, on the family who take her in as a companion to the daughters.

I can't resist a little further speculation: that lively young Edward Stanley has met Mary Wynne at his family friends the Halifaxes, and they have fallen in love. Mr. Stanley won't hear of such a match (nor would Frank Churchill's adoptive parents hear of his to Jane Fairfax, so he doesn't tell them). Mr. Stanley sends young Edward off on the grand tour in Europe, an experience calculated to cure him of his unsuitable attachment. In France Edward frets for Mary Wynne and home, and uses an injury to his favourite hunter as an excuse to dash back to England. The hunter having expired in the Devonshire family home, he takes a hackney coach to Chetwynde, where his parents and sister are staying with Kitty's Aunt Percival; finds Kitty dressed to go to a ball, and cheerfully accompanies her there. Finding her thoroughly congenial with her light-hearted reception and readiness in laughter, he decides off the cuff to pay her very notable attentions, both to shock her very shockable aunt and to satisfy his father of his being cured of Mary Wynne. His father is "perfectly convinced that Edward ought not to remain in England, and was resolved to hasten his leaving it as son as possible." But Edward, he finds, is "much less disposed towards returning to France, than to accompany [the family] in their projected tour" to the Lake District (279) – where, as we have yet to learn, he will be able to meet Mary Wynne, as she accompanies the Halifaxes on their tour. Meanwhile, to allay his father's anxiety about his attachment to Mary Wynne, as well as to amuse himself by exciting Mrs. Percival's anxieties about the dangers of Young Men, he pays marked attentions to Kitty.

> He would always sit by her in the room, appear dissatisfied if she left it … . Everything that she said, appeared to interest him; his Conversation was addressed to her alone, and she seemed to be the sole object of his attention. (283–4)

In fact, he lays it on with a trowel, as Frank Churchill does with Emma.

So where would this go?

I do not propose to provide a full plot summary of the finished novel; rather, in succumbing briefly to the lure of the fragment, to suggest the parallels with the situation and characters in *Emma*. The characters in "Catharine" are so well developed that hey invite such speculation about "What Next?" Q.D. Leavis has pictured Austen as a thrifty novelist who hated waste and therefore raided her early writings to serve as the skeletons for her later ones: so "Catharine" becomes

Northanger Abbey, "Lady Susan" *Mansfield Park*, "The Watsons" *Emma*, and so on (Leavis 62–5). My own procedure is somewhat different, in that I am drawing on the later work in order to speculate about possible directions that the early work might have taken.

Young Jane Austen, writes Margaret Anne Doody, was "not autobiographical" ("Introduction" xxiii). Kitty's history is not Jane's. A young writer of fiction, by definition, has less experience to draw on than a mature one. So where does she turn for her content? One resource is to draw on her reading instead, as young Austen did, extensively, in turning so frequently to parody and burlesque. Another, for more realistic fiction, is to draw on what she knows of the experience of her extended family experience; and as others have noticed, Austen incorporated the fate of her aunt Philadelphia Austen, who as a young woman was sent to Bengal to find a husband and a living, in the history of Kitty's friend Cecilia Wynne (Doody and Murray 391; Alexander, "Introduction" xxi). And then, in addition, she can draw on her own enthusiasms – English fiction, English history, and Gilpin on landscape – and *bêtes noires* – Queen Elizabeth as murderess – to share with her heroine as matter for conversation. In these ways we can read "Catharine, or the Bower" as Jane Austen's own "Picture of Youth" – her own youth, as well as Kitty's.

"Catharine, or the Bower," with its teenage heroine who often recalls her author, her quest for a true friend and satisfying conversation, and its tantalising similarities to the later novels, stands intriguingly at the cusp of Austen's development as author, from inspired and irreverent teenager to committed and attentive novelist.

Chapter 5
"Love and Freindship" in the Classroom[1]

I have already made it amply clear that I believe Austen's juvenilia deserve reading and studying. But given the constraints of time in courses on literature, "Do Austen's juvenilia belong in the classroom?" is a legitimate question. If you have a chance to teach *Pride and Prejudice* or *Mansfield Park*, dare you jettison it for a selection of items from *Volumes the First*, *Second*, and *Third*? Put this way, the question possibly requires the answer "No." I am too confirmed an admirer of the six great novels to miss any opportunity of teaching them when it arises. I have taught *Pride and Prejudice* to grades 10 and 12 and to first-year university students, and *Emma* in survey courses on the English novel. And from time to time I have been fortunate enough to teach all six novels in a specialised upper-level course, or in a graduate course. In these last cases, I make time for some of the juvenilia, and particularly for "Love and Freindship," as a way into the novels. Graduate students, who have some knowledge of the sentimental tradition that it parodies, are bowled over by it. And even in teaching Austen at the lower and less specialised levels, I usually get in "Love and Freindship," if only in the form of some selected readings, as a way into the Austen novel at hand. An instructor who worked with me in editing Austen's juvenilia for the Juvenilia Press regularly teaches "Love and Freindship" to first-year students before she launches them into *Pride and Prejudice*: She has found it a way to get past their nervousness at encountering so daunting a canonical work as the great novel which most have heard of but few have read. "Well, what do you know! The great Jane Austen didn't know how to spell "friendship"! – and they proceed encouraged.

Why "Love and Freindship" rather than the many other delectable items among Austen's juvenilia? In discussing teaching a text, one needs to pick one that has much to offer; and to me "Love and Freindship" is the most complete and accomplished single piece in the rich collection of Austen's youthful works. Unlike "Catharine, or the Bower" and many of the others, it is finished; as an example of epistolary fiction and of burlesque it relates usefully to much eighteenth-century fiction; and as a reaction to the extremes of sensibility and romanticism it invites an approach through the history of ideas.

Though teaching "Love and Freindship" as an adjunct to the more famous novels of Austen's maturity affords rich classroom opportunities, experience has convinced me that it is a work that can stand alone as a teaching text, and in various pedagogical contexts. A course in romanticism, for instance, could include it as a

---

[1] A version of part of this chapter was published as "Teaching 'Love and Freindship'" in *Jane Austen's Beginnings*, ed. J. David Grey. Ann Arbor: UMI Research Press, 1989, 135–51.

succinct critical text, since it is a marvellously pointed and intellectually acute reaction to romanticism, and a codification of its conventions. With its brevity and concentration, its control of diction and mastery of burlesque it would be a joyful addition to courses in composition and rhetoric at both basic and advanced levels. Sandra Gilbert and Susan Gubar chose "Love and Freindship" as the representative work by Jane Austen for *The Norton Anthology of Literature by Women*. That effectively spread the knowledge of this otherwise little-known but brilliant text, and demonstrated that it is an appropriate text for courses in women's literature. Moreover, since juvenilia studies have become a recognised area for research and teaching, it would provide the jewel in the crown of a course devoted to juvenilia.

As a text for teaching to young people, one great advantage it has, and shares with the other juvenilia, is that it is written by one of themselves. In teaching at high school and first-year levels, in particular, where the English instructor is apt to be faced by a number of students more or less resistant to literature, it is a shrewd move in the game to beat the generation gap by infiltrating the opposition forces with an author who shows so many signs of sharing *your* concerns, while being on *their* side of the gap. This kid with the marvellous control of language and assured command of an extensive vocabulary, this writer with an intense and exuberant involvement in other literature, is a mere teenager, a 14-year-old. Some sharp cookie. Like, totally awesome. Perhaps, suspects the resistant student who may yet become a convert, there is something to literature after all.

The approach one takes in teaching "Love and Freindship" will of course vary according to the context in which it is taught. If it is a part of a course on romanticism or the history of the novel, then the emphasis will naturally fall on the war of ideas and the burlesque of the novel of sensibility. If it is a text in a course in composition and rhetoric, clearly the language and narrative technique will be to the fore. And when I am teaching it as an adjunct to the teaching of Austen's other works, then it is useful to focus on the intimations of things to come, the themes and technical concerns that are to be developed in the great novels. By way of giving some coverage to all these possibilities, I will divide this essay into three parts, roughly on past, present, and future: one on the burlesque element as a reaction to literature that has gone before, one on "Love and Freindship" as a text standing on its own, and one on this little work as looking forward, a pointer to the novels yet to come. Finally I touch on a somewhat recondite topic, *editing* "Love and Freindship," which for me has also been a pedagogic endeavour.

Looking Back: The Burlesque

For the informed graduate student who comes to it via wide reading in the eighteenth-century novel and the novel of sensibility, "Love and Freindship" has a particular and unrivalled delight – something like that it must have had for its first readers, Jane Austen's sister and brothers, who were steeped in the unselected and uncanonical fiction of the day. To come to young Austen's reaction via *The Man of Feeling* or *The Fool of Quality*, or even *Clarissa* or *Evelina*, is to feel a bracing breeze of wit after a cloistered absorption in emotion.

But fortunately the wit is accessible to the less specialised student too, for you don't have to wade through *Laura and Augustus* and the other novels that are being parodied to get the point. (In the next chapter, however, I provide a shortcut to examining the relation of "Love and Freindship" to the texts it principally bounces off, *Laura and Augustus* and *Emily Montague*.) Their conventions and narrative procedures are brilliantly and unfairly generalised, selected, and lampooned for us. As A. Walton Litz pointed out, "The *Juvenilia* are remarkably self-sufficient, and most of the burlesque passages are self-explanatory" (Litz 18).

Even the unsophisticated student may learn from the text itself – from Sir Edward's speech, carefully planted early in the work – that it bounces off other texts, when Sir Edward reacts to the romantic effusions of his son: "Where, Edward in the name of wonder (said he) did you pick up this unmeaning Gibberish? You have been studying Novels I suspect" ("L&F" 108). For the reader uninitiated in the fiction Austen was burlesquing, it can become a stimulating exercise to deduce the characteristics of the novels young Edward has been studying.

How would an intelligent but not necessarily widely-read student respond to such a question on "Love and Freindship"? It reads, let us say, "Making clear the evidence on which you base your conclusions, deduce the major characteristics of the kinds of novel Sir Edward suspects his son of reading." First, the student would need to look carefully at what young Edward has just been saying. I quote here from his mini-autobiography, delivered on the first night of his acquaintance with Laura and her parents, which includes the dialogue with his father:

> "My Father … is a mean and mercenary wretch – it is only to such particular freinds as this Dear Party that I would thus betray his failings. – Your Virtues my amiable Polydore (addressing himself to my father) yours Dear Claudia and yours my Charming Laura call on me to repose in you, my Confidence." We bowed. "My Father, seduced by the false glare of Fortune and the Deluding Pomp of Title, insisted on my giving my hand to Lady Dorothea. No never exclaimed I. Lady Dorothea is lovely and Engaging; I prefer no woman to her; but know Sir, that I scorn to marry her in compliance with your wishes, No! Never shall it be said that I obliged my Father."
>
> We all admired the noble Manliness of his reply. (108)

The tirade received with such admiration by its later audience is designated "unmeaning Gibberish" by Sir Edward. This already points to two symmetrically opposed sets of values among the characters of the work; and with some close reading or some helpful guidance the student may align these values with Sense and Sensibility, in their extreme forms. Young Edward's values (as deducible from this passage alone) include a vaunted scorn for material considerations, an opposition on principle to fathers, a determination to be independent of parental guidance even at the cost of his own comfort and convenience, an extraordinary readiness to form instant intimacies beyond his family, and a strong propensity to talk about himself: we are already well on the way to the values of Sensibility (at least of Sensibility as here exaggerated and satirized), which are to be more elaborately adumbrated in the rest of "Love and Freindship"; and these are the values, clearly, that are enshrined in the novels that his father suspects Edward of reading. Since the same values are also articulated at large by the heroine, Laura, the student may expand from Edward's mini-narrative to his wife's larger one, and may move also from thematic concerns to technical ones. Laura, as heroine of sensibility, gives us a version of the novel of sensibility, with its routine gestures of sighing and swooning, prodigious coincidences, birth-mystery plot, embedded life-histories of different characters, and improbable layout in epistolary form. All this and much, much more (as the brochures say) the intelligent but unread student can deduce for herself from an attentive reading of the text, because of the vivid exaggeration of young Austen's parody.

The more fully initiated graduate student, meanwhile, may receive more recondite pleasure from the same passage, the pleasure of recognition. "Love and Freindship" is one more document in the ongoing eighteenth-century debates on true and false sensibility, marriages of interest and romance, the disinterestedness of true friendship, and the proper extent and limits of parental authority. Richardson's Clarissa Harlowe, for instance, had already delivered such a lecture as Sir Edward would have approved to her friend Anna, who was inclined to despise her sensible and eligible suitor because, like young Edward's Lady Dorothea, he was unexciting: "[You] have nothing to do [Clarissa tells her friend] but to fall in with a choice your mama has made for you, to which you have not, nor can have, a just objection: except the frowardness of our sex … makes it one that the choice was your mamma's … Perverse nature, we know, loves not to be prescribed to; although youth is not so well qualified … to choose for itself" (Letter 73, 291). Clarissa puts it mildly; her uncle Anthony's phrase, "a most horrid romantic perverseness" (Letter 32.4, 155), might be closer to describing young Edward's reaction to Lady Dorothea. For the well-read seeker after sources, of course, "Love and Freindship" provides a veritable Happy Hunting Ground. Where shall we find the original for the wonderful recognition scene, in which poor Lord St. Clair is reunited with four grandchildren (all by separate mothers, and unaware of each other) in as many minutes? (120–21). In Fielding's *Joseph Andrews* ("I have discovered my son, I have him again in my arms!" [IV 16, 293])? In Smollett's *Humphry Clinker* ("You see, gentlemen, how the sins of my youth rise up in judgement against me" [III Oct 4, 292])? In Sheridan's *The Critic*, as Walton Litz suggests? (Litz 21) Or (my candidate) in Frances Burney's *Evelina* ("Acknowledge thee, Caroline? – yes, with my heart's best blood I acknowledge thee!" – though this same estranged father has previously dismissed this applicant with an irony worthy of Mr. Bennet: "It is not three days since, that I had the pleasure of discovering a son; how many more sons and daughters may be brought to me, I am yet to learn, but I am already perfectly satisfied with the size of my family"? [*Evelina* 485, 411]). Fourteen-year-old Jane, familiar with these and many more, generalises and caps them all with Lord St. Clair's bevy of supernumerary grandchildren. Well may he enquire nervously, "But tell me (… looking fearfully towards the Door) tell me, have I any other Grand-children in the House" – and, after dealing out banknotes all round, beat a hasty and permanent retreat (121).

An undue emphasis on "Love and Freindship" as burlesque of other novels has the danger of giving the impression, particularly to the unsophisticated student, that Jane Austen despised the fiction of her day. And as we have seen, Henry Tilney can help here, with his readiness both to parody and admire *The Mysteries of Udolpho* (*NA* 106). The intimate relation of admiration with mockery needs to be understood as informing "Love and Freindship" too. Reading novels and critically reacting to them were clearly the great delights of young Jane Austen's life. And when we teach her youthful burlesque her delight needs to emerge as well as her mocking judgment.

Suppose that "Love and Freindship," instead of being written by a teenage girl for the small circle of her family, had been written by Byron – as it well might have been, in the same wicked mood in which he wrote "English Bards and Scotch Reviewers": it would surely have been published in its own day, and read, and laughed over, and quoted, and become part of the canon. B.C. Southam, who is careful to acknowledge the occasional and fugitive nature of Austen's juvenilia, nevertheless calls it "the most amusing and incisive of all eighteenth-century attacks upon sentimental fiction" (Southam, *Literary* 3); for acute perception of the flaws in a certain mode, and the limber articulation of them, are not only remarkable for a 14-year-old, they are remarkable for *anybody*. This document in the history of ideas is the product of a first-class mind as well as of an agile creative imagination. The tenets of the cult of sentimentality, many of which were common to the romantic movement, are marvellously grasped, dramatised, and reduced to absurdity. In fact young Austen uses the logical strategy of *reductio ad absurdum* with brilliant consistency. Each treasured position of the sentimentalist is identified, exaggerated, and pursued to the point where it becomes a reversal of itself. Laura, Edward, Sophia and Augustus, the adherents to the cult, are like a comic version of Milton's Satan, who can produce a fine intellectual argument in support of his insanely perverse proposition, "Evil, be thou my Good."

Romantic individualism, chiefly manifested here in the rejection of social sanctions as epitomised in parental advice, becomes ultimately self-annihilating; as we have seen, Edward can't consider marrying Lady Dorothea, even though he likes her, because his father advises it. In the same way other treasured watchwords of the sentimental cult are consistently turned upside down. Sensibility itself, the capacity to feel tenderly for others, becomes callousness: at the outset Laura admits that though her sensibility was at one time "too tremblingly alive to every affliction of my Freinds," she now feels for nobody's afflictions but her own (104). Sophia enacts this hyper-refinement of the emotions: "Alas, what would I not give to learn the fate of my Augustus! – to know if he is still in Newgate, or if he is yet hung. – But never shall I be able so far to conquer my tender sensibility as to enquire after him" (127). So overwhelming are her tender feelings for him that she deserts him when he most needs her.

Romantic reverence for the beauties of external nature becomes one more way of turning in upon the self:

> "What a beautifull Sky! (said I) How charmingly is the azure varied by those delicate streaks of white!"
>
> "Oh! my Laura (replied [Sophia] hastily withdrawing her Eyes from a momentary glance at the sky) do not thus distress me by calling my Attention to an object which so cruelly reminds me of my Augustus's blue Sattin Waistcoat striped with white!" (128)

Apparently absorption in emotion leaves no room for admiring the beauties of nature.[2]

"The world is too much with us," wrote Wordsworth, giving memorable voice to the romantic's rejection of a hypercivilised society and of things worldly; "late and soon, / Getting and spending, we lay waste our powers." Laura and her fellow romantics believe that they live according to the spirit of this rejection. Edward scorns his father, the representative of social authority, as "a mean and mercenary wretch," and expects to live the life of the lilies of the field, who toil not, neither do they spin. But as our students quickly notice, this innocent assumption that the world owes them a living leads directly to various acts of theft and embezzlement, and numbers of banknotes are "gracefully purloined" (116) with some skill by these untaught children of nature. Decades later, Dickens was to render this sinister reversal of a vaunted indifference to material things in the figure of Harold Skimpole, a character based on another romantic, Leigh Hunt. Skimpole confesses proudly "to two of the oldest infirmities in the world: one was, that he had no idea of time; the other, that he had no idea of money." He claims, "I covet nothing … . Possession is nothing to me." But he proceeds cheerfully on the assumption that others must support him, and like his forebears, Laura and her associates, he elevates his freeloading into a moral principle. "I almost feel as if *you* ought to be grateful to *me*," he tells his benefactor, "for giving you the opportunity of enjoying the luxury of generosity" (*Bleak House* ch. 6). Young Austen's Sophia can similarly turn the moral tables on her benefactor when, being caught in the act of "majestically removing" his banknotes to her own purse, she angrily calls their owner the "culprit" (96).

This pattern of turning romantic principles into their own reversal is most fully and inventively developed in the presentation of freedom of choice: Laura and company believe that they are free spirits, children of nature, living a life of spontaneous response, rejecting the code of the fathers, and expressing themselves

---

[2] Christine Alexander points out that the blue satin waistcoat is a reminiscence of Werther's in Goethe's *The Sorrows of Werther*, the obligatory reading for all adherents to sensibility, as Laura believes ("Introduction" xxx).

habitually by the "spontaneous overflow of powerful feelings" that is Wordsworth's definition of poetry. That is their conception of themselves. As Austen exposes them, however, we see them as the veritable slaves of their own convention of freedom. Their code is every bit as exacting as the patriarchal one. A large section of the population, according to their code, has "no soul" (112), and may therefore be dismissed as "that inferior order of Beings" (84). The category includes: anyone who has a steady income, or who thinks food and drink more nourishing than the "pleasing Pangs of Love" (111), or who does not admire *The Sorrows of Werther*, or who is named Bridget or Richard, or who is not above the middle size, or whose hair is not auburn. On the other hand, those who are like the heroines in the possession of "exalted Ideas, Delicate Feelings [and] refined Sensibilities" (131), belong to the body of the Elect, and have every right to plunder the sordid wretches who have money – money that may be "gracefully purloined" (116) or "majestically remove[ed]" (125) without any moral qualms.

All this comes most comically to the fore in the episode at Macdonald-Hall, where Laura and Sophia, who have hitherto been exiles from society, become authority figures themselves. The 15-year-old Janetta Macdonald proves malleable, and her new role models, with considerable zest, set about her conversion from Sense to Sensibility. She is engaged to Graham, but Laura and Sophia take things into their own hands. "They said he was Sensible, well-informed, and Agreable; we did not pretend to Judge of such trifles, but as we were convinced he had no soul, that he had never read the Sorrows of Werter, and that his Hair bore not the least resemblance to Auburn, we were certain that Janetta could feel no affection for him, or at least that she ought to feel none" (122). Laura and Sophia, with their own rigid notions of propriety, symmetrically reverse the requirements of such parents as Clarissa Harlowe's by detaching Janetta from the prudent suitor and marrying her to an opportunistic fortune-hunter.

To identify, exaggerate, and reduce to their own absurd opposites these tenets of the dying cult of sensibility, from which the new cult of romanticism, phoenix-like, was about to rise, and to do all this in the dramatic form of a brief narrative, is surely to have achieved something considerable, in the history of those movements, as well as to have produced a marvellously funny pastiche. "Love and Freindship" as burlesque, as a reaction to previous and contemporary texts, deserves a place in courses on the eighteenth century and romanticism.

The Text Itself

Although "Love and Freindship" inevitably makes its first impact as a burlesque, it also deserves attention for its own intrinsic value, and for its internal ironies. Students in a course on composition would have plenty to learn from the control of language and the narrative structure of this brief but eventful story.

The series of letters that constitutes "Love and Freindship" sets it up as a narrative of instruction. Isabel asks Laura, the friend of her youth, to recount "the

Misfortunes and Adventures of your Life" for the moral benefit of her daughter, Marianne (103). Laura quickly assumes that she is to appear in her own story as the positive moral example: "may the fortitude with which I have suffered the many Afflictions of my past Life, prove to her a useful Lesson," she prays (103–4). But the attentive student who matches the beginning with the ending will notice that Isabel is far from admiring the youthful Laura's conduct. When they meet in the stagecoach which coincidentally contains all the surviving personages of the story, Laura delivers an oral version of her life story, but Isabel tends to be disapproving. "Faultless as my Conduct had certainly been during the whole Course of my late Misfortunes and Adventures, she pretended to find fault with my Behaviour," notes Laura indignantly (135). Isabel, it appears, has gone through some moral evolution in the course of the narrative: having been once the bosom "Freind" of Laura and the chosen companion of her youth, she learns from her friend's experience and her recounting of it that Sense is morally preferable to Sensibility. Hence her scheme in eliciting Laura's written narrative is to provide her daughter Marianne with a *negative* example, not the positive one that Laura fondly assumes. Marianne as reader is to learn to *avoid* Laura's sentimental excesses, and is thus to be converted from Sensibility to Sense, as her mother was before her. Although young Austen doesn't labour the point – in fact she merely tosses it in – there are intricacies and ironic possibilities in this narrative setup that are worthy of a more elaborate tale.

Laura herself is immune from any moral benefit to be derived from her experience: the only moral she can draw from it is the one she relays from the dying Sophia, about the imprudence of wilful fainting fits (132). She remains satisfied that since "I had always behaved in a manner which reflected Honour on my Feelings & Refinement," she must be irreproachable, and so have nothing to learn (135).

The many interpolated narratives within Laura's narrative suggest that the young Jane was meditating (though certainly not solemnly) on narratology. What is narrative *for*? All the characters, whether on the side of Sense or Sensibility, clearly lap it up. On that memorable coach ride between Edinburgh and Stirling, the characters deliver autobiographies at an astonishing rate. First, at Sir Edward's entreaty, Laura tells the story of his son's death; next, Laura "related to them every other misfortune which had befallen me since we parted"; next, Isabel gives Laura "an accurate detail of every thing that had befallen her since our separation"; finally, Augusta supplies "the same information respecting herself, Sir Edward and Lady Dorothea" (135). Like that of the gossip-hungry writers of Letters the Second and Fourth in "A Collection of Letters," Laura's curiosity for such personal narratives is insatiable. After this marathon of telling and listening, while the others are regaling themselves with "Green tea and buttered toast," Laura seeks out her cousins, and "we feasted ourselves in a more refined and Sentimental Manner by a confidential Conversation" (137) – consisting, of course, in further "entertaining Narration" (140). Apparently Laura actually lives off people's lives and adventures. To keep her supplied with this verbal grist to her mill can be exhausting, and as we have seen her demand for Edward's adventures proves fatal, and he actually expires while he draws breath to tell his story.

What, besides a substitute for toast and tea, do Laura and the others get out of each other's stories? It seems that the morally approved characters, Sir Edward and his ilk, get moral enlargement and some matter for thought: the raw data can be sifted, interpreted, judged; it conduces to more than itself. But for the Sensibility crew, a life history is mere food for curiosity. Laura *telling* a story proposes to "gratify the curiosity of [Isabel's] daughter" (103); Laura *hearing* a story desires Isabel only "to satisfy my Curiosity" (135). For such people a story begins and ends with itself, or rather with *the* self, and no mental or moral growth is involved in the transmitting of it. The teller gratifies the self, and slakes the listener's curiosity (or the "degrading thirst after outrageous stimulation" that Wordsworth was to complain about in the preface to *Lyrical Ballads*). It's notable that the sensible Sir Edward wants Laura to tell him of his son Edward, a third party. But Laura makes Edward's death only an episode among her own adventures, for she can proceed no further than the I-thou narrative.

The two species, with their opposed sets of assumptions about appropriate behaviour and appropriate discourse, have their own distinct languages. And identifying these languages, or the kinds of *patois* common to a group, or particular to an individual, can be a useful exercise in a course in composition and rhetoric. The familiar conversation between Edward and his sister Augusta on "Victuals and Drink," which I have discussed before, is useful in the classroom too:

> "Never, never Augusta will I so demean myself. (said Edward). Support! What Support will Laura want which she can receive from him?"
>
> "Only those very insignificant ones of Victuals and Drink." (answered she).
>
> "Victuals and Drink! (replied my Husband in a most nobly contemptuous Manner) and dost thou then imagine that there is no other support for an exalted Mind (such as is my Laura's) than the mean and indelicate employment of Eating and Drinking?"
>
> "None that I know of, so efficacious." (returned Augusta). (111)

The whole conversation is longer, but even from this extract one can tell that the two interlocutors speak in two different registers; and if one's students in rhetoric can become sensitive to tonal register, much is gained. Edward adopts the grand style for the expression of his elevated emotions of scorn and indignation. Augusta calls him "you," but he calls her "thou," and his archaism is intended to capture the dignity of chivalric romance. His characteristic syntax is exclamatory ("Support!" "Victuals and Drink!") and histrionic. Augusta on the other hand is down-to-earth and colloquial, to match her practical concern with creature comforts. She speaks economically in sentence fragments, supplying only the noun phrases that answer his rhetorical questions (he *means* them to be rhetorical). And she, like her father, can handle irony ("None that I know of, so efficacious"), whereas it is characteristic of the adherents of sensibility that they are as incapable of using irony as of understanding it. Their speeches may of course be ironic for the *reader*, however. Here, for instance, Edward's outrage at the notion that Laura will need support from his father can be matched against the circumstances of the ending, when the widowed Laura retires on an allowance of £400 a year, supplied by Sir Edward (140).

An exercise in practical criticism of such a passage can alert students to different verbal styles. And because young Austen is here being deliberately crude and hyperbolic, even the unawakened first-year student can get the point. The marvellous nuances and finely discriminated tones in the quite recognizable speech patterns of John Thorpe, Mrs. Jennings, Mary Bennet, Mr. Woodhouse, and the rest ate yet to come. But meanwhile we still have broad burlesques by way of developing the student's ear, such as this exchange with 15-year-old Janetta Macdonald. She has been engaged by her father to sensible Graham, and she has no objection. But Laura and Sophia, hungry for romance, are determined to persuade her that Graham is being thrust upon her, that young Captain M'Kenzie is the one she *really* loves, and that he too must adore *her*. The languages of sense and sensibility are delightfully in counterpoint. Janetta says simply that she has no reason to suppose that M'Kenzie is interested in her:

> "That he certainly adores you (replied Sophia) there can be no doubt –. The Attachment must be reciprocal –. Did he never gaze on you with Admiration – tenderly press your hand – drop an involuntary tear – and leave the room abruptly?" "Never (replied she) that I remember – he has always left the room indeed when his visit has been ended, but has never gone away particularly abruptly or without making a bow." "Indeed my Love (said I) you must be mistaken – for it is absolutely impossible that he should ever have left you but with Confusion, Despair, and Precipitation –." (103–4)

It is a fine passage of indoctrination. Sophia and Laura come on as oracles, with vocabulary and syntax belonging to romantic convention: (the elegant inversion "That he certainly adores you … there can be no doubt" sounds much more impressive than "There can be no doubt that he certainly adores you.") According to their world-view a fierce and romantic passion – though just by a passing captain for a fifteen-year-old girl he hardly knows – is virtually a law of physics. That being the case, it must follow as the night the day that he will behave according to the strictest rules of romantic love, with rapt gaze, tender pressure of the hand, abrupt exits, and so forth. Janetta's innocent and literal comment that he has never left except when his visit is over, or without making his formal bow, provides an amusing though mundane counterpoint to Laura and Sophia's violent adjustments of reality to make it conform to their world-view. "Consider but for a moment Janetta, and you must be convinced how absurd it is to suppose that he could ever make a Bow, or behave like any other Person" (124). Any other world-view is simply an impossibility. Laura and Sophia exploit language to bamboozle the all-too-teachable Janetta into their way of seeing. The passage seems, indeed, like a parody in advance of Emma Woodhouse's manipulation of Harriet to make her believe that Mr. Elton is in love with her.

A full study of Austen's language is not possible here, but I touch on what seem to me useful starting points, by way of suggesting how much there is to follow up. One kind of sensitivity that is particularly surprising in so young a writer is her fine ear for what is hackneyed and outworn. Laura and Sophia talk in catchwords, in ready-made clichés: "She was all Sensibility and Feeling. We flew into each others arms and after having exchanged vows of mutual Freindship for the rest of our lives, instantly unfolded to each other the most inward Secrets of our Hearts" (114). So much is compacted into one sentence – the physical action, the content of the vows, the invoking of lifetimes, the unfolded secrets – that the sentence structure itself conveys the emptiness of the claims: the two heroines could as well be conducting their meeting by semaphore, like Girl Guides, waving successively the Sensibility flag, the Eternal Vow flag, and the Inmost Secret flag. And one of the sharp weapons in Austen's verbal armoury comes into wicked play: the adverb. The fact that those inmost secrets are unfolded "instantly" utterly devalues them.

The deliberate and incremental development of the action in the six novels calls for attention, and requires the reader to consider, to remember. The juvenilia, on the other hand, are rowdy, full of extravagant exaggeration, exuberant jokes, nonsense, slapstick, anarchic hurmour and gratuitous motion. The jokes come so thick and fast that it is hard to keep up with them. "Love and Freindship" is the kind of work that provokes belly laughs. And like other funny books – *Pickwick Papers* for instance, which Chesterton memorably aligned with "Love and Freindship" (xv) – it has a plot that is subordinated to laughter. It's easy to forget the sequence of the action of such works. Laura and her lovers and friends rocket about between London, Wales, and Scotland in a manner that is as difficult for the readers as for the characters themselves to keep track of. But this very chaos is intentional.

"It would be almost impossible to summarise the action of *Love and Freindship*," Litz pointed out, "since one of Jane Austen's aims was to satirise the intricate and unnatural plots of contemporary fiction" (Litz 19).

"Impossible to summarise"? Let me try. One way to keep track of the tale is to map the travels. The many journeys, the manic "loco-motion" that Chris Wiesenthal explores (Wiesenthal 57–60), add to the rapid, even dizzying pace, as well as to its humour. Edward arrives at Laura's home in the Vale of Uske on horseback, having taken a huge detour across southern England from Bedfordshire. Subsequently he and Laura abscond in his father's carriage; presently Laura and Sophia, in quest of their missing husbands, set out in a hired coach for London, hollering questions to passers-by when they get there, "If they had seen my Edward?" (118). On their way to Scotland to seek out Sophia's cousin Macdonald they encounter their grandfather, Lord St. Clair, in *his* "coroneted Coach" (120) When Macdonald throws them out, for once Laura and Sophia are on foot for about a mile and a half (how they carry the goods they have jus packed Laura does not reveal), and Laura tries to interest Sophia in the natural beauties around them.

Her dilemma in finding a subject of conversation without trampling on Sophia's delicate sensibility is "most fortunately releived by an accident truly apropos; it was the lucky overturning of a Gentleman's Phaeton … . It was a most fortunate Accident as it diverted the Attention of Sophia from the melancholy reflections which she had been before indulging" (128–9). How "fortunate" that a fatal accident in which both husbands are killed can alleviate the refined anguish of Sophia's hyper-developed sensibility!

Now comes the denouement of Sophia's imprudent fainting and Laura's "running mad." Immediately following Sophia's lamented demise Laura is picked up by a stage-coach bound for Edinburgh, on which all the characters are coincidentally gathered: the coachman and his wife Philippa (Edward's aunt); Edward's father, now married to Lady Dorothea, and his sister; and Laura's own long-lost friend Isabel and her daughter. Moreover, the coach is to remain on a relay between Stirling and Edinburgh, something like a perpetual motion machine. Laura keeps going, and going, and going … .

That is, a very high proportion of the action of this hectic narrative is on the road, in transit. Within all this movement are pointed locational jokes. Janetta and M'Kenzie, as encouraged by Laura and Sophia, elope "for Gretna-Green, which they chose for the celebration of their Nuptials" (125). But the whole point of eloping to Gretna Green from England was to cross the border and so avoid English laws forbidding the marriage of minors without parental consent; and since Janetta and M'Kenzie are already in Scotland, it's an empty gesture.

The wild and apparently gratuitous journeys, that is, turn out to be geographically consistent, and can be followed through a map of mainland Britain; and the various journeys and modes of transport are cunningly indicative of character. The tendency to stasis in the novels – the setting in a country village, and characters like Mr. Woodhouse who eschews travel not only for himself but for everyone else – is wildly and gleefully reversed, and we have the same delight in movement for its own sake that pertains in "The Beautifull Cassandra" ("She next ascended a Hackney Coach and ordered it to Hampstead, where she was no sooner arrived than she ordered the Coachman to turn round and drive her back again" [55]) – as well as in the other juvenilia.

I like to think that if "Love and Freindship" were made into a movie, it would be a "Road Movie" – like, say, *Rain Man* or *Thelma and Louise*, where vehicles and modes of transport are centre stage, and unity is supplied not by stasis but by the ever-changing scenery and the characters' shifting relations with it. Perhaps the subject for a creative Master's thesis could be to write the screenplay for a Road Movie to be called "*Laura and Sophia*." Surely it would put *Thelma and Louise* in the shade!

An "intricate and unnatural" plot? Yes, but it makes its own wild kind of sense.

If we talk of plotting, "Love and Freindship" provides a birth mystery plot of an intricacy to dazzle and amaze. And while examining "Love and Freindship" as a text standing on its own, I don't want to omit the importance of reading aloud as a classroom strategy. The Lord St. Clair episode provides an incomparable passage for reading as well as for practical criticism.

Reading Austen aloud is a rich and rewarding exercise, and we know she intended it to be so. Her work was often read to the family, and written with that in mind. A memorable scene from real life, which Austen provided in a letter to Cassandra, was a reading of *Pride and Prejudice*, which had just come to hand, fresh off the press. The Austens themselves were in on the secret of Jane's authorship, but they had a visitor, Miss Benn, who didn't know; so that the reading was fraught with some necessary family reticence. Austen was dissatisfied with her mother's rendering: "Tho' she perfectly understands the Characters herself, she cannot speak as they ought," she wrote (*Letters* 203). Clearly she had high standards for good, dramatic reading aloud, and her work, juvenilia included, often calls for voice.

The splendid scene of Lord St. Clair and his bevy of long-lost grandchildren, especially, lends itself to being read aloud. It is too long to quote in full, so a piece of it – albeit a long one – must suffice. Laura sees a "Venerable Stranger," and "an immediate Sympathy whispered to my Heart, that he was my Grandfather."

> I threw myself on my knees before him and besought him to acknowledge me as his Grand-Child. – He started, and after having attentively examined my features, raised me from the Ground and throwing his Grand-fatherly arms around my Neck, exclaimed, "Acknowledge thee! Yes dear resemblance of my Laurina & my Laurina's Daughter, sweet image of my Claudia and my Claudia's Mother, I do acknowledge thee as the Daughter of the one and the Grandaughter of the other." While he was thus tenderly embracing me, Sophia … entered the Room in search of me --. No sooner had she caught the eye of the venerable Peer, than he exclaimed with every mark of Astonishment – "Another Grandaughter! Yes, yes, I see you are the Daughter of my Laurina's eldest Girl; Your resemblance to the beauteous Matilda sufficiently proclaims it." … He folded her in his arms, and whilst they were tenderly embracing, the Door of the Apartment opened and a most beautifull Young Man appeared. On perceiving him Lord St. Clair started and retreating back a few paces, with uplifted Hands, said, "Another Grand-Child! What an unexpected Happiness is this! to discover in the space of 3 minutes, as many of my Descendants! … there wants now but the presence of Gustavus to compleat the Union of my Laurina's Grand-Children.
>
> "And here he is"; (said a Gracefull Youth who that instant entered the room). (120–21)

Here we have melodramatic action – falling on knees, tender embraces, retreating backwards with uplifted hands; high-flown dialogue with exclamations and "thees" and "thous"; and wildly improbable but conventional discoveries: all combining to make this a scene ready-made for hamming it up. And Lord St. Clair's conventional joy is nicely salted by the ironic note of his "looking fearfully towards the Door" in terror of yet another grandchild.

I had long admired the scene as a wonderfully nonsensical take-off of the birth mystery plot and the recognition scene. Those elaborate speeches about genealogies sound completely zany. All that "Acknowledge thee! Yes dear resemblance of my Laurina & my Laurina's Daughter" stuff had to be just gobbledegook. But then I discovered through close reading that in all this wild tangle of relationships there is actually order and consistency. Lord St. Clair's improbable family tree actually works (Figure 5.1). Moreover, in working out his and other families, I found that a chart demonstrates a balanced familial symmetry among the figures of Sensibility and Sense. In supplying this chart, I claim to be the first genealogist who has taken Lord St. Clair's family tree seriously.

In these family trees I have indicated the characters of Sense in straight caps, and the characters of Sensibility in italic caps. This makes it clear that while the heroine has a pedigree of unblemished Sensibility, the hero's family members are symmetrically divided. Perhaps Sensibility needs the opposition of Sense to define itself. Sir Edward and Philippa, brother and sister, represent Sense and Sensibility respectively; the same is true of the next generation, Augusta and Edward. Sophia (Sensibility) is likewise opposed to her cousin Macdonald (Sense). And there is a similar symmetry among the morally mobile younger generation. Young Janetta Macdonald, who begins by espousing Sense, is converted by Laura and Sophia to Sensibility, and the sequence of her two suitors, Graham and M'Kenzie, confirms this. Young Marianne, for whom the letters are written, is presumably mobile in the other direction (if her mother's plan works), being converted by the moral action of this narrative from Sensibility to Sense.

Like the apparently pointless travels, the wild implausibility of the birth mystery plot and its unlikely relationships turn out to be not random and chaotic, but neatly patterned, to reinforce the major thematic oppositions of the tale.

In the same way as the theme provides structure and pattern for the family tree, so the moral oppositions provide shape for the story. Browning is said to have claimed that if Jesus Christ had not existed, we would have had to invent him: the myth is so aesthetically apropos for the state in which humanity finds itself. Similarly, I sometimes think that if morality hadn't existed, Austen would have found a way to invent it: for those sharp antitheses (between sense and sensibility, or between the self-centred and the outward-looking, or between wisdom and folly), those clean oppositions in "Love and Freindship" and the major works too, are there not just for didactic purposes, but because they supply form, a tense and delightful aesthetic structure.

Looking Forward: Intimations of the Major Novels

To discover Sense and Sensibility as located in siblings is to lead to the relation of "Love and Freindship" to the major novels.

Laura's chosen friend, Sophia, from fainting in the grass as the evening dew is falling, contracts "a violent pain in her delicate limbs, accompanied with a

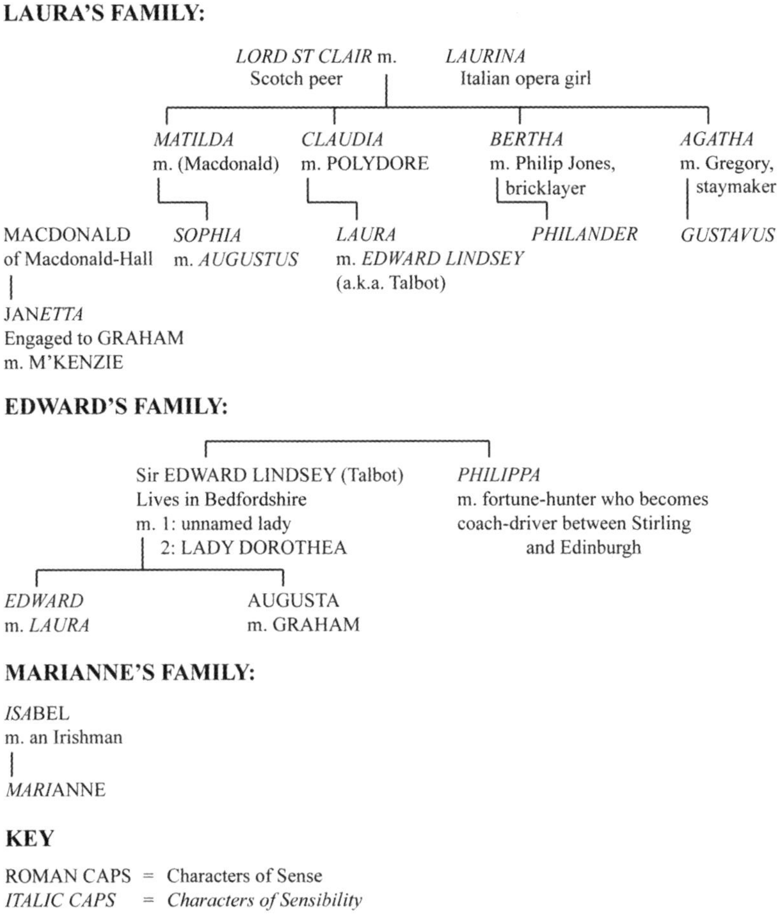

Fig. 5.1 Genealogies for "Love and Freindship" [diagram].

disagreeable Head-ake" (301), and presently dies, delivering the memorable advice – "Run mad as often as you chuse; but do not faint" (133) – that is the overt moral of "Love and Freindship." I like to recall that the recipient of this advice is called Marianne, for it is Marianne Dashwood in *Sense and Sensibility* who contracts a violent cold ("with a pain in her limbs") after a twilight walk in dew-wet grass that proves almost fatal. And the two Mariannes are both educated from Sensibility towards Sense. This is only one of dozens of connections between "Love and Freindship" and the major novels. And if one is teaching it as an adjunct to the teaching of Austen's major works, clearly the ongoing theme of Sense arid Sensibility makes the most obvious starting point. "Love and Freindship" leads most clearly and directly to *Sense and Sensibility*. But the contrast between Sense and Sensibility, varied as the rival claims of reason and emotion, remains a central structuring idea in all the novels. The conventions of the cult of Sensibility, without the sensibility itself, are insincerely adopted by Isabella Thorpe in *Northanger Abbey*, with her instant friendship and her claims of loving at first sight ("The very moment I beheld him – my heart was irrevocably gone" [*NA* 120]); Marianne Dashwood has the genuine article, and in her sensibility is sympathetically treated, though regarded as excessive in its manifestation. And Elinor, who has sense, is educated in the direction of sensibility. This movement is continued in *Pride and Prejudice*, which presents a woman and a society too apt to be governed by the head and to neglect the affairs of the heart. Fanny and Mary Crawford in *Mansfield Park* are recognizable variations on Marianne and Elinor. In *Emma* the theme goes underground, as it were, and emerges explicitly only at the end. Emma, with her eagerness, her out-spokenness and her readiness to promote romance, first strikes us as belonging on the sensibility side of the pale; while the undemonstrative Jane Fairfax, proper and controlled and apparently a cold fish, looks like the representative of sense. But by the end we have learned that Jane, guiltily cherishing a secret passion, is the uncontrolled romantic, while Emma, who hasn't even recognised whom she's in love with, emerges as strong in the head, but rather weak in the heart. Anne Elliot, we know, completes the pattern. "She had been forced into prudence in her youth, she learned romance as she grew older" (*P* 32). From "Love and Freindship" to *Persuasion* we can see Austen go through much the same evolution.

An alternative thread, first found in "Love and Freindship" and running as a strongly uniting theme through the other novels, starts with Sir Edward's pregnant conclusion, when faced with his son's romantic outburst, "You have been studying Novels I suspect" (108). This leads not only backward into the novels Austen was burlesquing, but forward into the novels she was to write herself. That is, we can go beyond the activities of parody and burlesque to the more interesting and dominant idea of literature as model for life. Austen's characters, like Don Quixote, are intently engaged in a quest to make experience conform to literary precedent. Again, students of the whole of Austen's oeuvre can trace this idea as developed with increasing subtlety through Catherine's Gothic fantasies in *Northanger Abbey*, and Marianne's sense of entrapment in hackneyed language and hackneyed responses at the very moments that she is practising them, to the elaborate fictions that Emma imposes on life. Many of Emma's most serious errors arise from the assumption that fictional conventions are transferable to life. Her preconception that Harriet Smith, of unknown parentage, is a fit wife for a gentleman is ultimately traceable to the same conventions that lane Austen parodied in the Lord St. Clair episode in "Love and Freindship": because there's a birth mystery about Harriet, Emma concludes she must be of noble parentage. The theme is dear to the hearts of Austen and other well-read novelists (Cervantes, Fielding, Sterne, Thackeray, George Eliot, and James come especially to mind), because it is born of a consuming love of books. These are writers who *live* their literature, and are wryly conscious of the propensity. And they are sophisticated, too, being fully aware, long before Oscar Wilde told the rest of the world, that

"Life imitates Art far more than Art imitates Life." Jane Austen's fictions, from her juvenilia on, demonstrate a constant and amused concern with the complex and sometimes hilarious interaction of life and literature.

"Love and Freindship" is a visible a step toward the mature novels in matters of technique as of theme. Austen's giant step from the eighteenth century to the nineteenth involved for her a weaning from the epistle. *Sir Charles Grandison* and *Evelina* were undoubtedly habit-forming, as we have seen: "Love and Freindship" ("a novel in a series of letters"), "Lesley Castle" ("An unfinished novel in letters"), "A Collection of Letters," and "Lady Susan" lead to "First Impressions" and "Elinor and Marianne," the lost first epistolary versions of mature novels. And in these novels themselves the letter continues to be of crucial importance.

What "Love and Freindship" shows in this evolution is Austen's power of self-examination. It is easy to slip into a convention; but a finely conscious artist in the making already has a weather eye on the potential absurdities in a medium. In the opening she brilliantly conflates two separate conventions in order to burlesque both. She combines the convention of the perfect heroine, necessarily described in the third person by an omniscient narrator, with the first-person narrator of the epistolary novel, with hilarious effect in the "Lovely as I was" passage. And in being not "written to the moment" as in Richardson, but recollected in tranquillity long afterwards, and delivered in arbitrarily chopped-off chunks, the letters draw attention to their own absurdity. Here is the self-critical creative mind at work. Full self-awareness belongs rather to sense than to sensibility, after all.

Editing "Love and Freindship"

The Juvenilia Press, as I explained in Chapter 2, began in the classroom, with an experimental edition of *Jack and Alice*,[3] produced mainly by the students. And when I invented the Press itself, *Love and Freindship* was one of the earliest editions with the Press's imprint, and the very first to display the Press's signature "look," as designed by Winston Pei of Black Riders Design. He was one of the students in the graduate course on Jane Austen that produced the edition. Student participation in the editing process has been part of the Press's mandate from the beginning; so in a chapter on teaching *Love and Freindship* it is relevant to discuss some of the issues that arose in the course of producing our edition of this most famous of Austen's juvenilia.

Students, even graduate students, don't usually get a chance to consider editing, never mind practise it; and as a result they tend to consider their classroom texts as God-given and problem-free. It is a revelation to them to discover, in practice, that a canonical text is not just a sequence of words that can be faithfully reproduced from year to year and stay the same. They learn that editors are making choices

[3] For the present purpose, I revert to italics for the titles of the individual works of Austen's juvenilia, since the Juvenilia Press editions of them are indeed independent little volumes.

all along the way, and that they can be good choices or bad. So perhaps the textual editing – as opposed to the other disciplines involved in producing a volume – is for them the most important and revealing part of the enterprise.

The group of students in the half-year course on Austen who undertook producing an edition of *Love and Freindship* with me came to the task with enthusiasm, and early in the project we divided the tasks, between textual editing, introduction, illustration, annotation, and bibliography.[4]

The textual editors, Christopher Wiebe and Winston Pei, started by seeking out a copy text: should it be Chesterton's first revelation of *Volume the Second* in 1922, or Chapman's *Minor Works* with B.C. Southam's revisions, or Doody and Murray's *"Catharine" and Other Writings*, or one of many other individual collections? (Peter Sabor's in the Cambridge edition of *The Works of Jane Austen*, the edition I use in this book, wasn't yet available.) In collating these possibilities Christopher Wiebe was shocked to find many textual variants. With proper scholarly indignation he wrote of "decades of laissez-faire and uneven editorial practices in terms of juvenile writings of canonical authors … I was surprised at the 'sloppiness' of some of the transcription (see the faux-pas with regards to capitalisation and punctuation)." Youthful idiosyncrasies of Austen's manuscript in spelling and the use of symbols such as "&" were sometimes preserved, sometimes corrected.

Having rejected existing editions as possible copy texts we opted for a return to Austen's manuscript in *Volume the Second*, in a microfilm from the British Library, with their permission. Our textual editor continued, with a passion that I have found textual editing often inspires:

> Call me brazen, but I am for all or nothing – either "correct" everything or transcribe it as it stands; it is the hazy shilly-shallying negotiations that seem unconscionable, indeed editorially negligent. I believe we must make a stand and faithfully transcribe, including retaining the "&" symbol, for in some cases Austen also uses the "and" form.
>
> I find myself surprisingly passionate![5]

So "make a stand" we did, and retained all the eccentricities of Austen's youthful manuscript; so our textual editor was able to record in his Note on the Text, "We have opted for minimal editorial intervention. Our edition is therefore closer to the manuscript than that of Doody and Murray, whose major intention was 'to supply the reader with a readily readable text' (10)."

---

[4] Let them be named: Pippa Brush took on writing the introduction and a number of the explanatory notes. Christopher Wiebe and Winston Pei devoted themselves to textual editing. Sherry Kleian contributed humorous illustrations, with a couple of them by me. And these and the rest of us divided the explanatory notes between us: Rachel Bennett, Shelley Galliah, Victoria Lamont, Marg McCutcheon, Richard Pickard, and Tania Smith.

[5] Letter from Christopher Wiebe, 16 May 1995.

Pippa Brush, who bravely took on the writing of the introduction, covered necessary ground on the rediscovery and publication of Austen's juvenilia, as well as focussing on the geographical meanderings of Laura and Sophia, and extracting the information that could be visually supplied in a map of England, Wales, and Scotland, showing "The Journeys of Love and Freindship" – discriminating "Edward's journey," with its looping between Bedfordshire and the Vale of Uske, from "Laura and Sophia's journey," and so on.

In her lively and unpretentious illustrations Sherry Klein added a comic-book dimension to Laura's story, with middle-aged Laura's memories appearing in a balloon above her as she writes. Not shy of anachronisms, she showed Laura hitch-hiking on the Edinburgh coach; and she supplied Laura with a cat to share her travels, which sticks out its tongue at Macdonald as it follows Laura, with packed suitcase, from Macdonald-Hall, and puts up an umbrella to shelter itself from the shower of Laura's tears at Sophia's death.

Learning to write a note that is usefully informative, strictly relevant to the item annotated, pointed, succinct, and if possible elegant and entertaining too: that is a discipline very much worth mastering. The notes (which in Juvenilia Press volumes can be quite copious) are very much a team enterprise, and can be divided by subject so that each annotator can to some extent specialise and become expert. One may take on language and definitions (for instance "Gibberish," "sensibility"); another travel and modes of transport ("coroneted Coach and 4," "Phaeton"); and connections to Austen's life and works ("Madame La Comtesse De Feuillide"); or reference to other literature ("Sorrows of Werter," and many recognizable take-offs of *Clarissa*, *Evelina*, *Laura and Augustus*). The famous line "We fainted Alternately on a Sofa" gets two notes to itself: one that pinpoints a possible source in Sheridan's *The Critic* of 1779, with the stage direction, "[*They faint alternately in each other's arms*]"; and another on "sofa," with a definition from Johnson's dictionary, and quotation from "I sing the Sofa" from Austen's favourite poet Cowper. Such notes not only inform the reader; the students who write them have often done considerable research before reducing their findings to a brief and apposite note that captures the essence of the information required.

Design came late in the day, after most of the rest of the volume – prefatory matter, text, illustrations, notes, and bibliography – had been put together, an ISBN number assigned, and the students were departing for the summer. We were fortunate that Winston Pei had already been accepted into a book design course at the Banff School of Fine Arts; and he took our text and illustrations, as well as Christine Alexander's edition of *Branwell's Blackwood's Magazine* (illustrated by her daughter), as his projects for the course. When he returned, he brought with him the two volumes fully designed and ready for the printer, distinct from each other in colour and cover image, but also visibly related as coming from the same press, the Juvenilia Press, no less. He had created our "look": and we have retained it through the years, and through some 50 volumes since. And we retained him as well, as our principal designer.

Last scene of all, that ends this strange eventful history, was indeed a "scene": we decided to adapt *Love and Freindship* for a reading on stage for the local chapter of the Jane Austen Society of North America. Tania Smith, our Laura, actually committed the whole of her part to memory, though the rest of us were content to read ours. As it happened, the two guys in the cast, Christopher and Winston, were both tall. At the moment when the Phaeton of Edward and Augustus overturns, both crashed to the floor in unison. "It was truly dramatic," as Jane Austen might have said (*MP* 390): and it drew a storm of applause there and then.

Those students came away from the course as certified experts on *Love and Freindship*, and on Austen too. *And* with a book to their credit.

"That [M'Kenzie] certainly adores you (replied Sophia) there can be no doubt" (123). Sophia is here in the process of detaching teachable young Janetta from her old suitor and attaching her to a new one, as Emma is later to do with Harriet Smith. The passage is pregnant with other concerns that are to be lasting in the Austen oeuvre: not only the propensity to arrange reality according to a preconceived pattern, as Emma the imaginist does, but also the indoctrination and manipulation of one human being by another. The impress of a formed consciousness upon a relatively unformed one is the stuff that some of the best novels, but especially Jane Austen's, are made of. The pedagogic enterprise is a dangerous and fascinating one, and it may turn out well, like Henry Tilney's with Catherine, or disastrously, like Sophia's with Janetta or Emma's with Harriet. "We all love to instruct," comments Elizabeth Bennet in a moment when she is aware her practice doesn't measure up to her preaching, "though we can teach only what is not worth knowing" (*PP* 380).

But to return to our own students, and our pedagogic enterprises on their behalf (and our own). There is only so much we can tell them: the rest they must discover for themselves. And "Love and Freindship" is a text that will do much towards teaching itself. Although it is the product of subtle perceptions, and shows a subtle artist in the making, it is itself gloriously obvious. And unlike the self-centred romantics it parodies, it leads attention beyond itself, by its reach for other literature, by its healthy mockery of the unending circle of self, and by its exuberant play of mind.

Chapter 6
"Love and Freindship" and its Targets

"Love and Freindship" and *Laura and Augustus*[1]

As we have seen, "Love and Freindship" can stand alone as a very funny burlesque, for one can readily deduce the kind of novel it bounces off. Nevertheless, it is worth examining it in relation to its satirical targets, to discover the artfulness of this teenager's response to novels that were familiar to her and her circle, though not to most of us in the twenty-first century. Of course there were many examples of the novel of sensibility, and Austen's parody is directed at more than one or two of them. But where a particular butt of her parody can be identified, a comparison of the texts can provide new insights into Austen's taste and artifice.

To start with a notable parallel: The tremblingly sensitive heroine of *Laura and Augustus*, an anonymous three-volume novel of 1784 sometimes attributed to Eliza Nugent Bromley, asks herself if she should have married the sordid wretch whom her father picked out for her, and answers her own question:

> No, my soul disdained such tyranny. The low-minded part of mankind imagine, that a direct submission is to be paid to a parent's every will. But if my conduct is rightly weighed, it will be found that a compliance would have more deserved blame, than praise.[2]

This heroine's self-congratulation on the matter of filial disobedience – here raised to the status of a moral principle – must surely remind readers of the now-familiar speech of Edward in "Love and Freindship," who scorns to marry the woman his father recommends:

> "No never exclaimed I. Lady Dorothea is lovely and Engaging; I prefer no woman to her; but Know Sir, that I scorn to marry her in compliance with your Wishes. No! Never shall it be said that I obliged my Father."
>
> We all admired the noble Manliness of his reply. ("L&F" 108)

---

[1] A version of this part of Chapter 6 appeared as an article in *Thalia: Studies in Literary Humor* 16.1–2 (1996). Since *Thalia* is now defunct, the copyright reverts to the author.

[2] *Laura and Augustus, an Authentic Story in a series of letters* by a young lady, 3 vols (London: printed for W. Cass, 1784), II, 99–100. The call number of the British Library copy, which is the one I consulted, is 1607/1997. Unfortunately this copy is missing pages 149–50 in the third volume. In what follows, I reference it as *L&A*, and "Love and Freindship" as "L&F."

To read the passages side by side is to appreciate all over again the brilliance of the 14-year-old Austen's parody. *Laura and Augustus* takes itself very seriously, and indeed the proper limit of submission to authority is a serious ethical issue. But the overstrained romantic rhetoric of the first passage ("my soul disdained such tyranny") invites parody; and its rather laboured generalizations about the "low-minded part of mankind" and clustering abstract nouns (tyranny, submission, compliance, blame, praise) make this a passage of rather routine moralizing. When young Jane takes over the proposition, she makes a dramatic scene, putting father and son in direct verbal conflict. She keeps the high-flown rhetoric ("No never exclaimed I"), and highlights the self-congratulatory tone, kindly providing an admiring audience so that we won't miss the point. And in creating scene and situation she carefully removes motivation (Lady Dorothea is no "sordid wretch," but quite personable and congenial), so that the proud denouncing of paternal authority becomes completely gratuitous. The first passage of partly justified moralizing is merely forgettable. Edward's grandly pointless defiance is richly comic and vividly memorable.

Marvin Mudrick first identified *Laura and Augustus, an Authentic Story in a series of letters*, as the major butt of Jane Austen's parody of the sentimental novel,[3] which is also subtitled as "A Novel in a Series of Letters." Since then, no one seems to have elaborated further on the parallels[4] – one reason, perhaps, being that copies of *Laura and Augustus* are hard to come by, as it has never been reprinted. However, we do not need to be deeply read in the novel of sensibility to get the point, as the major characteristics of the convention are hilariously identified, exaggerated, and parodied within "Love and Freindship." Still, the parallels are worth extracting, since they can remind us all over again of Austen's consummate art as a parodist. She may have been only 14 when she wrote it, but she was already a discerning reader, and a writer who could instinctively seize on what is potentially absurd, and turn it economically into laughing matter.

Laura and Augustus aspires to be an epistolary tragedy, and an updated version of *Romeo and Juliet*; and lest we miss the parallel, the hero's surname is Montague. Laura Levison, who arrives in Grenada in the West Indies at the outset of the novel, writes her experience to her dear friend Cecilia Byng, who is initially in England, but moves to the *East* Indies before Laura returns (so that the correspondence can be maintained). Laura is of good family, with Harlowe-like parents: like Clarissa, she has a socially ambitious father and a merely acquiescent mother. When Laura falls in love with a mere Lieutenant, her father will not hear of the match, and tries to marry her forcibly to the vile Mr. Boswell. She elopes with Augustus, and they

[3] Marvin Mudrick, *Jane Austen: Irony as Defense and Discovery*, 5–12. Mudrick briefly adumbrates the parallels with a view to extracting Austen's moral and aesthetic stance. My own emphasis is on her creation of humour out of pathos.

[4] An exception is the Juvenilia Press edition, *Love and Freindship*, ed. Juliet McMaster and others (Edmonton: Juvenilia Press, 1995), where in the notes we drew attention to some parallels.

are married, and duly cast off by her father. They are befriended and supported by a benevolent Mr. Worthy, they have a baby girl who is named Cecilia after the bosom friend and correspondent, and for a while they are blissfully happy. Then wicked Boswell has Laura abducted to another island, and Mr. Worthy is killed defending her. Augustus kills Boswell in a duel, and is therefore exiled. While sailing to England, the couple's ship is struck by lightning and burnt. The little family escapes, but they arrive in England with no more than the clothes on their backs; Laura's father remains inexorable; but they live happily in a small way while their health lasts. Then doctor's bills, unpaid rent, and over-reaction to the pathos of a dramatic production all begin to overwhelm them. Their woes are long drawn-out, and by the time a network of female friends is able to provide help, Augustus's health is shattered. As in *Clarissa*, help comes too late. Augustus dies, and Laura goes insane. The stern father is stricken by remorse at the sight of his demented daughter. Laura commits little Cecilia to her grandfather's care, and dies.

> For never was a story of more rue
> Than this of Laura and her Montague.
> (Adapted from *Romeo and Juliet*, V, 3)

What, never? Well, hardly ever.

This brief sketch of the plot of *Laura and Augustus* already supplies plenty of parallels with "Love and Freindship," including the names of two principal characters. In both novels, the heroine's marriage comes relatively early in the narrative; the father's tyranny is prominent; a delicate sensibility is a *sine qua non* of approval, and often invoked. The husband's death and heroine's madness provide the climax.

There are differences, to be sure. In setting, we do not get the global geography that makes the link between West Indies and East. But within the shores of mainland Great Britain, as we have seen, Austen allows her characters plenty of racketing about, with Edward's performing his 250-mile detour between Bedforshire and Wales.[5] Austen's Laura and Sophia certainly stray far beyond the "Country Village" that provides the norm as a setting for the novels. "Love and Freindship," like *Laura and Augustus*, flagrantly offends against the principle of unity of place.

This is not the *Shamela/Pamela* kind of parody, not a neat if exaggerated re-chronicling of essentially the same events, but a generalization from *Laura and Augustus* towards a more generic parody of what Mudrick calls the lachrymose novel.

Austen has chosen to highlight "freindship" over heterosexual love. In need of an on-stage "friend," she imports one from another source: Sophia. To have *two* heroines, one the bosom friend of the other, suits her comic purposes. And this friend is firmly on-stage.

---

5 See Pippa Brush, "Introduction" to the Juvenilia Press edition of *Love and Freindship*, xii.

Between the original Laura and Augustus, she inserts another couple: *her* Laura is married to Edward, and it is the "freind," Sophia, who is married to the Augustus of this story. The bosom friend has been promoted from Cecilia's status of correspondent, the mere recipient of Laura Levison's epistolary narrative, to co-protagonist. The correspondent in "Love and Freindship" is demoted from bosom friend to the mere daughter of the *last* bosom friend, now virtually cast off.

The doubling of the protagonist is a brilliant comic strategy. As with the shrewd move in inventing an audience for the defiant Edward in the let's-put-down-fathers scene, to provide Laura with an approving mirror image is to double and quadruple the comic effect. Each heroine acts and postures one against the other, and they mutually reinforce each other's absurdities.

The sensibility joke gains immeasurably from being performed as a *pas de deux*. Austen includes elaborate choreographing, as in the famous case of the heroines' fainting "Alternately on a Sofa" ("L&F" 114). Repetition and symmetrical pairing are part of the satisfying aesthetic structure. There are *two* lovely and sensitive heroines, two handsome and romantic husbands, two dashing long-lost cousins, two sets of "Cruel and Mercenary Parents" (116). The husbands perish together, the heroines faint and go mad in rhythmic counterpoint. Even the *corps de ballet*, the accumulating *other* characters, seem to move in a stylized and regimented manner, as in the famous recognition scene of Lord St. Clair and his long-lost grandchildren, or the gathering in the stage coach. In comparison, the characters and events of *Laura and Augustus* seem unorganized and messy.

It is the world-view of the heroine of sensibility that Austen parodies most resoundingly. The characters of *Laura and Augustus* recurrently congratulate each other on their tender sensibility. "You, my Cecilia," writes Laura, "have a mind replete with all those noble and generous sentiments, and a heart susceptible of all those delicate and refined feelings which are so great an ornament to human nature" (I 83–4). Laura's own susceptibility is as developed as anyone's, as her Augustus tenderly tells her when she weeps at the pathos of a play they both attend.

> "My Laura (cried the dear youth), thy soul I fear, possesses too great a share of sensibility, ever to render your happiness in this life permanent. Your heart, I doubt, my gentle love, is too sympathetically alive to every tale of woe." (III 14–15)

Such a passage was ripe for parody, and young Austen wickedly exchanges mutual congratulation for self-congratulation when her Laura boasts of "a sensibility too tremblingly alive" to the afflictions of others, but admits that though she is as sensitive as ever to her *own* afflictions, she has ceased to care for anyone else's. A nascent moralist who is alert to the narcissism and selfishness inherent in the cult of sensibility, Austen is nevertheless first and foremost a comic artist, who relishes the incongruity of elaborate self-praise in modesty's clothing.

A highly refined sensibility is the indispensable qualification for friendship – at least, friendship that deserves the name. Laura Levison meditates on friendship, and waxes philosophical: "For how few are there in the world, that know the just etymology of the word friendship! methinks 'tis a word that conveys so extensive a meaning, that there are few hearts capable of defining it … Delicate and refined feelings … alone can render friendship permanent" (*L&A* I 83–4). Austen catches the exclusive tone of such principles, and posits a world made up of sheep and goats; that is, those who have sensibility, and those who haven't. The characters of sensibility are instantly recognizable to each other. *Her* Laura, on the lookout for a "freind," swiftly passes over Lady Dorothea, who, "tho' Easy and Polite in her Address, … was of that inferior order of Beings with regard to Delicate feelings, tender Sentiments, and refined Sensibility" (112). On meeting the lovely Sophia, however, she immediately recognises the proper qualifications: "She was all Sensibility and Feeling. We flew into each others arms and … exchanged vows of mutual Freindship for the rest of our Lives" (114). It takes one to know one.

Cecilia in *Laura and Augustus* is anxious to show she is properly qualified. She writes tenderly to her absent friend: "For a month after the departure of my beloved companion, I wandered like a dove who has lost its mate. The fields, the groves, lost all their charms, and alike served but to nourish melancholy" (*L&A* I 9). Such a passage got the young Austen itching for specific examples of a melancholy so omnivorous that it will feed on anything, fields and groves included. This is the passage, I suspect, that prompted Austen's exchange where Sophia can't contemplate the streaked sky because it reminds her of Augustus's blue-and-white striped waistcoat ("L&F" 108). Again, Austen moves from abstract meditation to dramatic presentation.

Sophia's sensibility is so refined that it incapacitates her from taking any action to relieve the sufferings of Augustus, over whom she is grieving. Even Augustus's "blue sattin waistcoat striped with white" may be a reminiscence from Austen's parodic source, as well as from Goethe's *Werther*; with unusual specificity, Laura Levison tenderly records of *her* Augustus when he declares his love: "His waistcoat and breeches are white lustring, the waistcoat wrought in rose-buds, and fastened with bunches of silver" (*L&A* I 121).

It is the physiology of sensibility, amply chronicled in *Laura and Augustus*, that provides Austen with her richest comic material: the physical manifestations of tears, sighs, screams, faints, fits, and "running mad." *Laura and Augustus*, both in the main plot and in the many interpolated narratives, provides numerous examples of all these. It provides, indeed, enough on bodily processes to shock the delicate and shake the squeamish. Take the case of Adelaide, the mother of the "fair Eliza" who tells her own story. Two bosom friends have been separated when young. Years later, one of them meets a lady in distressed circumstances "in the pangs of childbirth":

> Good heavens! what words can express her amazement and horror, at beholding in the distressed female her lost friend Adelaide … She screamed, and fainted; her scream attracted the attention of my mother, who, on recognising her, was no less agitated than pleased. The sudden surprise, however, hastened her pains, and before the Countess was well recovered of her fit, I was presented to the world;

> my unhappy parent had but just power to recommend me to the protection of her friend, before death closed her eyes. (*L&A* I 44–5)

Birth pangs, screams, faints, fits, and death, all mutually aggravating, follow in quick succession; and one cannot help concluding, as young Jane Austen did, that a little less delicate susceptibility, and a little more application of practical common sense, might have been more efficacious. The same unfortunate Eliza, who later takes the veil, has her own troubles in her love life. Just after marrying the man of her dreams, the tender William, she learns that they are brother and sister. Naturally they both faint: "We lay eight days bereft of our senses," she records, with helpful specificity.

The pace of the main narrative is not so hectic; but there are some good fainting spells there too. For instance, upon Augustus's return from a duel, Laura cries faintly "'My Montague!' … and sunk into his arms. Her eyes closed, and her senses forsook her" (II 117). When he dies, her manifestations are still more dramatic. Distracted, she "screamed, threw herself upon his lifeless body, and fainted … . [F]or six hours, she was in successive fits" (III 135).

Young Jane Austen pounces most gleefully on the "eight days" and "six hours," the precision about time suggesting the competitive spirit of one eager to break a record. From the tenderly recorded physical pathology of sensibility, she leaps to the developed physical prowess of the athlete. While the original Laura foresees that she would "run distracted" (II 121), Austen's Laura, on the death of *her* husband, writes quite proudly of her vigour in running mad: "For two Hours did I rave thus madly and should not then have left off, as I was not in the least fatigued … " ("L&F" 100). Thus Austen richly exploits the implications of *running* mad as a vigorous physical activity (Wiesenthal 59).

A shrewd switch from the third to the first person serves Austen's comic purposes. The author of *Laura and Augustus* changes narrators towards the end of the epistolary narrative, so that the reader can look *at* the heroine, rather than through her eyes, and so absorb the pathos of her bereavement, madness, and ultimate death. But Austen's Laura, when going mad, keeps right on in the first person, noting her own symptoms not just with clinical detachment, but with pride:

> Sophia immediately sunk again into a swoon –. '*My* Greif' was more audible. My Voice faltered, My Eyes assumed a vacant Stare, my face became as pale as Death [was she looking in a mirror, one wonders?], and my Senses were considerably impaired – . ("L&F" 130)

The italic "*My* Greif" suggests again her competitive spirit. And the reader learns to appreciate the joke of the highly rational chronicling of periods of total irrationality.

Readers of "Love and Freindship" probably remember best this hilarious denouement, in which the two heroines are performing their competing routines of fainting and running mad: "For an Hour and a Quarter did we continue in this unfortunate Situation – Sophia fainting every moment and I running Mad as often"

(129). Sophia later succumbs to "galloping Consumption" (132); in *Laura and Augustus*, Montague is carried off by the same rough beast (*L&A*, III 50). But even at a gallop she cannot overtake Laura in her running mad, and has to concede defeat in her dying speech.

> "My beloved Laura (said she to me a few Hours before she died) take warning from my unhappy End and avoid the imprudent conduct which has occasioned it … Beware of fainting-fits … Though at the time they may be refreshing and Agreable yet beleive me they will in the end, if too often repeated and at improper seasons, prove destructive to your Constitution … . A frenzy fit is not one quarter so pernicious; it is an exercise to the Body and if not too violent, is I dare say conducive to Health in its consequences – Run mad as often as you chuse; but do not faint –." (132–3)

Choosing to run mad, like deciding not to faint, comically submits involuntary physical and psychological processes to deliberate decision. Austen cracks the same joke in *Northanger Abbey*, when she humorously questions the propriety of a young lady's dreaming of a gentleman "before the gentleman is first known to have dreamt of her" (*NA* 22).

Much of this grandly comic material from the denouement of "Love and Freindship" has its recognizable source in *Laura and Augustus*, although there the pathos is meant to be taken seriously. Austen mixes the elements of her source in new ways, in order to pluck comedy from tragedy.

Both Lauras have a mad speech. After Augustus Montague's death, his Laura is "divested of that delicate and refined understanding, for which she was once so distinguished," and cries on him to wait for her – as reported by a new narrator:

> "Ah, look, look! yonder where he goes! see how he smiles! he beckons me … . Hark!" cries she, holding up her finger – "hark! again do you not hear the music of the spheres! See how he rides on yonder cloud! how beautiful he looks! I come, I come, Augustus, thy Laura comes!" (*L&A*, III 137)

In making her Laura chronicle her own insanity young Austen turns the pathos inside out.

> 'Talk not to me of Phaetons (said I, raving in a frantic, incoherent manner) – Give me a violin –. I'll play to him and sooth him in his melancholy Hours – Beware ye gentle Nymphs of Cupid's Thunderbolts, avoid the piercing Shafts of Jupiter." ("L&F" 130)

(And then come the references to legs of mutton and cucumbers that I quoted earlier). Both mad heroines invoke the music that Shakespeare associates with madness and pathos in the cases of Lear and Ophelia; both heroines speak, almost by generic necessity, in iambic pentameters ("look! yonder where he goes! see how he smiles!" "Avoid the piercing Shafts of Jupiter"); but Austen's Laura includes those deflating culinary images that are never reconcilable with the heroic mode. Both produce respectably learned allusions to the music of the spheres and classical deities; but Austen's Laura gets in a muddle, and attributes Cupid's shafts to Jupiter, and Jupiter's thunderbolts to Cupid.[6] And again, Austen makes the brevity of her parody tell in her favour. Her Laura's mad speech, in total, is almost as long as the other Laura's. But the events leading up to it, including the account of the husband's death, are drastically telescoped, so we get the demented speech without any of the pathetic build-up. Her mode is boldly and briefly dramatic: we get all the plums, and none of the stodgy pudding.

Austen's "moral" to "Love and Freindship" is again a parodic triumph. While her Laura sensibly lays off being mad when reminded that "the Damps began to fall," and the day's work is done (130), the heroine of *Laura and Augustus* regains her wits by some timely weeping. The tears don't save her life, as her friends hoped, but they do seem to work as an effective vent to her dementia. Now she is able to talk rationally, and to deliver the fruits of her experience to her infant daughter. "May her mother's [memory]," she prays, "serve as a melancholy and useful lesson to her, to avoid the rock on which the unfortunate Laura split!" (III 151). The rock on which she split was her father's implacable resentment; so that in delivering her daughter to the care of that same implacable father, she is hardly making it easy for her daughter to avoid any rocks. The moral delivered by Austen's Sophia to avoid fainting – not to choose to do what is involuntary – sounds almost as pointless, and a lot funnier.

Many of the best comic passages in "Love and Freindship" have their recognizable parallels in *Laura and Augustus*. Even the memorable piece of self-referentiality, the put-down of novels as inappropriate models for life, has its moment in *Laura and Augustus*. The villain Boswell, on catching the clandestine lovers at their romantic assignation in a place they call "the Orange Grove," pours scorn on their literary romanticism. "This comes of people suffering their children to read those ridiculous books called novels," he scoffs – and is the more a villain for his literary barbarity (I 127). The wicked father produces similar sneers at the propensity of the young to strike heroic poses and to expect to live on love alone. When Laura refuses to part with Augustus, her father summarily dismisses her: "Take yourself off with your beggar's brat, and see if love will support you: you will find it, Madam heroine, I fancy damned slender diet" (II 149). This was no doubt the source for the exchange between Edward and his sister in "Love and Freindship" when he scorns "the mean and indelicate employment of Eating and Drinking," and she responds drily that it's still the most effective support she knows of (111).

Austen plays her own more developed self-referential games with Sir Edward's "You have been studying Novels I suspect" ("L&F" 108). Such suspicions are little short of criminal in the estimation of the fiction-nourished Laura, who

[6] Ellen Martin calls this "a mix-up that compromises Jupiter's power with passion and taints Cupid's passion with mastery," in "The Madness of Jane Austen: Metonymic Style and Literature's Resistance to Interpretation," *Jane Austen's Beginnings*, 84.

concludes of a man who "had never read the Sorrows of Werter" that he must consequently have "no soul" (122). Laura's most damning term of opprobrium is "illiterate." "What an illiterate villain must that Man be!" she reflects, of a stranger in a carriage, because he snores. It's not everyone who would connect literacy, or illiteracy either, with snoring. But Laura is right again, because the snorer turns out to be none other than Sir Edward, her Philistine father-in-law.

In this metafictional play at the intersection of "reality" and "fiction," Austen's Laura puts her money where her mouth is. "Love and Freindship," for all its burlesque of romantic fictions, is firmly subtitled "a novel"; whereas *Laura and Augustus* claims only to be "an authentic story."

Parody is a complex business, in which mockery co-exists with respect: – imitation being, as the proverb says, "the sincerest form of flattery." "Love and Freindship" is one of the parodies which have become more famous than the works they parody, and which have actually given the targets of their satire a new lease on life. *Laura and Augustus* is long forgotten, but "Love and Freindship" lives, and reflects some residual glory on its predecessor.

A good parody implies close and prolonged attention to the original. Young Austen, as the parallels show, knew her *Laura and Augustus* very well indeed. One can even find echoes of it, I believe, in the novels of her maturity. When a young man in *Laura and Augustus* finds himself between a fainting father and a hysterical bride – "to either side, he beheld the two dearest persons to him on earth, in the most distressed state" (I, 67) – it is hard not to recall Charles Musgrove on the Cobb in *Persuasion*, torn between his unconscious sister and "the hysterical agitations of his wife," in the most physically violent scene in Austen's novels (*P* 119). When Cecilia is urged to take a part in an amateur production of *The Jealous Wife*, but refuses (*L&A*, I 108), we are inevitably reminded of Fanny Price cajoled to play Cottager's wife in *Lovers' Vows*. And the whole issue of wicked and mercenary fathers, so fully taken over from *Laura and Augustus* by "Love and Freindship," is still to the fore in *Northanger Abbey*, where the narrator ends the book with the memorable appeal: "I leave it to be settled by whomsoever it may concern, whether the tendency of this work be altogether to recommend parental tyranny, or reward filial disobedience" (*NA* 261). For all Austen's early and sustained mockery, *Laura and Augustus* and its concerns had managed to install themselves very firmly in her literary consciousness. She is like her own hero, Henry Tilney, who is simultaneously a parodist and an admirer of *The Mysteries of Udolpho* and every good novel. Perhaps *Laura and Augustus* would not have qualified as "a good novel" in Austen's judgement, but she read it young, she remembered it well, and it became part of the way she defined her own fictional purposes by contrast.

A 14-year-old, at least one as shrewd as Jane Austen, has certain advantages as a parodist. The teenage parodist can cheerfully overlook nuance, subtlety, fine shading – things that the mature Austen is famous for – and go for vigorous mockery. Love is something the adults do, and the more they refine it and go on about it, the more the untouched teenager can ridicule it. Young Austen, writing from outside the involvements of sexual relations, is the spectator best qualified to make fun of the game. "Love and Freindship," it is true, *can* be read as a moral work, in which the apprentice novelist is working out the balance of sense and sensibility that is to occupy her in her mature work. But wonderfully uncomplicated physical energy overrides the embryonic moral pattern, and gusts of laughter do not submit to any moral scheme.

But where did *Sophia* come from, then?

"Love and Freindship" and *Emily Montague*

I believe she came from *The History of Emily Montague.*

In importing a second pair, Edward as Laura's love interest and Sophia as Laura's beloved "Freind" who is married to Augustus, Austen gave herself the opportunity for doubling the action and the jokes. But would she have wanted to dilute the parody by layers of plot and characters that were merely invented? I don't think so. And being on the lookout for another novel that invited parody, I came upon Frances Brooke's *The History of Emily Montague*. Another Montague? A clue, surely.

Historians of Canadian literature often call Frances Brooke's *The History of Emily Montague* of 1769 the first Canadian novel. Though it was published in England and written by an Englishwoman, the author Brooke spent the years 1763 to 1768 in Quebec, and drew extensively on her experience there for her novel, the first and best half of which is vividly set in Lower Canada (or Quebec, as we would call it now).

Emily Montague[7] is no mean literary achievement. It has a lively heroine, Arabella Fermor (there is further play on the allusion to the original of Pope's Belinda, although this Arabella is firmly Protestant) and a sentimental heroine, Emily Montague – a kind of contrast that recalls Richardson's vivacious Anna Howe and serious Clarissa Harlowe, as well as looking forward to Austen's Marianne and Elinor Dashwood and Elizabeth and Jane Bennet; it has a well-developed sense of location; and it incorporates strong female characters and a vigorous feminist stand. Again, it is an epistolary novel, and pays marked attention to the necessary hiatuses in communication between Lower Canada and England, allowing time not only for transatlantic sailing, but also for the winter freeze-up of the St. Lawrence River. That is, while Brooke takes on the epistolary convention with its frequent strains on credibility, she is business-like and convincing in following through on the consequences of her choice. Even today it is a good read, thanks to the vivacity of one heroine, the social and topographical interest of the story, and the rapid pace of the narrative.

---

[7] Frances Brooke, *The History of Emily Montague* [1769], A Critical Edition, ed. Laura Moss (Ottawa: The Tecumseh Press, 2001). References are to this edition and appear as *EM.*

Nevertheless, by the time Jane Austen took the pen into her hands in the late 1780s, a sentimental epistolary novel of 1769 inevitably seemed dated, and to "a mind lively and at ease" it must have called for parody. Young Austen, as I believe, answered the call, and *Emily Montatgue* seems to me a strong candidate as the novel most aptly parodied in her wild little fiction "Amelia Webster" from *Volume the First*, as well as a prominent target, along with *Laura and Augustus*, for "Love and Freindship."

Again, I shall address the parallels one by one. I am aware that it is not always easy for a reader to follow a set of parallels and variations paraded by a reader familiar with both texts, and that such a parade can become tedious. Pointing out parodic connections, moreover, can be perilously like explaining a joke. My defence is that we know there are many jokes in Austen's works that inevitably pass us by, as her literary and historical contexts recede from us; and that it can be enjoyable to rediscover them. So I proceed with the parade.

The brilliance of a parody such as "Love and Freindship," as we have seen, lies largely in the fact that it is wonderfully funny even if you don't know exactly what is being parodied, because Austen allows us to reconstruct the fictions she bounces off. A reader who does not know *The Mysteries of Udolpho* can still laugh at *Northanger Abbey*; but the reader who does know it finds an extra dimension of pleasure. And I suggest that knowledge of *Emily Montague*, as of *Laura and Augustus*, can enhance our enjoyment of Austen's teenage parodies, "Amelia Webster" and "Love and Freindship."

Frances Brooke's full-length epistolary novel *Emily Montague* contains the courtship and marriage of three separate couples: the heroine's to the hero, the secondary heroine's to the secondary hero, and the hero's sister to his friend. Exactly the same could be said of young Austen's minimalist epistolary novel, "Amelia Webster," though it occupies hardly two-and-a-half pages in the Cambridge edition. As with Austen's breathless dramatic version of *Sir Charles Grandison*, brevity is a major part of the joke.

Emily Montague is a novel to be taken more seriously than *Laura and Augustus*, and deserves better than to be studied only for what young Austen found laughable in it. Carl F. Klinck, in his introduction to the 1961 edition, aptly describes the rapid-fire pace of Brooke's epistolary romance:

> Her epistles are short, her paragraphs of minimum length, her transitions are telepathic; her sentences either balanced or uncomplicated; her flow rapid … Her wit is not mere affectation; it shows itself in brevity and aptness. (Klinck, iv)

The same certainly applies to the pace of Austen's "Amelia Webster," which might be described as romance by telegram. In fact the phrase in *Emily Montague* that first alerted me to a possible connection with "Amelia Webster" is a characteristic sign-off to the brief letters: "I have a thousand things to say to you, but … " – followed by explanation of an interruption (*EM* 36, 183). The formula recurs: "I have a thousand things to say, but am forced to steal this moment to write to you … . Adieu! Yours, Emily Montague" (213).

Young Jane Austen pounced on the absurdity of writing to say you don't have enough time to write. This is the whole of "Letter the 3d" in "Amelia Webster":

> DEAR MAUD
>
> Believe me I'm happy to hear of your Brother's arrival. I have a thousand things to tell you, but my paper will only permit me to add that I am yr affect. Friend, AMELIA WEBSTER (*J* 55)

Those "thousand things," apparently, have a hard time getting recorded. Michael Londry, the co-editor of the Juvenilia Press edition of "Amelia Webster," humorously speculates about the size of the paper that Amelia uses, and the size of her hand: Did Amelia write on "a ridiculously small card or paper," or perhaps in "a ridiculously large hand on a regular sheet of paper"?[8] The nonsensical text invites such bemused elaboration; and it mercilessly sends up an epistolary convention at the same time.

Colonel Edward Rivers, the hero of *Emily Montague*, falls for the heroine on a first meeting, even though he knows she is engaged to Another: "Lucy! [he writes to his sister] she is an angel … Only think of finding beauty, delicacy, sensibility, all that can charm in woman, hid in a wood in Canada!" (*EM* 15) Love at first sight is another convention that young Jane the parodist has fun with. As we have seen, Laura of "Love and Freindship" fell in love with her Edward the moment she saw him ("L&F" 80). In "Amelia Webster" she achieves a further clang of absurdity in imagining falling in love at long distance (distance being a precondition for an epistolary exchange). George Hervey writes to Amelia Webster:

> MADAM / An humble Admirer now addresses you – I saw you lovely Fair one as you passed on Monday last, before our House in your way to Bath. I saw you thro' a telescope and was so struck by your Charms that from that time to this I have not tasted human food. GEORGE HERVEY (59–60)

Love at first telescope sighting has never been so succinctly rendered.

Austen's familiar interconnections of the sexes through the friendships of their siblings – in *Northanger Abbey* alone we have C.atherine and James Morland, Isabella and John Thorpe, Eleanor and Henry Tilney – may also have its seed in *Emily Montague*. Colonel Rivers writes to his friend Temple of his recent engagement to Rivers' sister, "Nothing could make me so happy as an event that unites a sister I idolise to the friend on earth most dear to me" (*EM* 144). Again, young Austen wickedly parodies this bandying about of sisters as transferable property between the men. George Hervey writes summarily of his sisters to his friend Beverley as "both fine Girls – particularly Maud, who I think would suit you as a Wife well enough. What say you to this? She will have two thousand Pounds and as much more as you can get. If you don't marry her you will mortally offend GEORGE HERVEY" (58).

---

8 *"Amelia Webster" and "The Three Sisters"* (Edmonton: Juvenilia Press, 1993), 43.

Moreover, as I have intimated I believe Austen had *Emily Montague* in mind, as well as *Laura and Augustus*, as parodic butt when she wrote "Love and Freindship." In pondering this second source I can't help noticing that "Montague" is the surname shared by the hero of *Laura and Augustus* and the heroine of *Emily Montague*. Romeo's patronym was clearly a popular choice in the sentimental novel of the eighteenth century. And it seems likely that young Austen noticed that too. In her unfinished narrative "Sir William Mountague," as we have seen, the highly susceptible hero first falls in love with three sisters at once, and then proceeds to a staggering series of further engagements and amorous liaisons. Apparently it is in the Montague blood.

If from *Laura and Augustus* Austen got her heroine's and secondary hero's names, and the wilder manifestations of sensibility such as the tears, the frequent fainting, and the vigorous running mad, it was from *Emily Montague* that she got the idea of doubling the heroine to achieve *two* heroines with sensibilities "tremblingly alive" (a phrase that appears in *Emily Montague* too ["L&F" 104; *EM* 159]).

The two heroines of *Emily Montague*, Arabella and Emily, provide one model for the doubling. But an interpolated episode in this novel, much more tenderly sentimental than the main narrative and therefore inviting parody, seems closer still to providing an impulse for "Love and Freindship."

One of the points of the satire of Austen's burlesque is the comparatively high value in the novel of sensibility that is placed on "friendship" over against the more traditionally valued heterosexual love and marriage. The overturning of the Phaeton that leaves the two husbands "weltering in their blood" is called "an accident truly apropos," since it distracts Sophia from her melancholy musings. The vigorous response of fainting and running mad seems to be undertaken in a spirit rather of emulation than of grief. Laura's loss of her "freind" Sophia, occupies her more fully. Similarly, in the interpolated tale about the Sophia of *Emily Montague*, the narrator Fanny Williams is truly devoted to *her* Sophia, who has all the proper qualifications for a heroine of sensibility: "My Sophia [she writes] … has an air of youth, of softness, of sensibility, of blushing innocence, which seemed intended to inspire delicate passions alone" (310–11). And she is likewise contemptuous of Sophia's devious suitor and seducer, who recommends himself "by all those unmeaning, but flattering attentions, by which our credulous sex are so often misled" (311).

To Fanny, Sophia is "the friend of my soul, the best and most gentle of her sex"; to Sophia, Fanny is "the friend most dear to her on earth" (*EM* 314, 313). When Sophia is seduced and abandoned by an unscrupulous baronet, her father, "severe by nature … cast her from his heart and fortune for ever" (as fathers are apt to do in this kin of narrative [313]). When Fanny discovers her stricken friend, now at death's door, she "flew to her" (as Austen's Laura and Sophia "flew to each other's arms" ("L&F" 114). This Sophia "could only say, 'My Fanny! Is this possible,' and fainted away" (*EM* 313). And for this fine flourish of fainting and tears I present the parallel passages.

First, from *Emily Montague*: "Her eyes were fixed tenderly on me, she pressed my hand between hers, the tears stole silently down her cheeks" (313).

And now Austen's Sophia in "Love and Freindship": "I had wept over her every Day – had bathed her sweet face with my tears and had pressed her fair Hands continually in mine" (102).

Brooke's Sophia cannot resist moralizing on her deathbed: "The weakness of my heart has undone me; I am lost, abandoned by him on whom my soul doted" (314). Nor can Austen's, although in her famous "Beware of fainting fits" speech Sophia addresses more directly the perils of sensibility: "I die a Martyr to my greif for the loss of Augustus … . One fatal swoon has cost me my Life … . Beware of swoons Dear Laura" ("L&F" 132). With a deft hand Austen snatches the manifestations that hover on the brink of excess, and pushes them cheerfully over the top.

In each case "all this ruin [is] brought on by a sensibility of which the best minds alone are susceptible" (*EM* 315); in each case the surviving friend is stricken with overwhelming grief; and in each case – to shift from the sublime to the mundane – she is rescued from destitution by an annuity settled on her by a male relative of the dead husband.

The inserted episode of Fanny and Sophia occupies only one letter in *Emily Montague*, and does not interrupt the main narrative of *Emily Montague* for long. But the pitch of it is much higher, so to speak, than that of the main story, which is much more realistic and much less emotionally fraught.

There! I have convinced *myself*, at least, that, if Austen took her Laura and Augustus from *Laura and Augustus*, she found her Sophia in *Emily Montague*. As for Laura's Edward in "Love and Freindship": it's worth noting that Brooke's hero, the one who marries Emily Montague, is also an Edward: Edward Rivers. Young Austen merely juggled the names a little!

"Love and friendship" is a phrase fairly common in eighteenth-century discourse. In *Emily Montague* it appears twice (320, 330), and with notable emphasis. Close to the end of the novel, the male characters debate the rival claims of the two allegiances, and their similarity. Fitzgerald, now Arabella's husband, quotes: "Shenstone says admirably, 'That reconciliation is the tenderest part of love and friendship'" (*EM* 330). Though she might have plucked the phrase from many other places, it seems likely that Jane Austen took the title of her funniest juvenile work, as well as a second heroine's name and pathetic death-scene, from the first Canadian novel.

Critics of the Canadian novel have reason to admire *Emily Montague* for its vivid evocation of life in Lower Canada, the knowledge of native culture and customs, the social scene in the English military settlement, the specificity about winter clothing, sleigh rides on the St. Lawrence River, and scenery incorporating Montmorency Falls and the Ile d'Orléans. Not all of this, I suggest, passed Austen by.

The picture of Jane Austen in the New World is a might-have-been to linger over.[9] Like Keats, who claimed "Much have I travelled in the realms of gold" before he ever left English soil, Austen travelled vicariously, and through the books she read. Her marked preference for home-grown views – the "English verdure, English culture, English comfort" that characterise the scene near Mr. Knightley's Donwell Abbey (*E* 391) – makes it hardly surprising that she does not use the wilder landscapes and mixed cultures celebrated in *Emily Montague*. But the juvenilia, along with the influences on them, came before she had delimited her scene to those three or four families in a country village. And some of the wider-ranging geography of the juvenilia casts its shadow ahead to the mature novels. She never set a scene on the Plains of Abraham and never named Canada in her writings – though Newfoundland and its dogs get a look-in, both in the early fragment from *Volume the First*, "The Generous Curate" and in *Northanger Abbey*, were a Newfoundland puppy is the friend of Henry Tilney's solitude (*NA* 219). But the West Indian islands, the setting for much of that other fictional source for "Love and Freindship," *Laura and Augustus*, notably becomes the far-away place that Sir Thomas and Tom Bertram must travel to: and the Antigua references in *Mansfield Park* have sparked the burgeoning of postcolonial approaches to Jane Austen.

Though one doesn't need to have to have read *Laura and Augustus* and *Emily Montague* to enjoy "Love and Freindship," hunting out young Austen's parodic butts gives some sense of her as a reader as well as a writer and parodist. It is easy to imagine the Austen family settling down to read one or the other lachrymose novel aloud; perhaps Mrs. or Mr. Austen providing the voice while Cassandra and Jane "worked" at their needlework. "Not *more* tears!" or "What, fainting *again*?" they might have commented, laughing. And then in due course 14-year-old Jane retired to her room and her writing desk, to work on her own lachrymose novel – much more sympathetic to fathers and to good sense, much funnier, and delighting in the very excesses of the trembling sensibilities of her heroines; laughing to herself as she wrote about Laura and Sophia, Edward and Augustus, and the coach rattling between Stirling and Edinburgh that she was to remember even decades later.

---

9 I am indebted to Lindsey McMaster for stimulating discussion on this issue.

Chapter 7
Partial, Prejudiced, and Proud: *Pride and Prejudice* and the Juvenilia

I have claimed already that Jane Austen's juvenilia form a group of works successful in their own right, with their own cheerful and humorous world-view, by a teenager brilliantly creative and with an astonishing gift for language. But as we have seen, they also lead in many quite audible ways to the novels of her maturity. "First Impressions," written when Austen was in her early twenties, no doubt would have felt quite close in tone to some of the juvenilia. And we know it was read often in the Austen family, and seems to have been just as "light & bright & sparkling" as *Pride and Prejudice* itself. Austen wrote about its popularity in the family circle, with her own brand of humour: "I should not let Martha read 'First Impressions' again upon any account," she wrote to Cassandra in 1799. " … She is very cunning, but I saw through her design: she means to publish it from Memory, & one more perusal must enable her to do it" (*Letters* 441). Even if publishing it from memory was an exaggeration, it seems family members read it and reread it, both singly and aloud to one another. We can hear the voice of the same youngster who wrote delightedly about the "threescore Editions" that "The Beautifull Cassandra" and "The History of England" have run to (*MW* 193). Austen can revel in popularity, either actual or imagined, and joke about it too.

We will never know how close *Pride and Prejudice* is to "First Impressions," or how different. But for those who know the juvenilia well, part of the pleasure in reading *Pride and Prejudice* is the recognition of that adolescent who still mischievously peers through the now treasured lines of the adult novel. In some ways Austen brings her own early work and memories with her, reluctant, it seems, to leave them behind entirely. In some ways too, she is consciously putting away childish things.

In this chapter I shall be exploring some of the items she brought forward, and also the ones she chose to revise.

> Mr Watts is a single man in possession of a good fortune who is in want of a wife, and Mrs. Stanhope is a mother of a family of girls who is very much in want of a son-in-law.[1]

This short blurb we devised for the Juvenilia Press edition of "The Three Sisters," to draw attention to it as a sort of *ur*-version of *Pride and Prejudice*. We progress from the three Stanhope sisters to the five Bennet ones; from a desperate and greedy husband-hunt by Mary Stanhope to Mrs. Bennet's undisguised pursuit of suitors for her daughters, with material possessions figuring largely in both quests.

[1] The edition was edited by Joseph Wiesenfarth, Laura Minelli, and Kristin Smith.

It has been an old popular complaint against Jane Austen that she has only one plot: "All the novels are just about how the woman gets her man." It's a crude and reductive generalization. But insofar as it may be considered true, it is certainly *Pride and Prejudice* that best fits that pattern. "Five love-hungry beauties in search of husbands!" ran the ad for the 1940 movie of *Pride and Prejudice* starring Greer Garson and Laurence Olivier. But the explicit husband-hunting in *Pride and Prejudice* is principally performed by Mrs. Bennet on behalf of her daughters, rather than by the girls themselves (though Lydia certainly runs her mother a close second). In the other novels there is much less about the quest for a rich husband – or indeed almost *any* husband! – and the emphasis is rather on love and its impediments. Though minor characters like Sir John Middleton may joke about Marianne's "setting [her] cap" at Willoughby, he draws a strong reproof for his crude expression from Marianne herself (*SS* 54). In fact none of the heroines actively pursues a husband – nor would she be a heroine if she did. Charlotte Lucas does visibly set out to catch Mr. Collins, and she is treated sympathetically, but is not approved. Girls visibly in quest of good matches, such as Isabella Thorpe, Nancy and Lucy Steele, and Elizabeth Elliot, are consigned to minor roles and not approved.

Next after *Pride and Prejudice*, the mature work with a strong focus on the husband-hunt is *The Watsons*. Here the desperate need for a husband, especially for girls in families on the edge of gentility, is sympathetically treated. Elizabeth Watson, now considered by many in her circle as an old maid, speaks poignantly: "It is very bad to grow old & be poor and laughed at" (*LM* 82) – precisely Miss Bates's fate in *Emma*. Elizabeth Watson considers her sister Emma to be too "refined" in declaring she would "rather be [a] Teacher at a school (and I can think of nothing worse) than marry a Man I did not like." For her part Elizabeth Watson declares pragmatically, "I think I could like any good-humoured Man with a comfortable income." Even she, however, admits "I should not like marrying a disagreeable man" (*LM* 83). A sufficiently generous reservation, one might think.

In short, though the sensitive issue of the need for a husband is present in all the novels, the active hunting for a husband figures prominently only in *Pride and Prejudice* (where is it performed by the mother, not the marriageable girls), *The Watsons* (which is unfinished) and "The Three Sisters," where the marriageable girl herself is the principal huntress. In the juvenilia young Jane could take the gloves off, and be broad and satirical. The principal character, Mary, scorns her mother's more genteel tactics, and manages the business herself; though not without some qualms about her suitor's characteristics.

"The Three Sisters" opens with Mary Stanhope's letter to her confidential friend, announcing in triumph the proposal of marriage she has received. "It is the first I have ever had and I hardly know how to value it enough," she crows (*J* 74). Delighted to be asked, she relishes the power that the question gives her, and seems quite ready to prolong it. She gives Mr. Watts "an equivocal answer" so that she can keep him dangling while she considers the matter, which for her is far from a simple one.

In her letter, as she considers the advantages and disadvantages, she swings first one way and then another. Among the *dis*advantages: he is "old … very plain *so* plain that I cannot bear to look at him … extremely disagreable … ill tempered and peevish extremely jealous … stingy" (74). Quite enough, one would have thought, to prompt a refusal. Moreover, Mr. Watts shows a Collins-like readiness to switch between Mary and her sisters. "I am by no means guided by a particular preference for you above your Sisters," he tells her; "It is equally the Same to me which I marry of the three" (82). Rather than being put off by this un-suitor-like adaptability, Mary finds it a strong motive to snap him up, since she can't bear to think of her younger sisters' marrying before her. Her sisters are no help in this regard, as they connive at keeping her on tenterhooks as to whether they would accept him or not. While the youngest of the three, Georgiana, is somewhat like Elizabeth Bennet in her use of irony, as well as in her resolution, "I never would marry Mr Watts were Beggary the only alternative" (79), she is manipulative and unscrupulous, and has little compunction about tricking her sister into a miserable marriage.[2] Young Austen is not yet ready to present a sympathetic heroine, who is a mixture of good and bad but who strives for self-knowledge. In "The Three Sisters" she preserves the satiric edge.

Among the advantages: Mary Stanhope's more readily understandable motive for wanting to marry the disgusting Mr. Watts, of course, is the same as Charlotte Lucas's in accepting Mr. Collins – "the pure and disinterested desire of an establishment" (*PP* 137). "He has a large fortune and will make great Settlements on me; but then [and here she throws in a *dis*advantage] he is very healthy" (74). And Mary is a good deal more greedy than Charlotte Lucas. To establish a parallel I quote again from her list of *desiderata* in the marriage state:

> "Remember the pinmoney; two hundred a year … . And Remember I am to have a new Carriage hung as high as the Duttons', and blue spotted with silver; and I shall expect a new Saddle horse, a suit of fine lace, and an infinite number of the most valuable Jewels … This is not all … You must have two more Footmen to attend me, two Women to wait on me, must always let me do just as I please and make a very good husband."
>
> Here she stopped, I beleive rather out of breath. (64–5)

Mary's lust after pin money and other material goods recalls Mrs. Bennet's greed for status items for her daughters. "Oh! my sweetest Lizzy!" she gushes, when she hears of Elizabeth's engagement to Darcy, "how rich and how great you will be! What pin-money, what jewels, what carriages you will have!" (*PP* 419)

Another characteristic that Mary Stanhope shares with Mrs. Bennet is her almost obsessive self-contradiction. Incapable of weighing the benefits against the disadvantages, she is simply swept one way and another by impulse. As she writes her letter, she is firmly declarative – on both sides of the question. "I wont have

---

[2] See Louisa Maestrelli and Kristin Smith, "Introduction" to the Juvenilia Press edition of *The Three Sisters*, xi–xii.

him I declare. He said he should come again tomorrow and take my final answer, so I believe I must get him while I can … ” (75). No wonder her mother complains, “What you say one moment you unsay the next” (76). And much the same could be said of Mrs. Bennet. “I told you in the library, you know,” she says to Elizabeth about the Collins affair, “that I should never speak to you again, and you will find me as good as my word” (*PP* 126) – and yet here she is, speaking to Elizabeth. Austen specifies “in the library” to make sure we get the point: that her declaration about never speaking to Elizabeth again was in the past, and that she is already infringing it even as she repeats it.

As we have seen, this self-contradiction is quite a motif in Austen’s writings, both in her youth and her maturity. In the juvenilia she presents figures like Mary Stanhope who simply want everything and haven’t the sense or the self-knowledge to sort out priorities and incompatibilities. They are determined to eat their cake and have it too. For the reader it is an exercise in discrimination to pursue a progress from the greedy characters like Mary, the omnivorous Sir William Mountague, and the endlessly taking Gower of “Evelyn,” to Kitty of “Catharine,” who realistically vacillates over the state of her heart, to Mrs. Bennet with her hard-wired inconsistency, to a complex character like Elizabeth Bennet. She too can be caught in similar self-deception and inconsistency.

Elizabeth’s precious and chosen “prejudice,” after all, calls for full self-discovery and analysis, by readers as well as by the complex character herself. Darcy says shrewdly to her before Colonel Fitzwilliam, “I have had the pleasure of your acquaintance long enough to know, that you find great enjoyment in occasionally professing opinions which in fact are not your own” (*PP* 195). We are told that Elizabeth “laughed heartily at this picture of herself.” But in fact Darcy is quite right. She *does* profess opinions which are not her own – as when, for instance, she tells him on the dance floor, “I have always seen a great similarity in the turn of our minds. – We are each of an unsocial, taciturn disposition, unwilling to speak, unless we expect to say something that will amaze the whole room” (103). Of course she is making this up as she goes along – it’s part of the playfulness that Darcy finds so piquant. Stolidly literal himself, he keeps track of her flights of fancy. Elizabeth scorns her mother and the Meryton gossips for first adoring Wickham and then denouncing him, for first hating Darcy and then adoring him. But she herself must go through the same evolution. In fact in many ways she is responsible for the community’s misconceptions, since she was in the vanguard of them herself. One might say that the difference between Mary Stanhope and Mrs. Bennet on the one hand, and Elizabeth on the other, is that the former contradict themselves in contiguous sentences, but Elizabeth takes the duration of most of the novel to reform her thinking. And of course another crucial difference is that Elizabeth is self-aware and they are not. At one point, when Lydia sneers that Wickham could never have cared three straws about Miss King – “such a nasty little freckled thing” – Elizabeth winces “to think that, however incapable of such coarseness of *expression* herself, the coarseness of the *sentiment* was little other than her own breast had formerly harboured and fancied liberal!” (244). The hugely self-interested characters like Mary Stanhope and Mrs. Bennet aren't capable of examining their own behaviour in this way. But Jane Austen as a teenager was already exploring the myriad ways in which the human character can deceive itself.

There are other intimations of *Pride and Prejudice* in "The Three Sisters." When it looks as though Mr. Watts may go elsewhere for a wife, Mary wishes she had "a Father or a Brother because then they should fight him" (77) As I explained in the chapter on illustrating the juvenilia, this little flight of fancy inspired my illustration of something that didn't actually happen – Mr. Watts facing a putative brother of Mary's in a duel, and then nimbly making his escape. Mrs. Bennet has her own imaginings: "Here's Mr. Bennet gone away," she cries melodramatically, "and I know he will fight Wickham, wherever he meets him and then he will be killed, and what is to become of us all?" (*PP* 317) But when she knows her husband is coming home, she characteristically reverses her position: "Sure he will not leave London before he has found them. Who is to fight Wickham, and make him marry her, if he comes away?" (329)

Mary's obsession with pin-money and clothing is another motif in the juvenilia that carries over to the novels. The female interest in clothing is natural and forgivable,[3] and of course Jane Austen herself was as fond of a pretty bonnet as the next girl, and in decorating a bonnet was ready to debate the issue of whether "it is more natural to have flowers grow out of the head than fruit" (*Letters* 44). In "The Beautifull Cassandra" the heroine falls in love with a bonnet in preference to the highly eligible viscount – a preference quite understandable in a 15-year-old. But Austen cares about priorities; and when Mary Stanhope is ready to sacrifice marital happiness for generous pin-money, or Isabella Thorpe, trying to recapture her estranged fiancé, is easily distracted by the spring fashions, and "hats the most frightful you can imagine," we learn to recognise "shallow artifice" (*NA* 222, 224). In *Pride and Prejudice* Lydia is like her mother in her susceptibility to a red coat, and her characteristic activity is to buy a hideous bonnet in order to take it apart and make it up again. Lydia's letter announcing her elopement with Wickham is outrageously frivolous throughout; but the capstone is her instruction on forwarding her clothes: "I wish you would tell Sally to mend a great slit in my worked muslin gown, before they are packed up" (*PP* 321). We don't need to linger long over *that* piece of sartorial symbolism. Lydia is Lydia still!

It is not only the young who care about clothing. Mr. Collins warns Elizabeth not to be too fine when she dresses for dinner at Rosings. "Lady Catherine will not think the worse of you for being simply dressed," he tells her. "She likes to have the distinction of rank preserved" (*PP* 182). It's a revealing passage. Lady Catherine, it seems, looks back to the sumptuary laws, which regulated, among other things, who might wear what. These laws, long outdated, were intended to control wasteful expenditure on dress; but they were appropriated by the upper

---

3 See Penelope Byrd, *Jane Austen Fashion: Fashion and Needlework in the Works of Jane Austen* (Ludlow: Excellent Press, 1999), 14. First published as *A Frivolous Distinction: Fashion and Needlework in the Works of Jane Austen* (Bath: Bath City Council, 1979), and frequently reprinted.

classes to be the means of preserving class hierarchy and making it visible. In a memorable passage in *Northanger Abbey*, the narrator comments, "Dress is at all times a frivolous distinction, and excessive solicitude about it often destroys its own aim" (*NA* 71). How Lady Catherine would bridle to hear her treasured "distinction of rank" downgraded to a merely "frivolous distinction."

If in "The Three Sisters" we have an early version of the social situation of *Pride and Prejudice*, in "A Collection of Letters," we have a clear ancestress of Lady Catherine, as critics have often noticed.[4] Maria, "A young Lady in distress'd Circumstances" (*J* 197), is particularly interesting in that she is a first-person narrator (though the epistolary set-up masks that effect). If Austen had decided to graft the rest of Maria's story onto this fragment, perhaps we would have had Austen's nearest approach to *Jane Eyre*!

Maria's "distress'd Circumstances" require her to accept a ride to a ball in Lady Greville's carriage. This *grande dame* is quite as rudely presumptuous, and just as eager to have the distinction of rank preserved in dress, as our own dear Lady Catherine:

> "So Miss Maria [her ladyship greets her as she gets into the carriage] you seem very smart to night – *My* poor Girls will appear quite to disadvantage by *you* … Have you got a new Gown on?
>
> "Yes Ma'am," replied I with as much indifference as I could assume.
>
> "Aye, and a fine one too I think – (feeling it, as by her permission I seated myself by her) I dare say it is all very smart – But I must own, for you know I always speak my mind, that I think it quite a needless piece of expence – Why could not you have worn your old striped one?" (198).

There is a moment when we plainly glimpse the mature Jane Austen in the young image. When Elizabeth, in withholding her age from Lady Catherine, "suspect[s] herself to be the first creature who had ever dared to trifle with so much dignified impertinence" (*PP* 187). But the young Jane Austen had already done some outrageous trifling of her own in exposing the "dignified impertinence" of Lady Greville.

I hardly need to point out the parallels, so much of Lady Catherine is already there in this fragment: not only the objection to fine clothing in people she considers her inferiors, but the bossy assumption that people should always take her advice, the arrogant tone, and the intrusive questions on personal matters.

"You know I always speak my mind," says Lady Greville. "My character has ever been celebrated for its sincerity and frankness," declares Lady Catherine, a little more elaborately (*PP* 391). Both are egocentrically talking of themselves

---

4 For instance, A. Walton Litz in *Jane Austen: A Study of her Artistic Development*, 38–9; Q.D. Leavis, "Jane Austen: A Critical Theory," 67–8, 28–9. Margaret Anne Doody and Douglas Murray also draw attention to the parallels in their edition of *Catharine and Other Writings* (Oxford: Oxford University Press, 1993), 334–6.

while they purport to be addressing neutral matters; and both, in claiming their frankness as a virtue, are masking their actual rudeness.

The parallel doesn't end there. The next day Lady Greville comes in her carriage and summons Maria to talk to her at the window. When her daughter says sympathetically, "I am afraid you find it very cold Maria," Lady Greville agrees:

> "Yes, it is an horrible East wind … I assure you I can hardly bear the window down – But you are used to be blown about [by] the wind Miss Maria & that is what has made your Complexion so ruddy and coarse. You young Ladies who cannot often ride in a Carriage never mind what weather you trudge in, or how the wind shews your legs … But some sort of people have no feelings either of cold or Delicacy." (J 202)

It's a bit much to summon the girl out into the wind and then abuse her for indelicacy! While the mature Austen doesn't present anything quite so broad, she comes very close. It's Lady Catherine's daughter who summons Charlotte Collins outside to her carriage window, prompting Elizabeth's remark, "She is abominably rude to keep Charlotte out of doors in all this wind" (*PP* 130). And as for the indelicacy of allowing the wind to show your legs – perhaps there is a memory of that in Miss Bingley's strictures on Elizabeth's blowsy looks and muddy petticoat after her walk to Netherfield. But it is toned down from the juvenilia.

Clearly there were some things in the juvenilia that Jane Austen couldn't bear to leave behind. But a piece like this from "A Collection of Letters," which is so close to what she chose to rework for her own darling child *Pride and Prejudice*, interestingly illustrates the differences as well as the likenesses between the youthful work and the mature. Lady Catherine, with her arrogance, inquisitive cross-questioning, and intrusive instructions, does indeed embody "dignified impertinence." But she doesn't actually finger the fabric of Elizabeth's dress, as Lady Greville does Maria's. Miss de Bourgh does thoughtlessly keep Charlotte out in the wind at the carriage window, prompting Elizabeth's comment on her abominable rudeness; but she doesn't first summon her and then comment on how the wind makes the light muslins of the day cling to the contours of her legs. The broad satire and physical jokes of the juvenilia are toned down for the more realistic novel, and a more shockable readership. But the same comic spirit informs both works.

Similarly, though Mrs. Bennet shares a world-view and many sentiments with Mary Stanhope, she doesn't actually enumerate the luxuries she expects the husband to provide, as Mary does. We gain in probability, but perhaps we lose some enjoyable specificity.

"A Collection of Letters" seems to be a set of experiments, and this "Letter the Third," particularly, reads not like skeleton notes towards a novel (or extended fiction) but like a fully fleshed-out scene, complete in all its details, that has been snatched out of a larger work – except that the larger work isn't there. It has no beginning or suggested outcome; but what is there is already vivid and striking, with the back-story of the heroine already suggested. Maria, we learn from dialogue, is the daughter of a wine merchant, and now lives in a small way with her widowed mother – "in distress'd Circumstances," as the title informs us (197). Like Kitty of "Catharine, or the Bower," she must endure snobbish references to her background in trade. (Kitty is an heiress living with a maiden aunt, but her father too was in trade, so the Dudleys look down on her.) Like the Watson girls, Maria must be indebted to a richer family to host her for the night of a ball. In all three unfinished works, a ball provides the social focus of the narrative.

Since the Lady Greville episode is brought forward to *Pride and Prejudice* in such recognizable ways, I look for other connections and differences. Lady Greville has two daughters. One of them, the elder, is very much her mother's daughter (at one of Lady Greville's insulting sallies "She laughed excessively, as she always does at her Mothers wit" [151]). The younger, Ellen, is much pleasanter, and on Maria's side. The two rolled into one, apparently, cancel each other out, for poor Anne de Bourgh is a relative nonentity. But in both cases the Lady's daughter it to some extent the heroine's rival. Lady Greville objects to Maria's new ball gown partly because, she says, "*My* poor Girls will appear quite to disadvantage by *you*": and she is indignant to see Mr. Bernard, who is apparently a "catch," dancing with Maria. In this case, however, her indignation is mild compared with Lady Catherine's outrage at the notion of Elizabeth Bennet's polluting "the shades of Pemberley" (*PP* 396).

It is possible to follow through an inheritance from Austen's experimental fragments to the published novels, in the matter of a structurally all-important ball. "Letter the Third" strikes a keynote first, with Maria's journey with Lady Greville and her daughters to a ball where Maria has her chance to dance with the desirable partner of the evening. "Catharine, or the Bower" also features an important ball, where the carriage ride *to* the ball is equally significant, as the handsome but irresponsible Edward Stanley makes his striking first impression, and the heroine is again subject to snobbish criticism from her social superiors. Then comes *The Watsons*, where again the journey to the ball (this time just two girls in a cart) and the ball itself are both structural parts of the action, and where again the heroine is of visibly lower status than the grand people around her. (One wonders how much of this derived from Austen's own experience.) The issue of early eating hours for unfashionable families, and late arrival and late eating hours for the fashionable ones, appears again.

Pride and Prejudice seems to come next in the sequence, in that the first assembly, where Darcy speaks slightingly of Elizabeth, sets the action going. However, the significant journey *to* the ball does not appear. In *Northanger Abbey* again we have two significant balls, including Tilney's classic analogy between the dance and marriage – and two significant carriage rides with suitors both unwelcome and welcome. In *Sense and Sensibility* there is no significant ball scene until the late one where Willoughby slights Marianne; in *Mansfield Park* and *Emma* there are important balls, but they come late in the action; and in *Persuasion* there is no ball at all. On the one occasion where an impromptu dance is arranged, the heroine merely plays the piano, with tears in her eyes, while the hero dances with someone else. Evidently as Austen grew older, and occasions for dancing diminished, the ball scene seems to have lost some of its appeal as a road to courtship and marriage. But *Pride and Prejudice* belongs with the early fictions, and the inheritance from them is clear.

If "The Three Sisters" provides intimations of the social situation in *Pride and Prejudice*, and Lady Greville of "A Collection of Letters" gives us a preview of Lady Catherine, "The History of England" connects significantly with the mature novel's theme. Young Austen as historian explores and dramatises the operation of "prejudice." At the outset of the history she cheerfully confesses:

> I suppose you know all about the Wars between [Henry the 6th] and the Duke of York who was of the right side; If you do not, you had better read some other History, for I shall not be very diffuse in this, meaning by it only to vent my Spleen *against*, and shew my Hatred *to* all those people whose parties or principles do not suit with mine, and not to give information. (*J* 178)

So she takes up the cudgels in defence of her afflicted heroine, Mary Queen of Scots, and denounces the villainess who had her executed, Queen Elizabeth. And a very entertaining job she makes of it. Despite her cheerful admission of her intense partisanship, she denounces the same fault in others. Of the Protestants who find fault with Mary for sticking to Catholicism, this historian claims, "This is a striking proof of *their* narrow Souls & prejudiced Judgements who accuse her" (184). She sounds like Elizabeth Bennet at the Netherfield ball, who accuses Miss Bingley of the very fault she is most guilty of herself, "wilful ignorance" about Wickham's wrongs (*PP* 106).

The author of the "History" is clearly proud of her partisanship. Although much later Jane Austen told the Regent's Librarian, James Stanier Clarke, that she could not write a "Historical Romance" to save her life (*Letters* 312), when she writes here of Mary Queen of Scots she pulls out all the romantic stops. "This bewitching Princess," she calls her: "Abused, reproached and vilified by all, what must her noble Mind have suffered when informed that Elizabeth had given orders for her Death! Yet she bore it with a most unshaken fortitude … " and so on. Likewise she revels in turning Queen Elizabeth and her ministers into villains for "this blot, this everlasting blot upon their Understanding and their character" (184). Hardly the impartial tone of the conscientious historian! She actually lines up her allies on the side of her martyred heroine, "whose only friend then was the Duke of Norfolk, and whose only ones now are Mr Whitaker, Mrs Lefroy, Mrs Knight and myself" (184).[5]

---

5 "Mr Whitaker" was John Whitaker, author of *Mary Queen of Scots Vindicated* (1787), and so clearly on the "right" side of the debate. Mrs. Lefroy was a close friend of young Jane Austen, and Mrs. Knight, also much older than her, was the adoptive mother of Jane Austen's brother Edward. See Pater Sabor's edition of the *Juvenilia* in *The Cambridge Edition of the Works of Jane Austen*, 465.

Opinionated? Definitely. And as we have seen, vilifying Queen Elizabeth was a conversational resource for young Jane as for her characters, too, as in "Catharine," where we find Kitty challenging the adults on the matter. The debate was evidently young Austen's hobby horse, and she made the most of it.

Elizabeth Bennet is opinionated too, and proud of it. From the moment she overhears Darcy's arrogant dismissal of her charms, "She is tolerable; but not handsome enough to tempt *me*" she proceeds to "[tell] the story … with great spirit among her friends" (*PP* 12), gathering allies, and an audience to share her views.

Wickham, with his damaging testimony on Darcy, is a godsend. For Elizabeth is not simply mistaken about the relative merits of Darcy and Wickham. She has *chosen* to dislike the one and champion the other, as Austen did in the case of Queen Elizabeth and Mary Queen of Scots. With less humour than the young Jane, indeed with a degree of self-righteousness and self-congratulation, Elizabeth makes her partisanship quite a mission.[6] When she reports what she has heard from Wickham to Jane, Jane is shocked: "It is difficult indeed – it is distressing. – One does not know what to think." "I beg your pardon; – one knows exactly what to think," is Elizabeth's super-arrogant response (*PP* 96). She has become the self-appointed authority on the matter, and she won't tolerate any questioning of her status as expert, even from Jane. Like the young historian of "The History of England," she can make capital of a set of prejudices.

In her title page for "The History of England" young Austen identifies the author: "By a *partial, prejudiced* and ignorant Historian" (*J* 176, my italics). Those who know both texts well will catch the echo:

> Of neither Darcy nor Wickham could she think, without feeling that she had been blind, *partial, prejudiced*, absurd. (*PP* 230, my italics)

Elizabeth goes on to tell herself, "I have courted prepossession and ignorance [here she includes reference to the missing element of "ignorance" in the author's self-description in "The History"], and driven reason away, where either were concerned. Till this moment, I never knew myself" (*PP* 230).

Courted prepossession and ignorance; *driven reason away*: there is the emphasis on her chosen self-delusion. Later Elizabeth admits to Jane, "I meant to be uncommonly clever in taking so decided a dislike to [Mr. Darcy], without any reason. It is such a spur to one's genius, such an opening for wit to have a dislike of that kind" (*PP* 250). No doubt young Jane, with her championing of Mary Queen of Scots and her pointed dislike of Queen Elizabeth, meant to be uncommonly clever too – and indeed she was so, and made full use of the openings for wit that her partiality and prejudice afforded her. But declared prejudice over figures long dead, in a playful parody of history, is one thing; deliberate and advertised side-taking with young men very much alive is another. And when as a mature author she wrote her realistic novel about partiality and prejudice, Jane Austen

[6] I have written at more length on Elizabeth's obsessive pursuit of an idea in "*Pride and Prejudice*: Acting by Design," 30–35.

no doubt capitalized on curbing her youthful exuberance and setting it in a moral light. What if everyone believed you, and you turned out to be wrong? she perhaps asked her younger self. The boisterously chosen partisanship of the author of "The History of England" is updated as a model for her more responsible later heroine.

I am positing that the mature Austen remembered very well her clever parody of history, her vaunted partiality and prejudice. No doubt she had had an appreciative audience back then who had laughed heartily at her cheerful admission of ignorance, her sallies about "saving … *myself* the trouble of writing what I do not perfectly recollect" (180), and especially her exaggerated partisanship. "Mrs Lefroy [and] Mrs Knight," the friends she names as her allies in making a heroine of Mary Queen of Scots, would have been delighted to figure in her clever funny history. She was uncommonly clever. She *meant* to be uncommonly clever.

To me the repetition of those words "partial, prejudiced" from the title page of "The History of England" to Elizabeth's hour of self-discovery after reading Darcy's letter is no accidental echo, but Austen's deliberate reference to her earlier work and her earlier self. She looked back on a certain vanity she had felt, a pride in her youthful composition, and on mature consideration recognised it as a dangerous characteristic in a clever heroine who becomes enamoured of her own cleverness.

It's surely no accident that she gives the heroine of this new history the name of the villainess in her last, Elizabeth.

Was Jane Austen scolding her younger self? – when in *Pride and Prejudice* she turned serious and examined the damage that could be wrought by the kind of chosen prejudice that activated the young author of "The History of England" and her lively heroine Elizabeth? I don't mean to claim that she renounced the clever young author of the playful history; rather that she chose to explore the moral implications of the emphatic and cheerful side-taking that she had practised so amusingly in her youthful "History." If some part of her repented the vigorous and uncompromising stand she took, it was a recognition that play, even – or perhaps especially – *clever* play, can be dangerous. At most her "repentance" would be of the order of Mr. Bennet's when he recognises the error of his ways in being a merely playful rather than a moral father: sincere, but transitory: "Let me once in my life feel how much I have been to blame. I am not afraid of being overpowered by the impression. It will pass away soon enough" (*PP* 330).

There are many moments through the novels where the laughing face of young Jane peers through the more serious prose of Jane Austen the novelist. We know that the Austen family and close associates knew the juvenilia well, and could make private jokes about them. When Austen found she know several of the people on the crowded coach on the way to visit her brother Henry in London, she could write to Cassandra, "It put me in mind of my own coach between Edinburgh and Stirling" (*Letters* 270). As late as 1814 she could still refer to that minor incident in "Love and Freindship" where the characters are collected on the coach, and expect Cassandra to pick up the reference without effort or explanation. "My own coach," she writes affectionately, making a possession of the content of her writing. Her juvenilia were her own darling children too.

In the same way, I believe, other little pieces of the juvenilia that probably started as private family jokes find their way into *Pride and Prejudice*. Let me pause on blue coats. In "Frederic and Elfrida," that cheerful little take-off on courtship and propriety, "the lovely Charlotte," as we have seen, receives two proposals of marriage in quick succession, and accepts them both. The first is from "an aged gentleman" in an "old pink Coat"; but she much prefers the second suitor, "a young and Handsome Gentleman with a new blue coat," for "[t]here was a something in the appearance of the second Stranger, that influenced Charlotte in his favour" (*J* 8–9). Perhaps the blue coat had something to do with it. (Young Austen enjoyed poking fun at the moralists' position that no virtuous young lady would be influenced by physical good looks in a suitor.) Poor Charlotte! Since she can't oblige both suitors, she throws herself in the river.

But the blue coat survives Charlotte's sad demise, as in Augustus's "blue Sattin Waistcoat striped with white" in "Love and Freindship" (128). We know Austen paid attention to coat colour in men: Of Tom Lefroy she wrote to Cassandra, "He has but *one* fault … – it is that his morning coat is a great deal too light" (*Letters* 2). So it is no surprise that when Bingley first visits Mr. Bennet at Longbourn, and the girls watch eagerly from an upper window, they are excited to discern that he wears – you guessed it – a blue coat (*PP* 9). And when Lydia is about to be married, and her aunt is lecturing her, Lydia admits, "I did not hear above one word in ten, for I was thinking, you may suppose, of my dear Wickham. I longed to know whether he would be married in his blue coat" (*PP* 352). We can surely imagine that there had been some late-night giggles shared by Jane and Cassandra over this or that handsome hunk's blue coat; and some later laughter too, when Jane included memories of youthful jokes in her published novel.

To skim though a few more of the many echoes from Austen's teenage works to *Pride and Prejudice*: The instant intimacies that are so notable a part of "Love and Freindship" look forward not just to Isabella Thorpe's self-interested "friendship at first sight" for Catherine, but also to Miss Bingley and Mrs. Hurst's "taking up" Jane Bennet for their own amusement (and then dropping her again when the intimacy doesn't suit them). In "Jack and Alice," the resourceful Lucy proposes to the beautiful Charles Adams, and receives "an angry and peremptory refusal, but thinking it might be rather the effect of his modesty than any thing else, I pressed him again on the subject" (*J* 24). Shades of Mr. Collins! – but with the added joke of the reversal of the sexes.

To move from matters of character and theme to plot structure: two early pieces appear contiguously in *Volume the First*, the three page epistolary "well written tale," "Amelia Webster" and the mini-drama, "The Visit." In both, brevity is the main part of the joke. And in both we see, from the beginning to the culmination, no less than three different courtships. At the end of "Amelia Webster" we have the three marriages announced in the newspaper. "The Visit" ends with a more fully dramatised scene (though still at a lightning pace). After the vile dinner including "fried Cowheel & Onion" (who would have thought such a menu would have such an aphrodisiac effect?) we have this touching conclusion:

> LORD FITZGERALD And now my amiable Sophia condescend to marry me.
>
> [*He takes her hand and leads her to the front*]
>
> STANLY. Oh! Cloe could I but hope you would make me blessed –
>
> CLOE. I will. [*They advance.*]
>
> MISS FITZGERALD. Since you Willoughby are the only one left, I cannot refuse your earnest solicitations – There is my Hand.
>
> LADY HAMPTON. And may you all be Happy!
>
> FINIS (68)

It is a wild romp, not to be taken seriously. But in examining *Emily Montague* of 1769, which as we have seen was a novel parodied in "Love and Freindship." and "Amelia Webster," I realized young Jane has followed a recurring plot structure: in a novel of courtship it takes three couples to make up a satisfactory conclusion. And sure enough that's what we have in *Pride and Prejudice*: Lydia and Wickham, Jane and Bingley, Elizabeth and Darcy. I can't resist pursuing this matter of satisfactory plot structure a little further: In *Sense and Sensibility* we have Lucy and Robert Ferrars, Elinor and Edward, Marianne and Colonel Brandon; in *Emma* Harriet and Robert Martin, Jane Fairfax and Frank, Emma and Knightley. Not to mention – but I'll mention it anyway – Henrietta and Charles Hayter, Louisa and Benwick, Anne and Wentworth. It takes the jokily abbreviated telegraphic works to define a recurring pattern.

It's one more instance, I believe, of the spill-over from the exuberant youthful works to *Pride and Prejudice*. With this pattern in mind, it is tempting to speculate on how some of the unfinished pieces – "Catharine," or "Letter the Third," or "Lesley Castle" – might have found their consummations. So, briefly and tentatively, I take licence to sketch what I see as the likely trajectories of these three unfinished pieces from the juvenilia.

Speculations on Endings

"Catharine, or the Bower" I have already discussed, noting that Edward Stanley, despite being the first man who awakens Kitty's sexual interest, doesn't seem worthy of being he principal love interest. Charming as he is, Edward is more like the heroine's alternative suitor, Wickham or Frank Churchill. And I settled it that he is already secretly in love with the heroine's lost friend Mary Wynne, who was surely destined to come back into the narrative. Her steady sense and intelligence will be like Jane Fairfax's in going some way towards reforming him. And again as in the Fairfax/Churchill match, the young man will not be worthy of her; but she loves him anyway.

Edward's flighty sister Camilla is a major character in what we have of "Catharine," and she must inevitably be half of the second match. And the other half? – perhaps the pleasant Sir Henry Devereux who proposes to come on the expedition to the Lake District with her (250); but my money is on is on that "Horrid Wretch" Sir Peter (255), despite his gout; for the gout could be a much slighter infirmity, like Colonel Brandon's rheumatism for which he wears a flannel waistcoat (*SS* 45). Camilla cares about status, and his baronetcy will clearly be tempting to her. Sir Peter also plans to come on the trip to the Lakes, so he will have the opportunity to fall for her charms, and to propose. It will be a comic affair, perhaps like Mary Stanhope's marriage to Mr. Watts, or Lucy Steele's to Robert Ferrars – or, indeed, Charlotte Lucas's to Mr. Collins; though one would hope for a better chance of happiness for Camilla.

As for Kitty herself: I believe she will re-encounter her childhood friend Charles Wynne. His preference for the church and actual profession in the navy (258) connects him with Austen's brothers, as well as with other heroes like Edmund and Wentworth. And I congratulate myself in arranging this matter according to precedent, for Kitty *did* know Charles Wynne before she meets the dangerous Edward. Back then, he would have been more like an older brother – like Mr. Knightley, in fact, who is Emma's brother-in-law. Once grown up and sexually aware, Kitty will ultimately find that he is the lover and husband for her. And I leave it open for Austen to have returned to insert an early scene from childhood – like the one in *Mansfield Park* where Edmund helps Fanny to write a letter to her brother William, and rules her lines for her – before the young author wound up "Catharine, or the Bower" to send to the publisher.

"Lesley Castle," now: Three matches? Lady Lesley gets her hooks into Sir George Lesley so early in the epistolary sequence that that match doesn't count as one of the three wind-up couples. But her brother, William Fitzgerald, is promptly smitten with the willowy Matilda Lesley, and her sister confirms, "I am certain she likes the fellow" (175). So that makes Match Number One. Matilda's sister Margaret, in the last letter of the fragment, admits to an instant attraction: "The elegant address of Mr Clifford, his polished Manners and delightful Bow, at once confirmed my attachment," she writes (173). So that is Match Number Two. Match the Third involves the Lesley sibling, young Lesley, whose wife, early on, "left him, her Child and reputation … in company with Danvers and dishonour" (143). He finds comfort on the continent, turns Catholic, obtains a Papal Bull to annul his first marriage, and "Marries a Neapolitan Lady of great Rank and Fortune" (174). But this leaves the melancholy Eloisa Lutterell, whose fiancé was killed in a riding accident, without consolation. I am tempted to argue that a marriage on the continent doesn't count, and to find a way to get her and the forsaken Lesley together. But that would be cheating.

As for the culinary-minded Charlotte Lutterell: she is like Emma in claiming she doesn't mean to marry. But I believe that *un*like Emma she will indeed stay single. Perhaps, though, she will have a pleasant Platonic relationship with a distinguished and dedicated Chef.

"Letter the Third" provides much less to go on. But surely Maria will make a match with the eligible Mr. Bernard, who dances with her at the ball (as Emma Watson of *The Watsons* will marry Mr. Howard, her partner at *her* ball). Perhaps Lady Greville's daughters, the arrogant Miss Greville and her sympathetic sister Ellen will each provide half of two further pairings, to make up the regulation three matches.

There, I have settled it all: three matches per unfinished tale. And along the way I have discovered the lure of the fragment. There have been several "completions" of *The Watsons* and *Sanditon*. But I have enjoyed free rein with these fragments from the juvenilia.

"That ["Lesley Castle"] is unfinished, I greive," young Austen wrote to her brother Henry in her dedication; "yet I fear that from me, it will always remain so" (142). I claim that that gives the rest of us an opportunity, even an invitation, to do the finishing. But that way lies … another book.

It is time to return to my main business, the connections between *Pride and Prejudice* and the Juvenilia. Young Austen, as we know, was already a master of language, a commander of the *mot juste* and the sharp turn of syntax. And as we find aspects of situation, character, theme, and plot structure recurring from the juvenilia to the novel, so I also hear verbal echoes. In "Jack and Alice," written when Austen was only 13, Lady Williams has a fine if confusing flow of rhetoric, with an exactness of syntax that points up the absurd content of her speech. When her houseguest Lucy receives a rival invitation, "Lady Williams insisted on her going – declared that she would never forgive her if she did not, and that she should never survive it if she did" (*J* 27). The limber and witty balance of "if you do not … ; if you do. … " recalls Mr. Bennet: "An unhappy alternative is before you, Elizabeth … Your mother will never see you again if you do not marry Mr. Collins, and I will never see you again if you *do*" (*PP* 125).

When that same Lady Williams discourses on the "many rare and charming qualities" of Alice, including drunkenness and bad temper – "tho' I am very partial to her, and perhaps am blinded by my affection, to her real defects" (*J 26*), I hear Mrs. Bennet on Charlotte Lucas: "Not that *I* think Charlotte so *very* plain – but then she is our particular friend" (*PP* 48).

In the chapter on dialogue in the juvenilia I demonstrated Austen's strategy of giving us the absurd and laughable speeches – say those of Charles Adams or Mary Stanhope or Laura – verbatim and at length, while the merely sensible rejoinders are summarized. So (in the scenes where they appear together) we get more speech of Mrs. Bennet than Mr. Bennet, more of Lady Catherine than Darcy, and so on. It was Austen's strategy of clustering the tastiest morsels of speech – the comic, the outrageous, the absurd – for maximum effect, and merely skimming over what is merely sensible and ordinary. She wants to make her dialogue sparkle on the page. *Pride and Prejudice* collects and concentrates the piquant and the ridiculous, both in the number of broadly comic characters and in their speech. It is part of the "light & bright & sparkling" texture of this novel.

In a topic like mine it is easy to get carried away by numbers, and to multiply individual parallels at the expense of large concerns. And it must be conceded that the many pieces of juvenilia, for all their local brilliance, can't achieve the large effects available in a sustained work. But certain large features of the early works *as a collection* carry over into *Pride and Prejudice* – more than into any of the other five novels. In the early writings there is an energy, an exuberance, a *jouissance* that flashes through the wild and impossible tales, scraps, and unfinished pieces with their scintillating verbal felicities: Laura and Sophia fainting "Alternately on a Sofa," for instance (*J* 114), or Alice's iambic lament over Lucy, who has just had her leg broken by the man-trap on Charles Adams's estate: "Oh! cruel Charles to wound the hearts and legs of all the fair" (*J* 25): or Sophia's instructions to her friend Laura, "Run mad as often as you chuse; but do not faint" – which Patricia Rozema used as a kind of refrain in her movie of *Mansfield Park*.

And we find these qualities too in *Pride and Prejudice*, in its physically vigorous heroine, in the array of brilliantly comic minor characters, and in the celebration of laughter; in Mr. Bennet's delight in the absurd, which teaches us how to enjoy it too; in Elizabeth's dearly loving a laugh (62); in the coming together of a couple opposed, like Beatrice and Benedick in their "merry war." There are moments in *Pride and Prejudice* that make you want to stand up and cheer:

> "I do not pretend to possess equal frankness with your ladyship. *You* may ask questions, which *I* shall not choose to answer." (*PP* 392)

> "If any young men come for Mary or Kitty, send them in, for I am quite at leisure." (*PP* 419)

We all have our favourites.

With the slapstick jokes of the colliding bodies, the wild improbabilities, the comic figures, and deliciously exaggerated parody and satire, all presented in what is already "the best chosen language" (*NA* 31), the early works provide belly laughs. Jane Austen's more mature wit and controlled expression prompt rather the appreciative smile. But both are informed by a comic spirit that can delight and transport us. No other novel ends quite so triumphantly happily as *Pride and Prejudice*. And I like to think that part of that triumph is the lambent spirit of the young Jane that co-exists with the mature but still sparkling mature author at so many points. Let's say *Pride and Prejudice* and the juvenilia are like Jane and Elizabeth Bennet, as Elizabeth describes them at the end: "I am happier even than Jane: she only smiles, I laugh" (424).

Works Cited

Alcott, Louisa May. *Little Women* (1868). Ed. Elaine Showalter. New York: Penguin, 1989.

Alexander, Christine. "Introduction" to *Love and Freindship and Other Youthful Writings by Jane Austen*. London: Penguin Books, 2014. ix–xlv.

Alexander, Christine, and Juliet McMaster, eds. *The Child Writer from Austen to Woolf*. Cambridge: Cambridge University Press, 2006.

Amis, Kingsley. "What Became of Jane Austen?" *Spectator* 6745 (4 October 1957): 339–40. Reprinted in *Jane Austen: A Collection of Critical Essays*. Ed. Ian Watt. Englewood Cliffs, N.J.: Prentice-Hall, 1965. 141–4.

Ashford, Daisy. *Daisy Ashford: Her Book*. Ed. Irvin S. Cobb. New York: George H. Doran, 1920.

Austen, Jane. *"Amelia Webster" and "The Three Sisters."* Ed. Juliet McMaster et al. Edmonton: Juvenilia Press, 1993.

———. *The Beautifull Cassandra*. Ed. and illus. Juliet McMaster. Victoria, Canada: Sono Nis Press, 1993, 2005. [With music: http://www.jasna.org/publications/cassandra/index/htm.]

———. *Evelyn*. Ed. Peter Sabor et al. Edmonton: Juvenilia Press.

———. *Frederic and Elfrida*. Ed. Peter Sabor et al. Edmonton: Juvenilia Press, 2002.

———. *The History of England*. Ed. Jan Fergus et al. Edmonton: Juvenilia Press, 1995.

———. *Jack and Alice*. Ed. Joseph Wiesenfarth et al. Edmonton: Juvenilia Press, 2000.

———. *Jane Austen's Letters*. Collected and edited by Deirdre Le Faye. Oxford: Oxford University Press, 1995.

———. *Jane Austen's Letters to her Sister Cassandra and Others*. Ed. R.W. Chapman. 2nd ed. London: Oxford University Press, 1964.

———. *Jane Austen's Men*. Ed. Sylvia Hunt et al. Sydney: Juvenilia Press, 2005.

———. *Jane Austen's "Sir Charles Grandison."* Ed. Brian Southam. Oxford: Clarendon Press, 1980.

———. *Lady Susan*. Ed. Christine Alexander and David Owen. Sydney: Juvenilia Press, 2005.

———. *Lesley Castle*. Ed. Jan Fergus et al. Edmonton: Juvenilia Press, 1999.

———. *Love and Freindship*. Ed. Juliet McMaster et al. Edmonton: Juvenilia Press, 1995.

———. *Love and Freindship and Other Youthful Writings by Jane Austen*. Ed. Christine Alexander. London: Penguin Books, 2014.

———. *Minor Works*. Volume VI of *The Works of Jane Austen*. Ed. R.W. Chapman, with further revisions by B.C. Southam. Oxford: Oxford University Press, 1987. Reprint.

———. *Three Mini-Dramas*. Ed. Juliet McMaster, Lesley Peterson, et al. Sydney: Juvenilia Press, 2006.

———. *The Three Sisters*. Ed. Joseph Wiesenfarth et al. Sydney: Juvenilia Press, 2004.

———. *Volume the First, Volume the Second, Volume the Third* (facsimile edition). With introductions and transcriptions by Kathryn Sutherland. 3 vols. New York: Abbeville Press Publishers, 2013.

———. *The Works of Jane Austen*. Ed. R.W. Chapman. 5 vols. 3rd ed. Oxford: Oxford University Press. 1996.

Austen-Leigh, James Edward. *A Memoir of Jane Austen, to Which is Added Lady Susan*. London: Richard Bentley and Son, 1872.

Austen-Leigh, Joan. "The Juvenilia: A Family 'View.'" In *Jane Austen's Beginnings: The Juvenilia and Lady Susan*. Ed. J. David Grey. Ann Arbor: UMI Research Press, 1989. 174–80.

Babb, Howard S. *Jane Austen: The Fabric of Dialogue*. Columbus: Ohio State University Press, 1967.

Barbauld, Anna Letitia. "On the Origin and Progress of Novel-Writing." *British Novelists*. 50 vols. London: Printed for F.C. and J. Rivington, 1810. I, 1–62.

Blank, Antje. "Dress." In *Jane Austen in Context*. Ed. Janet Todd. Cambridge: Cambridge University Press, 2005. 234–351.

Breton, Rob, ed. *From Seven to Seventeen: Poems of John Ruskin*. Sydney: Juvenilia Press, 2012.

[Bromley, Eliza Nugent]. *Laura and Augustus: An Authentic Story in a Series of Letters*. 3 vols. London: Printed for W. Cass, 1784.

Brontë, Charlotte. "Charlotte Brontë on Jane Austen." In *Jane Austen: The Critical Heritage*. Ed. B.C. Southam. London: Routledge and Kegan Paul, 1968. 126–8.

———. *An Edition of the Early Writings of Charlotte Brontë*. 3 vols. Ed. Christine Alexander. Oxford, Basil Blackwood, 1991.

———. *The Search After Hapiness* [sic] (1824). London: Harville Press, 1969.

Brooke, Frances. *The History of Emily Montague* (1769). New Canadian Library no. 27. Toronto: McClelland and Steward, 1961.

———. *The History of Emily Montague*, A Critical Edition. Ed. Laura Moss. Ottawa: The Tecumseh Press, 2001.

Brownstein, Rachel. "Endless Imitation: Austen's and Byron's Juvenilia." In *The Child Writer from Austen to Woolf*. Ed. Christine Alexander and Juliet McMaster. Cambridge: Cambridge University Press, 2005. 122–37.

Brush, Pippa. "Introduction" to *Love and Freindship*. Ed. Juliet McMaster et al. Edmonton: Juvenilia Press, 1995. vii–xii.

Bulwer, John. *Chirologia, or the Natural Language of the Hand* ... (1764). Ed. James W. Cleary. Carbondale and Edwardsville: Southern Illinois University Press, 1973.

Burney, Frances. *Camilla, or A Picture of Youth* (1796). Ed. Edward A. Bloom and Lillian D. Bloom. Oxford: Oxford University Press, 1983.

———. *Cecilia, or Memoirs of an Heiress* (1782). Ed. Peter Sabor and Margaret Anne Doody. Oxford: Oxford University Press, 1988.

———. *The Complete Plays of Frances Burney*. Vol. 1 *Comedies*. Ed. Peter Sabor. Montreal and Kingston: McGill-Queen's University Press, 1995.

———. *Evelina* (1778). Ed. Edward A. Bloom and Lillian D. Bloom. Oxford: Oxford University Press, 1968.

Burrows, John. "Style." In *The Cambridge Companion to Jane Austen*. Ed. Edward Copeland and Juliet McMaster. Cambridge: Cambridge University Press, 1997. 170–88.

Byrne, Paula. "Ungentle Jane." Review of *Volume the First*, *Volume the Second*, and *Volume the Third* by Jane Austen, with introductions by Kathryn Sutherland, and *Love and Freindship and Other Youthful Writings* by Jane Austen, ed. Christine Alexander. *TLS*, 18 February 2015.

Chesterton, G.K. "Preface" to Jane Austen's *Love and Freindship*. New York: Frederick Stokes, 1922. vii–xvi.

Chesterton, G.K., ed. *"Love and Freindship" and Other Early Texts by Jane Austen*. New York: Frederick A. Stokes, 1922.

Copeland, Edward, and Juliet McMaster, eds. *The Cambridge Companion to Jane Austen*. Cambridge: Cambridge University Press, 1997.

Dickens, Charles. *Bleak House* (1852–1853). The New Oxford Illustrated Dickens. Oxford: Oxford University Press, 1948.

Doody, Margaret Anne. *Frances Burney: The Life in the Works*. New Brunswick, N.J.: Rutgers University Press, 1988.

———. "Jane Austen, that Disconcerting 'Child.'" In *The Child Writer from Austen to Woolf*. Ed. Christine Alexander and Juliet McMaster. Cambridge: Cambridge University Press, 2005. 101–21.

———. "A Regency Walking Dress and Other Disguises: Jane Austen and the Big Novel." *Persuasions* 16 (1994): 69–84.

Eliot, George (Mary Ann Evans). *Edward Neville* (1834). Ed. Juliet McMaster et al. Edmonton: Juvenilia Press, 1995.

Fergus, Jan. "Introduction" to Jane Austen's *The History of England*. Edmonton: Juvenilia Press, 1995. i–xii.

———. "Introduction" to Jane Austen's *Lesley Castle*. Edmonton: Juvenilia Press, 1998. viii–xvii.

Farrell, Kaitlyn. "A Dog's World: The Significance of Canine Companions in Hogarth's *Marriage A-la-Mode*." *British Art Journal* 14.2 (Autumn 2013): 35–8.

Fielding, Henry. *Joseph Andrews* and *Shamela*. Ed. Martin C. Battestin. Riverside Edition. Boston: Houghton Mifflin, 1981.

Forster, E.M. *Aspects of the Novel* (1937). Harmondsworth: Penguin Books, 1962.

Gay, Penny. *Jane Austen and the Theatre*. Cambridge: Cambridge University Press, 2002.

Gilbert, Sandra M., and Susan Gubar. *The Madwoman in the Attic*. New Haven and London: Yale University Press, 1979.

———. *The Norton Anthology of Literature by Women*. New York: Norton, 1985.

Grey, J. David, ed. *Jane Austen's Beginnings: The Juvenilia and* Lady Susan. Ann Arbor: UMI Research Press, 1989.

Grundy, Isobel. "*Persuasion*: or, The Triumph of Cheerfulness." In *Jane Austen's Business: Her World and Her Profession*. Ed. Juliet McMaster and Bruce Stovel. London: Macmillan, 1996. 3–16.

———. "Why Do They Talk so Much? How Can We Stand it?" In *The Talk in Jane Austen*. Ed. Bruce Stovel and Lynn Weinlos Gregg. Edmonton: University of Alberta Press, 2002. 73–89.

Hartnick, Karen L. "Introduction" to *Henry and Eliza*. Edmonton: Juvenilia Press, 1996. xiii–xix.

Herrle, Jeffrey. "Introduction" to *Catharine, or the Bower* by Jane Austen. Edmonton: Juvenilia Press, 1996. vii–xiv.

Hill, Reginald. "Jane Austen: A Voyage of Discovery." *Persuasions* 19 (1997): 77–92.

James, Henry. "The Lesson of Balzac" (1905). In *Literary Criticism: French Writers, Other European Writers; Prefaces to the New York Edition*. Ed. Leon Edel. New York: The Library of America, 1984. 115–38.

———. "Preface" to *The Ambassadors*. New York: Charles Scribners, 1909. Reprinted Augustus M. Kelley, 1971. v–xxiii.

Kipling, Rudyard. "The Janeites." http://www.jasna.org/membership/janeites.html.

Johnson, Claudia L. "'The Kingdom at Sixes and Sevens': Politics and the Juvenilia." In *Jane Austen's Beginnings*. Ed. J. David Grey. Ann Arbor: UMI Research Press, 1989. 45–58.

Johnson, Claudia L., and Clara Tuite, eds. *A Companion to Jane Austen*. Oxford: Wiley-Blackwell, 2009.

Klinck, Carl F. "Introduction." *The History of Emily Montague*. New Canadian Library. Vol. 27. Toronto: McClelland and Steward, 1961.

Kortes-Papp, Victoria. "Introduction" to Jane Austen's *Evelyn*. Ed. Peter Sabor et al. Edmonton: Juvenilia Press, 1999. ix–xv.

Lambdin, Laura Cooper, and Robert James Lambdin, eds. *A Companion to Jane Austen Studies*. Westport: Greenwood Press, 2000: 173–90.

Laura and Augustus: An Authentic Story in a Series of Letters by a young lady. 3 vols. London: Printed for W. Cass, 1784. [Sometimes attributed to Eliza Nugent Bromley.]

Leavis, Q.D. "Jane Austen: A Critical Theory." *Collected Essays*, Volume 2: *The Englishness of the English Novel*. Ed. G. Singh. Cambridge: Cambridge University Press, 1983. 61–126.

Le Faye, Deirdre, ed. *Jane Austen's Letters*. Oxford: Oxford University Press, 1995.

Litz, A. Walton. *Jane Austen: A Study of her Artistic Development*. London: Chatto and Windus, 1963.

———. "The Juvenilia." *Jane Austen's Beginnings*. Ed. J. David Grey. Ann Arbor: UMI Research Press, 1982. 1–6.

Londry, Michael, ed. *"Amelia Webster" and "The Three Sisters"* by Jane Austen. Edmonton: Juvenilia Press, 1993.

McMaster, Juliet, ed. *The Beautifull Cassandra*, by Jane Austen. Victoria: Sono Nis Press, 1993.

———. *Jane Austen the Novelist: Essays Past and Present*. London: Macmillan, 1996.

———. "Mrs. Elton and Other Verbal Aggressors." In *The Talk in Jane Austen*. Ed. Bruce Stovel and Lynn Weinlos Gregg. Edmonton: University of Alberta Press, 2002. 41–56.

———. "*Pride and Prejudice*: Acting by Design." In *The Novel from Sterne to James*. Ed. Juliet and Rowland McMaster. London: Macmillan, 1981. 19–36.

———. *Reading the Body in the Eighteenth-Century Novel*. London: Palgrave Macmillan, 2004.

———. "The Secret Languages of *Emma*." *Persuasions* 13 (1991): 119–31.

———. "The Talkers and Listeners of *Mansfield Park*." *Persuasions* 17 (1995): 77–89.

———. "Talking About Talking." In *Approaches to Teaching* Pride and Prejudice. Ed. Marcia McClintock Folsom. New York: The Modern Language Association of America, 1993. 167–73.

Martin, Ellen. "The Madness of Jane Austen: Metonymic Style and Literature's Resistance to Interpretation." *Jane Austen's Beginnings*. Ed. J. David Grey. Ann Arbor: UMI Research Press, 1989. 83–94.

Mudrick, Marvin. *Jane Austen: Irony as Defense and Discovery*. Berkeley and Los Angeles: University of California Press, 1952.

Opie, Iona and Peter. *The Oxford Dictionary of Nursey Rhymes*. Oxford: Clarendon Press, 1951.

Richardson, Samuel. *Clarissa*. Ed. Angus Ross. Harmondsworth: Penguin, 1985.

Ruskin, John. *From Seven to Seventeen: Poems of John Ruskin*. Ed. Rob Breton et al. Sydney: Juvenilia Press, 2012.

———. *Modern Painters*. The Works of John Ruskin. Ed. E.T. Cook and Alexander Wedderburn. London: George Allen, 1903–1912.

Sabor, Peter. "Brotherly and Sisterly Dedications in Jane Austen's Juvenilia." *Persuasions* 31 (2009): 33–46.

———. "Introduction" to *Juvenilia*. Ed. Peter Sabor, in *The Cambridge Edition of the Works of Jane Austen*. Cambridge: Cambridge University Press, 2006: xxiii–lxvii.

———. "Note on the Text." In *Jane Austen's Evelyn*. Ed. Peter Sabor et al. Edmonton: Juvenilia Press, 1999. xvi–xx.

Sendak, Maurice. *In the Night Kitchen*. New York: Harper and Row, 1970.

———. *Outside Over There*. New York: Harper and Row, 1981.

———. *Where the Wild Things Are*. New York: Harper and Row, 1963.

Smollett, Tobias. *Humphry Clinker* (1771). Ed. James L. Thorson. New York: W.W. Norton, 1983.

Southam, B.C. "Introduction." In *Jane Austen's "Sir Charles Grandison."* Ed. Brian Southam. Oxford: Clarendon Press, 1980.1–34.

———. *Jane Austen's Literary Manuscripts*. Oxford: Clarendon Press, 1964. 1–36.

———. Review of *Lady Susan* in *News Letter* of the Jane Austen Society, No. 27. 19–20.

Southam, B.C., ed. *Jane Austen: The Critical Heritage*. London: Routledge and Kegan Paul, 1968.

Spacks, Patricia Meyer. "Plots and Possibilities: Jane Austen's Juvenilia." In *Jane Austen's Beginnings*. Ed. J. David Grey. Ann Arbor: UMI Research Press, 1989. 125–34.

Sutherland, Kathryn. "Introduction" to *Volume the First*, by Jane Austen. New York: Abbeville Press Publishers, 2013. 5–14.

Tave, Stuart M. *Some Words of Jane Austen*. Chicago: University of Chicago Press, 1973.

Thackeray, William Makepeace. *The Oxford Thackeray*. Ed. George Saintsbury. 17 vols. London: Oxford University Press, 1908.

Todd, Janet, ed. *Jane Austen in Context*. Cambridge: Cambridge University Press, 2005.

Tomalin, Claire. *Jane Austen: A Life*. London: Penguin Books, 1997.

Wiesenfarth, Joseph, et al, eds. *The Three Sisters*, by Jane Austen. Sydney: Juvenilia Press, 2004.

Wiesenthal, Chris. *Figuring Madness in Nineteenth-Century Fiction*. Houndmills and Basingstoke: Macmillan, 1997.

Index

Separate entries are supplied for each item of Jane Austen's juvenilia, as well as for the six novels, two fragments, and her letters. Other authors are indexed by name, with subheadings for their works and characters. Sustained discussion is indicated by page numbers in *italics*, illustrations by page numbers in **bold**.